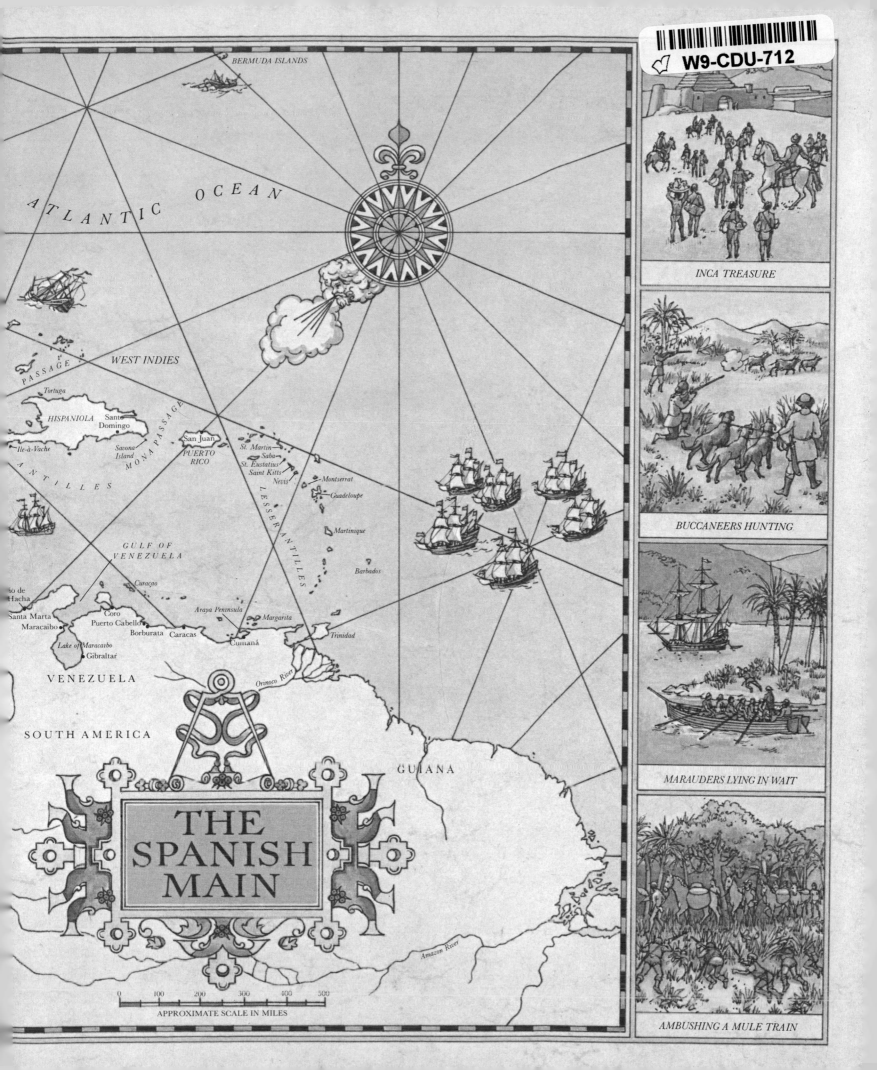

ATLANTIC OCEAN

BERMUDA ISLANDS

WEST INDIES

PASSAGE

Tortuga

HISPANIOLA
Santo Domingo

Ile-à-Vache

Savona Island

MONA PASSAGE

San Juan
PUERTO RICO

St. Martin
Saba
St. Eustatius
Saint Kitts
Nevis

Montserrat

Guadeloupe

Martinique

Barbados

LESSER ANTILLES

ANTILLES

GULF OF VENEZUELA

Curaçao

Araya Peninsula

Margarita

Río de Hacha

Santa Marta
Maracaibo

Coro
Puerto Cabello
Borburata
Caracas

Cumaná

Trinidad

Lake of Maracaibo
Gibraltar

VENEZUELA

Orinoco River

SOUTH AMERICA

GUIANA

THE SPANISH MAIN

Amazon River

0   100   200   300   400   500

APPROXIMATE SCALE IN MILES

INCA TREASURE

BUCCANEERS HUNTING

MARAUDERS LYING IN WAIT

AMBUSHING A MULE TRAIN

The Seafarers   THE SPANISH MAIN

TIME
LIFE ®
BOOKS

Other Publications:

THE GOOD COOK
THE ENCYCLOPEDIA OF COLLECTIBLES
THE GREAT CITIES
WORLD WAR II
HOME REPAIR AND IMPROVEMENT
THE WORLD'S WILD PLACES
THE TIME-LIFE LIBRARY OF BOATING
HUMAN BEHAVIOR
THE ART OF SEWING
THE OLD WEST
THE EMERGENCE OF MAN
THE AMERICAN WILDERNESS
THE TIME-LIFE ENCYCLOPEDIA OF GARDENING
LIFE LIBRARY OF PHOTOGRAPHY
THIS FABULOUS CENTURY
FOODS OF THE WORLD
TIME-LIFE LIBRARY OF AMERICA
TIME-LIFE LIBRARY OF ART
GREAT AGES OF MAN
LIFE SCIENCE LIBRARY
THE LIFE HISTORY OF THE UNITED STATES
TIME READING PROGRAM
LIFE NATURE LIBRARY
LIFE WORLD LIBRARY
FAMILY LIBRARY:
    HOW THINGS WORK IN YOUR HOME
    THE TIME-LIFE BOOK OF THE FAMILY CAR
    THE TIME-LIFE FAMILY LEGAL GUIDE
    THE TIME-LIFE BOOK OF FAMILY FINANCE

The Cover: French privateers load their
boat with plunder from a Spanish
settlement on the island of Cuba in this 1590
engraving by Theodore de Bry. The
settlers, accustomed to attacks by the
many water-borne marauders who
prowled the Spanish Main, had carried
most of their valuables into the hills, and
the French, angered by the paucity of
their haul, vengefully torched the town.

The Title Page: A brass butt cap and trigger
guard adorn the rich wood stock of this
flintlock pistol, once owned by Nicholas
van Horn, a Dutch buccaneer who plied
the Spanish Main in the late 17th Century.

The Seafarers

THE SPANISH MAIN

by Peter Wood
AND THE EDITORS OF TIME-LIFE BOOKS

TIME-LIFE BOOKS, ALEXANDRIA, VIRGINIA

Time-Life Books Inc.
is a wholly owned subsidiary of
TIME INCORPORATED

FOUNDER: Henry R. Luce 1898-1967

Editor-in-Chief: Henry Anatole Grunwald
Chairman of the Board: Andrew Heiskell
President: James R. Shepley
Editorial Director: Ralph Graves
Vice Chairman: Arthur Temple

TIME-LIFE BOOKS INC.

MANAGING EDITOR: Jerry Korn
Executive Editor: David Maness
Assistant Managing Editors: Dale M. Brown (planning),
George Constable, Jim Hicks (acting), Martin Mann,
John Paul Porter
Art Director: Tom Suzuki
Chief of Research: David L. Harrison
Director of Photography: Robert G. Mason
Senior Text Editor: Diana Hirsh
Assistant Art Director: Arnold C. Holeywell
Assistant Chief of Research: Carolyn L. Sackett
Assistant Director of Photography: Dolores A. Littles

CHAIRMAN: Joan D. Manley
President: John D. McSweeney
Executive Vice Presidents: Carl G. Jaeger,
John Steven Maxwell, David J. Walsh
Vice Presidents: Nicholas Benton (public relations),
John L. Canova (sales), Nicholas J. C. Ingleton (Asia),
James L. Mercer (Europe/South Pacific), Herbert Sorkin
(production), Paul R. Stewart (promotion),
Peter G. Barnes
Personnel Director: Beatrice T. Dobie
Consumer Affairs Director: Carol Flaumenhaft
Comptroller: George Artandi

The Seafarers

Editorial Staff for The Spanish Main:
Editor: George G. Daniels
Designer: Herbert H. Quarmby
Text Editors: Stuart Gannes, Anne Horan,
Sterling Seagrave
Staff Writers: Russell Adams, Michael Blumenthal,
Susan Feller, Gus Hedberg, Mark M. Steele
Chief Researcher: Charlotte A. Quinn
Researchers: Peggy L. Sawyer, Philip Brandt George,
Mindy A. Daniels, W. Mark Hamilton, Trudy W. Pearson,
Jeremy Ross, James R. Stengel
Art Assistant: Michelle René Clay
Editorial Assistant: Ellen P. Keir

Editorial Production
Production Editor: Douglas B. Graham
Operations Manager: Gennaro C. Esposito,
Gordon E. Buck (assistant)
Assistant Production Editor: Feliciano Madrid
Quality Control: Robert L. Young (director), James J. Cox
(assistant), Michael G. Wight (associate)
Art Coordinator: Anne B. Landry
Copy Staff: Susan B. Galloway (chief), Sheirazada Hann,
Celia Beattie
Picture Department: Nancy Cromwell Scott
Traffic: Jeanne Potter

Correspondents: Elisabeth Kraemer (Bonn); Margot
Hapgood, Dorothy Bacon, Lesley Coleman (London);
Susan Jonas, Lucy T. Voulgaris (New York); Maria
Vincenza Aloisi, Josephine du Brusle (Paris); Ann
Natanson (Rome).
Valuable assistance was also provided by: Janny Hovinga
(Amsterdam); June Carlyn Erlick (Bogotá); Enid Farmer
(Boston); Caroline Alcock, Judy Aspinall, Pat Stimpson
(London); Jane Walker (Madrid); Douglas Tunstall
(Málaga); Bernard Diederich (Mexico City); Carolyn T.
Chubet, Miriam Hsia (New York); Mimi Murphy (Rome).

The editors are indebted to Champ Clark, Martha
Reichard George, Barbara Hicks and Lois Gilman for their
help in the preparation of this book.

The Author:
Peter Wood first saw what once was the Spanish Main as a messboy on a banana boat plying between Florida and Central America. Since then he has made many visits to the Caribbean, including a stint with a film crew photographing the old Spanish fortifications of Cartagena in Colombia, before they were dwarfed by high-rise hotels. He has contributed to numerous magazines and written several books, including Caribbean Isles in The American Wilderness series for Time-Life Books.

The Consultants:
John Horace Parry, Professor of Oceanic History at Harvard University, was educated at Cambridge University, where he took his Ph.D. He served in the Royal Navy during World War II, rising to the rank of commander. He has written many books, including The Discovery of South America, The Spanish Seaborne Empire, Trade and Dominion and Europe and a Wider World.

William Avery Baker, a naval architect and engineer, spent 30 years with the Shipbuilding Division of Bethlehem Steel Corporation, designing vessels of all sizes, from tugs to supertankers. He is curator of the Hart Nautical Museum at the Massachusetts Institute of Technology, where he took his degree. He is also author of The Engine Powered Vessel, a history of ships from the first paddle-wheeler to the first commercial nuclear ship, the Savannah.

For information about any Time-Life book, please write:
Reader Information, Time-Life Books,
541 North Fairbanks Court, Chicago, Illinois 60611.

Library of Congress Cataloging in Publication Data
Wood, Peter, 1930-
   The Spanish Main.
   (The Seafarers)
   Bibliography: p.
   Includes index.
   1. Spanish Main—History.   I. Time-Life Books.
II. Title.   III. Series.
F2175.W66   972.9   79-14919
ISBN 0-8094-2721-4
ISBN 0-8094-2720-6 lib. bdg.

Contents

The ruthless conquest
of a golden Aztec Empire

Early in the 16th Century the mighty Aztec civilization of Mexico was at its zenith—with a population of nearly a million, a host of fabulous gods and a rich ruling class of nobles, priests and bureaucrats. With their army the Aztec overlords preyed upon 25 million subjects from whom they extorted an immense tribute in gold, silver and other treasure. And they expected greater riches still: Aztec priests prophesied that the god Quetzalcoatl would reappear from the east, toward which he had departed long ago on a raft of snakes, and would bring good fortune with him. Instead, from the east in 1519 came the Spaniard Hernán Cortés.

Cortés, the archetypal Spanish conquistador—the word simply means conqueror—embarked from Cuba as captain general of an expedition to seize Mexico. His 600 soldiers—16 of them on horseback—were armed with muskets, crossbows and swords. Cunning and ruthless, lusting after gold and glory, Cortés and his men first subdued the coastal tribes, defeating some and coercing others. Then, helped by an Indian mistress who was his interpreter, Cortés duped his way into the lakebound stronghold of the Aztec capital, Tenochtitlán, and made a hostage of the Aztec Emperor Moctezuma. Within the next three years, as depicted in the 17th Century paintings here and on the following pages, the Spaniards destroyed the Aztec nation.

At the end of this era of intrigue, carnage and plunder, the Aztec treasure was sent to Spain, where Cortés, as one chronicler wrote, was "held in as much esteem as was Alexander in Macedonia and Julius Caesar among the Romans."

Cortés would be followed through decades of conquest by men hammered from the same Spanish steel. Francisco Pizarro, Pedro de Alvarado, Gonzalo Ximénez de Quesada and other conquistadors would discover, butcher and plunder the Carib of the West Indies, the Maya of Yucatan, the Chibcha of Colombia and the Inca of Peru.

The Caribbean and the Gulf of Mexico would become a Spanish lake, the mainland and islands bordering it a Spanish empire larger than all Europe. But this Spanish Main, as it came to be called, would seethe with conflict for centuries. For the Spaniards who had looted the New World would fall prey in turn to French, Dutch and English buccaneers, adventurers and royal servants—rogues and gentlemen every bit as bold and crafty as Cortés. The victors over the Indians would become the victims of fellow Europeans.

Slashing with his sword under the red flag of Castile and Leon, Hernán Cortés leads one of his first attacks against Mexican coastal Indians. The Indians were horrified by their first sight of men on horseback, thinking they were two-headed, four-legged monsters. Not far from an imaginary Spanish castle in the background, friars are busy converting the heathens. The legend in the corner describes the scene and lists the major figures.

N. 4

BOLCAN DE MEXICO
Nº 3

Cleverly exploiting the Aztec belief
the coming of a divine leader, Corte
Emperor Moctezuma, whose feet are
protected from touching the ground
whose own people must not look
upon his face. Standing beside Cort
his mistress, Malinche, an Indian
princess instrumental in winning fo
Spaniards thousands of Aztec-hatir
Indian allies. The Emperor invited t
Spaniards to be guests in his palace
and showered them with gold and si
only to be made their prisoner in ret

After being held captive for more than
six months in his own palace in
Tenochtitlán, Moctezuma (upper right),
fearing for his life, pleads with his people
to stop fighting so the Spaniards
can escape with the Aztec treasure.
Outraged by Moctezuma's submission, the
Aztec rebel, pelting their monarch
with stones and arrows—wounding him
so grievously that he soon died.

12

Fleeing the Aztec capital during the night against overwhelming numbers, the Spaniards hack their way across the causeways of the surrounding lake. A bridge they had planned to use was destroyed by the Aztec, and many of the conquistadors drowned because of gold strapped to their bodies. Cortés lost hundreds of Spanish soldiers and at least 2,000 Indian allies. Spaniards ever after called it la noche triste—"the sad night."

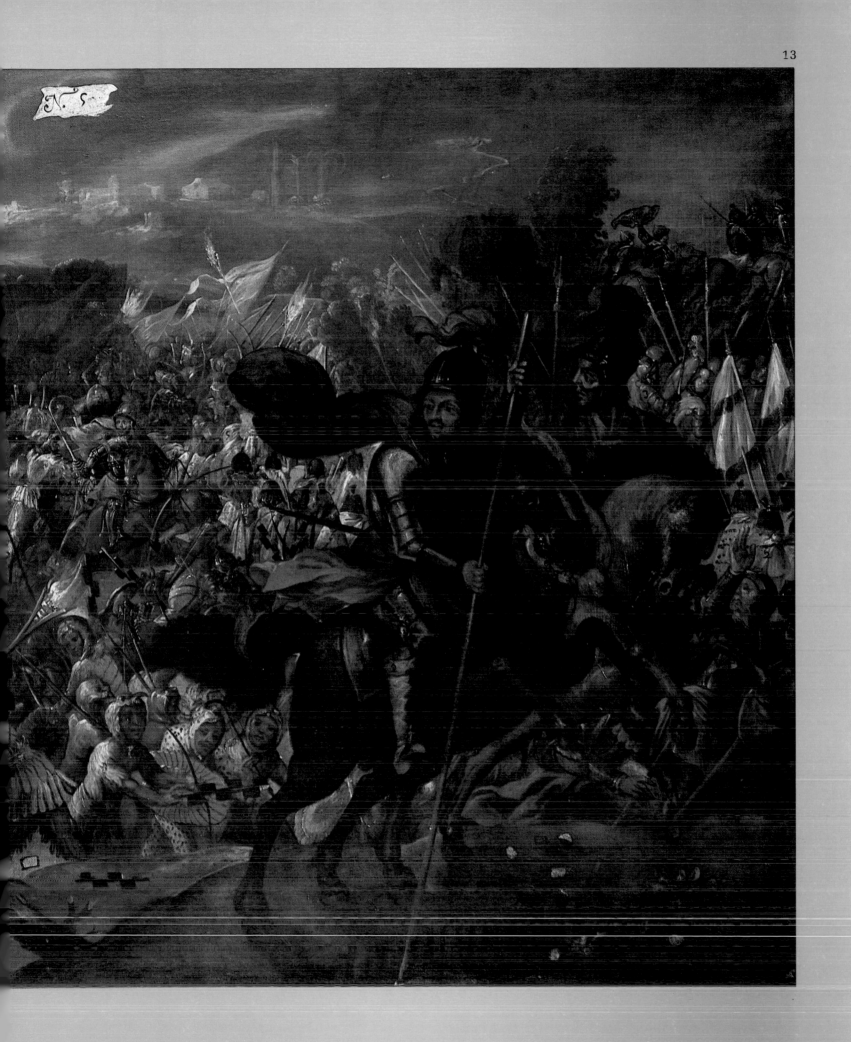

14

A year later, after a siege lasting three months, Cortés avenges la noche triste by assaulting the Aztec capital. Spaniards and their allies charge the causeways as others attack in launches across the protecting lake. In preparation for this campaign, Cortés had returned to the coast to regroup his forces with new recruits from Cuba and Spain, and had built 13 small ships that were carried to the lake by 8,000 Indians. More than 100,000 Aztec were slain, and the gold heart of their Empire was ripped out.

DE MEXICO POR CORTES. N.7

Ultimo conbate de mexico
por Cortes y los suyos por las tres calça
que van anota, y por la laguna len vo
gantos aquiendaum en decerca lo sin ha
sor. Guia Pedro de Aluarado el vltimo de
Cholola, y por las banderas de la Marcada

Fernan Cortes ———— 1
Calçada de S. Anton ——— 1
Christoual de Oli ——— 2
Pedro de Aluarado ——— 3
Calçada de Tacuba ——— 3
Gonçalo de Sandoual ——— 4
Calçada de Guadalupe ——— 4
Sacerdotes del Idolo ——— 5
Guachilobos que va a la Batalla — 6

Chapter 1

The first challenges to the lords of the Main

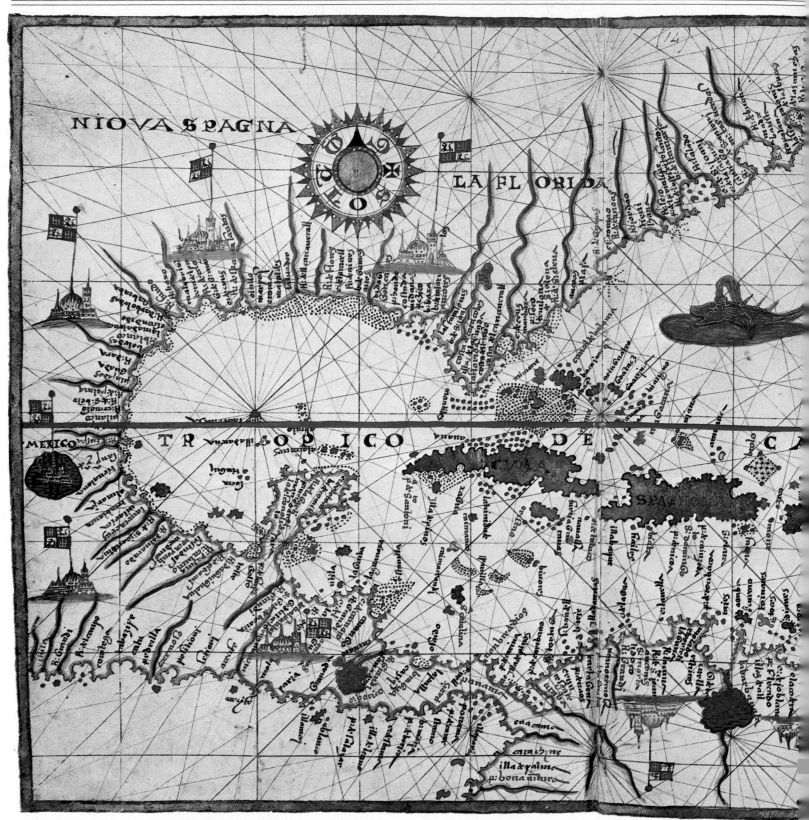

Bisected by the Tropic of Cancer, Spain's New World empire appears in some detail in this 16th Century map. The southern coasts and the main islands of the Caribbean are rendered with fair accuracy, but fidelity fades toward North America.

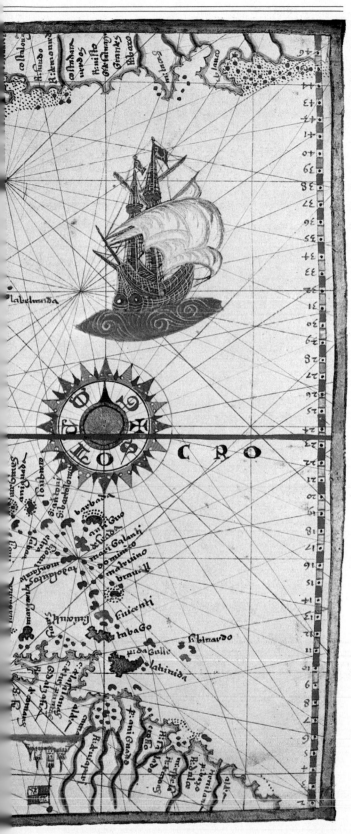

 haping a course from the New World to home in the spring of 1523, the three Spanish caravels rode low in the water, wallowing through the Atlantic swells. And well they might. Crowding their holds on this historic voyage was a staggering first installment on the wealth of Spain's new American empire. The shipment had been dispatched by conquistador Hernán Cortés and, although it included only a small portion of the plunder he had extracted from the Aztec in Mexico, there were literally tons of it: gold, silver, emeralds, pearls, topazes, magnificently carved masks set with rare gems, plumed cloaks, once the glory of Aztec priests, fashioned from the iridescent green tail plumage of the sacred quetzal bird. There were Aztec rings, shields, helmets, statues of New World animals, vases and mirrors of polished obsidian.

On board the flagship of the little fleet was the one-fifth share of the loot owed by Cortés to King Carlos I of Spain, who had recently been proclaimed Holy Roman Emperor Charles V. The King's treasure, Cortés wrote Carlos, included "things so marvelous that they cannot be described in writing, nor can they be understood without seeing them." Also on board were living gifts and curiosities for the court: Indian slaves, macaws with red, yellow and blue wings, talking green parrots, and all manner of exotic jungle animals, including cats that the Spaniards referred to collectively as *tigres*—small spotted ocelots and large, ferocious pumas and jaguars confined in stout wooden cages. In addition, the Spaniards had loaded aboard large amounts of such New World products as sugar, cow hides and corn.

The great cargo added to the natural clumsiness of the plump caravels, and progress was slow. As week followed interminable week, weather and sickness took their toll, and a number of bizarre misfortunes afflicted the fleet. In the midst of a storm one night, waves smashed the wooden bars of a cage on the flagship's deck and one of the jaguars escaped to terrorize the crew. The maddened beast tore an arm off one sailor, ripped a leg off a marine and clawed open the shoulders of another man. Two of the three men died before the animal finally leaped overboard into the storm-tossed sea. The officers and crew elected to shoot the other jaguar in the broken cage before it could escape as well.

The vessels took three months to reach the mid-ocean Azores, and then more ill fortune occurred. Captain Quiñones, the fleet commander, quarreled with another officer over the favors of an island harlot, and the jealous rival cleaved his captain's head in two with a cutlass. The crew pitched Quiñones' body overboard for the harbor sharks to dispose of, and sluiced his brains from the deck with wooden buckets of salt water. Captain Avila, in command of another caravel, took charge of the fleet and finally set sail from the Azores in early June, bound for Cape St. Vincent at the southwestern tip of the Iberian Peninsula, from there to lay a course along the coast of Portugal to the safety of Seville.

Avila had been warned in the Azores that a number of French corsairs were known to be in the Cape St. Vincent area, lying in wait for the Spanish treasure fleet. But by the end of June the caravels were within 10 leagues of the cape, and no enemy Frenchmen had appeared. The long, hard voyage was almost over. The pleasures of Seville were only a few days away. Captain Avila and his sailors began to breathe a little easier.

Then suddenly, high on the flagship's masthead, a lookout was startled out of his reverie by the sight of a sail bearing down across his fleet's bows. Five other ships were racing in close behind it. With sinking hearts the Spaniards recognized the vessels as those of French corsairs. Desperately, Captain Avila ordered his crews to man their weapons. But the treasure fleet's guns were few and poorly served.

Foaming across the Spanish bows, the French corsairs let go broadside after broadside, holing one caravel and dismasting a second. The third turned and fled downwind toward the southern horizon. After a brief but futile battle, the two crippled Spaniards—one of them the flagship carrying the King's treasure—were grappled and boarded. Their crews quickly surrendered as the Frenchmen swarmed over the railings.

Whatever rumors the French had heard about the treasure of Cortés, the reality was infinitely more dazzling. Taking an inventory of the caravels' holds, the attackers found that the Aztec pearls alone weighed 680 pounds; there were 500 pounds of gold dust in bags, three huge cases of gold ingots plus numerous other cases filled with silver ingots, and coffers of jewels. The Frenchmen transferred the loot to their own vessels, and then, as swiftly as they had swept out of the blue, they were gone—leaving the Spanish caravels to make their miserable way home.

When the ship that had escaped reached Seville with news of the terrible loss, all Spain was horrified. The anguish and rage mounted when the two plundered caravels anchored in Seville's Guadalquivir River. For then King Carlos learned the identity of the corsairs—and understood that they were in effect agents of his rival Francis I, King of France. The leader was Jean Florin, a renowned sea fighter in the employ of Jean Ango, Viscount of Dieppe. Ango was an immensely wealthy banker with close connections at the court of Francis I. For some years Francis had been chafing at Carlos' claim to absolute dominion over the New World, and he had sworn to help himself to its riches. Francis had thus bestowed his blessings on Ango's plan to outfit a fleet of privateers that would seize whatever Spanish wealth might come their way.

Now Francis had found his reward in a royal share of a treasure to make even a king blink in amazement. And Carlos had had his first bitter taste of the anger and frustration that accompanied the loss of New World treasure to a predaceous enemy, a taste that would become all too familiar to Spanish kings, captains and entrepreneurs over the centuries to follow. For the French corsairs' seizure of Cortés' treasure fleet was only the merest beginning, the opening scene in a long drama of conflict, of entrenched wealth versus lusting interlopers, of imperial Spain versus a host of inspired and determined enemies.

Spain's New World empire, vast and still growing, soon would encompass not only the Caribbean Sea and the Mexican mainland, but also Central America and South America, with their fabulously wealthy Indian civilizations. This sprawling dominion surrounding the Caribbean basin was known as the Spanish Main. At first the term was used only for the continental mainland, but it soon came to include the ring of islands bordering the Caribbean and the Gulf of Mexico, from Trinidad in the south to Cuba and the Straits of Florida in the north, and eventually it

Francis I, the shrewd and courtly King of France, ignored a papal edict in 1493 giving Spain exclusive dominion over the treasures of the Caribbean. He believed that Frenchmen had every right to take what they could from the area, and when the Spanish King bitterly complained of French incursions, Francis snapped: "The sun shines for me as for the Spaniard."

was also applied to the waters that stretched between the colonial lands.

The wealth that Spain extracted from this enormous empire might truly be said to beggar Rome. In the first century of conquest the weight of gold from South America alone amounted to something on the order of 10.5 million troy ounces, or 750,000 pounds—more than a third of all the gold produced in the entire world during those years. And once the looting had exhausted the accumulated riches of South America and Mexico, the Spaniards found vast new treasure-troves in the earth— whole mountains of silver at Potosí on the Andean plateau and Guana-juato in Mexico—and began mining them furiously with slave labor.

Yet just as the Spaniards ravaged and subjugated the various Indian peoples of the Antilles, Mexico, Colombia and Peru for these riches, so too over the next 200 years were the Spanish themselves bedeviled by predators of every stripe.

In the wake of the corsair Jean Florin came the legendary privateers and buccaneers John Hawkins, Francis Drake, Rock Brasiliano, Francis L'Ollonnais, John Esquemeling, Pierre Le Grand, Henry Morgan, Jean Baptiste du Casse and countless others. Sometimes in the royal service of England or France, at other times on their own account, these gentlemen and scoundrels fell upon the Spanish Main just as Spain seemed at the pinnacle of her power. Abetting them were countless rogues and riffraff who had fled the Old World for the New and established themselves as colonies of outcasts among the islands. The great privateers and bucca-neers made good use of them, as they did of the Spaniards' runaway African slaves. The marauders' exploits, often culminating in fantastic seaborne raids on the centers of Spanish wealth, were among the boldest and most daring in all the annals of adventure. And they proved how hollow was the Spanish claim to monopoly over all the New World.

From the very beginning the Spaniards had no doubt that they had been given a holy mission to explore and seize the riches across the western sea. But at first they were disappointed. They had expected to find the treasures of fabled Cathay and the Orient—not an endless string of islands and dark tropical coastlines peopled by half-naked Indians. In four voyages of exploration between 1492 and 1502, Christopher Colum-bus discovered the Bahamas and the verdant island of Cuba. He founded the first Spanish settlement in the New World on the island of Hispanio-la, viewed the coast of South America at the mouth of the Orinoco River and sailed beneath the great green jungled mountains of Venezuela. He was the first European to lay eyes on Jamaica, and he traveled along the lush coast of Central America as far as Honduras. But he did not find much gold, and he did not realize his cherished dream of a passage to the storied wealth of the Orient. And so he was deemed a failure.

The Spaniard chosen to oversee the settling of these newly discovered territories was the knight Nicolás de Ovando, who sailed for the New World in 1502 with 2,500 men. On Hispaniola he organized production of alluvial gold and mined small gold veins in the interior with disap-pointing results. But Ovando wisely devoted most of his energies to agriculture, bringing animals and plants from the Old World. Sugar cane flourished, and soon large plantations developed a heavy demand for slaves, both Indian and African. Tobacco, which was native to the New World, followed sugar as a foundation of the island economy. And the breeding of cattle, horses, donkeys and mules proved vital as the Spaniards expanded their dominion through the islands to the mainland.

By 1510 a Spanish colony had been established on the mainland coast of South America just east of the Isthmus of Panama. It soon faltered because of hostile Indian tribes, hunger and disease, and the survivors fled to a second colony that had been founded on the Atlantic side of the Isthmus itself. This colony, Nombre de Dios, had been christened by weary Spaniards who, upon arriving, had exclaimed, "Let us stop here, in the name of God." It would soon be famed throughout the civilized world. But in 1510 it was merely a blockhouse and a village of huts next to a fine natural harbor.

The leader of the colonists in Panama was the explorer Vasco Núñez de Balboa. In 1513, following Indian trails and stories of a great southern sea, Balboa led a small group of Spaniards 50 miles across the continental divide and took possession of the Pacific Ocean for the crown of Castile. In the course of his wanderings Balboa heard of fabulous golden empires in the mountains to the south. But his good fortune was short-lived. Before word of his Pacific discovery reached Spain, an impatient King Ferdinand had already christened Panama the Castilla del Oro, or Golden Castile, and had dispatched another man to govern the pivotal colony and spearhead the quest for wealth in Balboa's stead.

Balboa's rival was Pedro Arias de Avila, at 70 a remarkably elderly knight to be sent as commander of Spain's first large-scale settlement on the New World mainland. Arias was extraordinary in more ways than age. A few years before, he had collapsed of some unrecorded illness and had been laid to rest in a coffin. As he was about to be lowered into his grave, a tearful servant who was embracing the casket was astonished to hear movement inside. Incredibly, Arias was breathing and very much alive. Thereafter he ordered an annual Requiem Mass sung for him in the cathedral at Torrejón, and stood in his own unused grave to listen to it. He took his coffin everywhere he went, even to the New World.

Cunning, jealous and not a man of conspicuous moral fiber, Arias immediately began to plague Balboa. He refused to grant him men for further exploration, stripped him of all his property and belittled his accomplishments in letters to the Spanish court. Finally, Arias ordered Balboa arrested on trumped-up charges of sedition and treason, and after a summary trial had him beheaded.

Arias imported 1,500 footloose and cutthroat settlers to Panama, many of them soldiers of fortune who had served in various Spanish campaigns around Europe. They affected the title hidalgos—literally "sons of something"—to declare themselves persons of some substance compared with the peasantry of Spain, although the substance often consisted of little more than the foppish garments, sway-backed horse and broken lance caricatured almost a century later by Cervantes in his satirical novel, *Don Quixote*. They did not know how to dig the soil, grow their own food, tend flocks, pick fruit, or make and market goods. Like medieval knights, they knew only how to fight, and sometimes they did not know that very well. Their greatest ambition was to lead a life of

Embodying the artistry of the Inca craftsmen, silver figurines like this llama were first brought to Spain by Pizarro in 1528 to impress King Carlos I's court with the wealth and prospective plunder of the Peruvian Indian Empire. But Pizarro and his fellows melted such priceless artifacts into more easily transportable ingots when they got down to the serious business of looting.

The greatest single asset of the Spanish Main, this veritable mountain of silver in the Andean hills of Peru at Potosí was discovered in 1545 by a shepherd who found nodules of the precious metal lying in a clump of pasture grass. Shown here in a 1584 drawing, the mine included a primitive refinery (foreground), to which packtrains of llamas carried the ore for raking, washing and smelting.

wealth and ease on rich plantations worked by droves of slaves. Their appetites were whetted by tantalizing rumors of gold and silver easily taken from the docile inhabitants of the lands across the Atlantic.

An agent for the King described Arias' hidalgo immigrants as they prepared to sail on April 11, 1514. "A very impressive lot, very well dressed, none owning less than a jacket of silk and many one of brocade. It is said in Seville that never was such an assembly of fair and goodly men seen in Spain."

By the time the armada reached Panama, the agent reported, the men felt not so fair and goodly: "Being in a very wet country of swamps and overflowed land from which dense and sickly vapors rise, the men began to die and there died two thirds of them, though dressed in silks and brocades. Those who survived, ill as they were and thinking themselves lost, joined in raids on Indians, robbing and killing."

This slaughter of the Indians was to be a terrible chapter in the conquest of the Spanish Main. At first the Indians received the hidalgos in friendship, bringing the hungry men meat, fish and fruits. But the hidalgos, believing themselves agents of God, responded by ordering the

Indians to convert immediately to Christianity. The orders, of course, were announced in Spanish, which the Indians did not comprehend. The Spaniards concluded that the Indians refused to be converted; therefore it became legal to enslave them: "The Spaniards attacked the Indian huts at night, robbed them, turned dogs on the inhabitants, consigned them to flames and carried them off in chains as slaves," the King's agent reported.

All the while, the Spaniards themselves continued to die. Ironically, though they did suffer severely from tropical fevers, the worst disease had come with them from Spain. It was a form of sleeping sickness they called *modorra*, meaning "drowsy." Hundreds of men died of it.

Most Spaniards came to regard the whole Caribbean coast of Panama as pestilential. They soon started exploring the higher lands of the continental divide and crossed over to the drier and more hospitable Pacific side, where they founded the city of Panama. Wherever they traveled the Spaniards continued to meet each new Indian tribe with brutality and oppression. A Spanish chronicler in Panama reported: "The captains and men who left for those parts were accustomed to bringing back large gangs of people in fetters and all the gold they could find. The captains divided the Indians they had taken among the soldiers; the gold they took to Darien. This having been amassed and smelted, each received his share as did the officials and the bishop and also the Governor." The chronicler noted that the slaves did not last long: "As they came over so long a road worn out and broken by the great loads they carried, and the country differed from their own, and was not healthy, all died."

Similar tragedies were occurring on the islands of the Greater Antilles, where settlement was proceeding apace. As the first island to be settled after Columbus' discovery, Hispaniola became and remained the cultural and administrative center of the New World throughout the 16th Century. But the other big northern islands—Cuba, Puerto Rico and Jamaica—soon drew large numbers of colonists (the Lesser Antilles in the south were generally ignored by the Spaniards).

The Arawak Indians of the northern islands were peaceful, hospitable people who had no natural enemies except the annual hurricanes and the ferocious Carib cannibals who lived on the South American coast and on the smaller islands south of Puerto Rico. Long before the Spaniards came, the Carib were raiding Arawak settlements, slaughtering and eating the men and carrying off the women. When the Spaniards arrived the Arawak at first regarded the strange-looking white men with awe, believing them to be celestial beings. They meekly submitted as the Spanish swiftly placed large numbers of them in servitude, where they, like the Panamanians, soon began to die. According to legend, an Arawak chief rebelled in 1511 and decided to test the superstition that white Europeans could not be killed. Following the chief's orders, two Indians seized a Spanish planter named Diego Sacedo on the island of Puerto Rico, dragged him to the Guanroba River and held his head under water for several hours. Then they stood guard over his body for two days to make certain that he did not return to life.

Once the Spaniards were reduced to the status of mere mortals, the Arawak stood and fought against Spanish raiding parties. But the clubs

Attended by a slave, this flamboyantly dressed soldier of fortune, or hidalgo, was typical of the dandified Spanish adventurers who flocked to the New World in search of wealth. Dismissed by one observer as "young ruffians with colored stockings," they were nonetheless the cutting edge of Spanish conquest.

of the Indians were no match for the harquebuses, cannon and steel blades of the Spaniards. The enslaved Arawak were worked to death on tobacco and sugar plantations and in gold fields that yielded little wealth. Others committed suicide, and many perished of diseases brought from the Old World, against which they had no natural resistance. When the Spaniards arrived in the Caribbean there were perhaps as many as one million Arawak on the large islands; within 30 years there were virtually none.

Unable to enslave the fierce and cannibalistic Carib, the Spaniards simply exterminated all who did not flee into the hills or back to the South American mainland, where whites had not yet gained a foothold. History does not record how many were slain or died of disease.

Frustrated in their efforts to make the Indians a steady supply of slave labor, the colonists next turned to the blacks of West Africa. At first the Africans were brought to the New World from Portugal and Spain, where they had been taken by Portuguese slave traders who captured or purchased them in Africa. Their survival rate under the rigors of slavery was higher than that of the Indians, and the demand for labor in the Spanish Indies soon caused a heavy human traffic from Spain and Portugal, and directly to the New World from Portuguese slaving centers in West Africa. It was a lucrative business, and it attracted Dutch and British traders, who offered colonists the opportunity to buy African slaves on the sly, without paying the 30-ducat head tax imposed by the Spanish government's Casa de Contratación, or Trade House, in Seville.

By the middle of the 16th Century's second decade, a relatively rich and growing plantation society existed in the Greater Antilles, where transplanted hidalgos made up a new colonial aristocracy employing slave labor to produce sugar, tobacco, hides, cacao and a diminishing amount of alluvial gold. But none of this had made Spaniards forget their yearning for a direct western route to the Orient with all its wealth. And then came Mexico and the treasure of the Aztec.

In February 1517 a small group of Spaniards led by Hernández de Córdoba sailed west from Cuba, seeking a passage to the Orient. Landing on the Yucatan Peninsula, they encountered Maya Indians who whetted their appetites with tales of a rich and mighty civilization to the northwest waiting to be plundered. The Spanish adventurers rushed back to Havana with the news and in a matter of months the Governor had equipped a small fleet to sail west to the Mexican coast and investigate the extent of the tales. The fleet returned to Havana with stories of an emperor named Moctezuma and a world of gold and jewels for the taking. A new armada was prepared under the captaincy of yet another Spanish vagabond, Hernán Cortés—and within three years after he reached Mexico in 1519, Cortés and his conquistadors had overrun the mighty Aztec and begun a process of conquest that would not stop until Spaniards had overwhelmed almost the entire continent.

One of the first to follow Cortés was his lieutenant, the ruthless Pedro de Alvarado, who had distinguished himself in the destruction of the Aztec. Moving southward from Mexico, Alvarado and his conquistadors defeated the Quiché and Cachiquel peoples in Guatemala, and stripped them of their treasure. Alvarado then overwhelmed the Pipil civilization

A "Black Legend" from a friar's tale

An English translation of Friar Las Casas' tale

Few Spaniards were overly concerned by the manner in which the wealth of the New World was secured for their Empire, but there was one voice that cried out over the brutalities inflicted by the conquistadors. It was that of Bartolomé de Las Casas, a Dominican friar whose writings spawned the "Black Legend" of cruelty that was to haunt Spain for centuries.

Las Casas journeyed to Hispaniola in 1502 as a young settler bent on making his fortune. But being a profoundly religious man, he entered the priesthood around 1512. Two years later, he suddenly realized that "everything we had done to the Indians was nothing but tyranny and barbarism," and he made it his goal to right the wrongs.

Over the next half century Friar Las Casas made 14 trips through Europe and America, writing and preaching and urging the passage of laws for the Indians' protection. The friar's best-known work, written in 1542, was the *Very Brief Account of the Devastation of the Indies*; in it he described "Spaniards who acted like ravening beasts, killing, terrorizing, afflicting, torturing and destroying the native peoples, with the strangest and most varied new methods of cruelty."

While the 99-page volume had an effect on Spain's King Charles V, and led to new laws to improve conditions, the laws were largely ignored in the overseas empire. In any case, the book gave ammunition to Spain's enemies. Translations appeared in French, illustrated with the watercolors shown opposite and below, then in Italian, Dutch and English.

One Englishman who invoked the grisly acts portrayed in these books was the adventurer Walter Raleigh, who in 1596 asked Queen Elizabeth to annex the territory of Guiana. By so doing, Raleigh assured the Queen, she would free the Indians "from the intolerable tyranny of the Spaniards."

An Indian nobleman slowly burns to death on Hispaniola as his Spanish torturers feed the fire beneath him in this illustration from a 16th Century French edition of the eyewitness account by Friar Bartolomé de Las Casas. The conquerors kept the fire burning low, Las Casas explained, "so that little by little, as those captives screamed in despair and torment, their souls would leave them."

A chieftain named Hatuey burns at the stake in Cuba for attempting to flee from the Spaniards, as a Franciscan friar entreats him to convert to Christianity and thereby avoid eternal damnation. Las Casas reported that the courageous Hatuey replied that he would prefer to go to hell.

Conquistadors hurl Guatemalan rebels into pits filled with sharp-pointed sticks. The pits were originally dug and camouflaged by the Indians themselves to ambush Spaniards on horseback, but when the Spanish perceived the traps they turned the ruse against its perpetrators.

Dripping blood from the stumps of their severed hands, Hispaniolans flee their tormentors, who let them live as examples to other Indians. Sometimes, said Las Casas, the Spaniards hung the hands around the victims' necks, "saying, 'Go now, carry the message.' "

in neighboring El Salvador and by 1530 held sway over most of Central America between Panama and Mexico. As on the Antilles, agriculture flourished in the region but there was little gold or silver. In 1534 the impetuous Alvarado left in disgust and sailed down the Pacific Coast to Ecuador to join a rush that was already under way to loot a new-found civilization richer even than that of the Aztec—the golden Empire of the Inca.

But Alvarado acted too late to play a dominant role in this contest. A roughhewn old Spanish rogue named Francisco Pizarro was already there and firmly in control. Pizarro was the illegitimate and illiterate son of an impoverished soldier and as a child had tended pigs in Estremadura, a province on the border of Portugal. After a misspent youth, he became a soldier and eventually sailed for the West Indies and the Spanish Main. Pizarro was nearly 40 years old by the time he reached Panama, and he was in Balboa's company when the explorer first sighted the Pacific Ocean. With a few Indian slaves to do his bidding, Pizarro settled in Panama and might have ended his days developing a small plantation. But Panama was rife with rumors of incredible treasures somewhere to the south in the Andean mountain chain, and Pizarro was restless for glory.

With the help of a friendly priest, who persuaded some rich settlers to back Pizarro's ventures, the old soldier made two voyages south along the coast to Ecuador. These trips produced so little that Pizarro came to be regarded in Panama as an aging lunatic. But he would not give up. In 1528 he sailed for Spain to seek fresh funds and royal support from King Carlos. Pizarro caught the young monarch in an enthusiastic frame of mind. For six years the conquest of Mexico had poured forth phenomenal loot. It was said at court that Carlos actually danced an uncontrolled jig of joy each time royal agents informed him of the arrival of a new fleet of galleons. At the time of Pizarro's visit Cortés himself was back in Spain, bringing more treasure. The King was ready to encourage any project that might yield yet another extraordinary trove of heathen gold.

The monarch declared Pizarro lifelong Governor, captain general and royal advance agent for Peru, and sent him on his way to immortality. Back in Panama in 1530, Pizarro used the royal blessing to recruit and equip 180 men, and sailed with his tiny force down the Gulf of Panama and into the Bay of San Mateo on the coast of Ecuador. Marching quickly inland, he raided a startled Inca town, looted it of gold, silver and emeralds, and sent some of his men back to Panama with the booty so his agents could inspire more volunteers.

Meanwhile Pizarro's band hacked its way through jungle to the Gulf of Guayaquil and into northern Peru's sun-baked desert, until they reached the coastal town of Tumbes. Here Pizarro's troops, diminished by battles and illness, were reinforced by a fresh group of conquistadors led by Hernando de Soto, who had sailed south from Panama. Together they struck inland, on horseback and in full armor, into the barren Andes and the heart of the Inca Empire.

The drama about to unfold produced the second great hoard of riches from the Spanish Main, ultimately surpassing even that of Mexico. Unlike the relatively powerful Aztec, the Inca were fragmented and vulnerable. The last Emperor had divided his realm between his rightful son, Huascar, and his illegitimate son, Atahuallpa, causing civil war on the eve of the Spanish invasion. Atahuallpa was victorious, and imprisoned Huascar, but the struggle had left the Inca in a weakened condition at a crucial moment.

Pizarro's and de Soto's combined force of 168 men, armed with a number of cannon, made their grueling way across the coastal desert and up the bare mountain range to an altitude of three miles, where men and horses gasped for breath. Pizarro knew they were being watched; the men kept on their armor and struggled through the mountains for 55 days, until they reached the Incan city of Cajamarca. The place was virtually deserted. At the approach of this strange band of men and beasts, most of the inhabitants had fled to a nearby camp where Atahuallpa was guarded by 30,000 warriors. From a few villagers who had remained behind, Pizarro learned of the mighty force that awaited him and of the puzzlement and apprehension that the Indians felt. The Inca could easily have fallen upon the exhausted Spaniards and wiped them out. But they hesitated, not knowing the strangers' intentions, and remained frozen in place around their Emperor.

Pizarro sent de Soto and 35 horsemen to invite Atahuallpa to a meeting in the empty town. The Indian monarch agreed to a meeting and the next day was carried on a gilded litter into the city with an escort of 5,000 unarmed warriors and nobles. Pizarro's tiny force was hidden in strategic positions around the central square. Only a Dominican friar appeared before the Emperor to read a proclamation, which was clumsily translated by an Indian interpreter, demanding that the Inca Empire submit to the King of Spain. The priest then tried to put a prayer book in the Emperor's hands, but Atahuallpa contemptuously threw it to the ground. As if by that signal, the Spaniards suddenly opened fire, their horsemen charging and cannon booming. Thousands of Inca warriors were slain and Atahuallpa was captured.

But Pizarro's treachery was not ended. The Inca ruler offered to buy his freedom by filling with gold the room where he was imprisoned and filling a similar room with silver. The Spaniards readily agreed. After the rooms were filled, Pizarro's men melted down the priceless Inca statues, jewelry, plaques, vessels, plates, goblets, fountains and replicas of plants and animals into more manageable ingots. The gold came to a weight of 13,000 pounds, and the silver totaled 25,000 pounds. Then Pizarro condemned Atahuallpa to death. The Inca was told that he would be burned as a heretic if he did not convert to Christianity; if he did he would merely be strangled. Atahuallpa accepted baptism and was immediately throttled.

Pizarro and his men were now rich beyond belief. The royal fifth was dispatched to King Carlos without delay, and soon there came a torrent of conquistadors and settlers down the coast from Panama. Like the Arawak, Carib, Aztec and other indigenous American peoples, so were the Inca systematically slaughtered and enslaved throughout Ecuador, Peru and then Chile. Meanwhile other Spaniards discovered and overwhelmed the Chibcha Indians of Colombia—also rich in gold and in the most precious of all stones, the magnificent green emerald. On the Co-

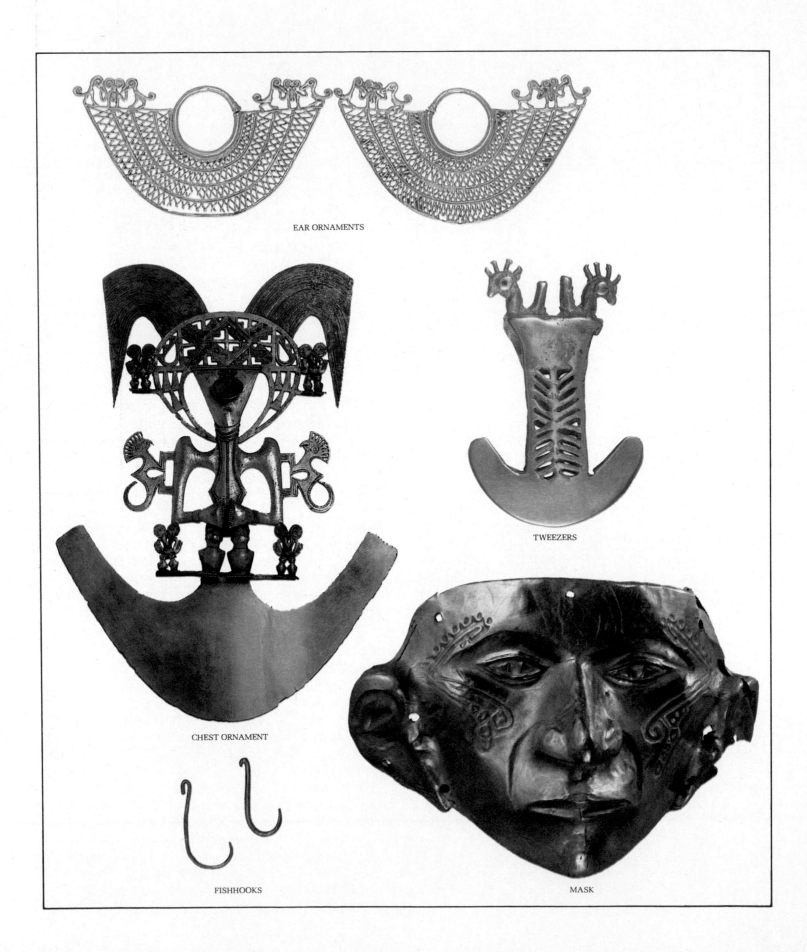

EAR ORNAMENTS

TWEEZERS

CHEST ORNAMENT

FISHHOOKS

MASK

Goldsmiths of the New World Indian civilizations fashioned a dazzling array of finely crafted objects, such as these artifacts from Colombia. The fishhooks were most likely ceremonial, but the tweezers were probably made for the everyday use of a wealthy tribal chief.

lombian coast the port of Cartagena was founded, and the loot from the Inca and the Chibcha poured down out of the Andes into the harbor at Cartagena or along mule tracks through the Darien jungles to Panama.

Now came the task of transporting all this great treasure back to the countinghouses of Seville, and in many ways that was more difficult than capturing it in the first place. In the early days of the Spanish Main, the seaborne traffic between the mother country and her newfound empire was haphazard at best. Individual ships or small fleets set sail when they pleased and on whatever course struck their captains' fancy.

But these were strange and dangerous waters for the Spanish captains. The Caribbean was an easy sea to enter but a difficult one to leave. The islands of the Greater and Lesser Antilles guarded the northern and eastern flanks of the Caribbean basin, and the northeasterly trade winds blew, month in and month out, at a steady 15 to 25 knots, varying no more than a compass point in direction. A vessel coming from Europe could easily speed through the passages between the islands, but for an eastward-bound vessel seeking to travel against the trades it was another matter entirely.

The ocean currents abetted the winds. Atlantic water pushed over the coral and volcanic sill of the Antilles shelf and moved westward at a steady two or three knots until it reached the coast of Central America. Then it turned northward to drive through the channel between Cuba and the Yucatan Peninsula into the Gulf of Mexico. There, warmed by the tropical sun and swelled with runoff from the great basin between the Rocky Mountains and the Appalachians, the currents swept along the Cuban coast and squeezed through the 90-mile strait between Cuba and Florida, powering the great Gulf Stream along the North American coast back toward Europe. So powerful was this current that it sometimes reached a velocity of five knots.

Eventually, experienced captains learned how to take advantage of these conditions. But in the early years all this had to be discovered by trial and catastrophe. Spanish seafarers found themselves trapped by hurricanes in narrow cuts, tossed upon uncharted reefs and hurled on vast sandbars from which there was no escape. These and other perils took a frightful toll.

Not the least of these dangers were the ever-present privateers and pirates; the approaches to Europe fairly swarmed with them. The English, the Dutch, and above all the French, since France and Spain were incessantly at war, took a cut at Spanish shipping. In 1533 a French privateer operating in the Atlantic captured a Spanish prize that was foolishly sailing alone and was so richly laden that even the French cabin boys received shares amounting to 800 gold ducats apiece. And the greater the traffic became, the more marauders arrived to feed on it. Most of the attacks took place off the approaches to Europe, where any man with a ship full of bravos could assault a hapless merchantman caught alone after a storm, or race in and cut a fat galleon out of an unescorted flotilla. Some of the raiders made the journey south down to the Canary Islands to prey on outbound Spanish vessels with their cargoes of wine and manufactured goods.

Because hundreds of ships never reached their destinations, the Spanish eventually decided to impose some order on the traffic with the New World. Beginning in 1543, they dispatched two major fleets to the Main each year. One sailed in April or May destined for Veracruz, terminus of the treasure trail leading down from the Mexican highlands. It was accompanied by ships bound for ports in the Greater Antilles and along the coast of Central America. There were often as many as 30 vessels in this flotilla. Outward-bound, they carried consignments of Old World products—wine, olive oil and manufactured goods such as glass, books, paper, clothing and utensils—to Spanish settlers in the New World. Warships were stationed at the fringes of the fleet to discourage attacks by pirates and privateers.

A second fleet usually left Seville in August, timed to reach the Caribbean in late autumn after the hurricane season. This fleet, consisting of assorted merchantmen guarded by some half a dozen warships, was headed for Panama and the coast of South America. A few of its ships went directly to Cartagena, at the northern extremity of the southern continent. But the bulk of the autumn fleet first put in at Nombre de Dios, the primary treasure port on the Caribbean coast of the Isthmus of Panama. This was where the great treasures from Peru arrived after an overland journey from the Pacific, across the narrow neck of Panama to the waiting galleons (pages 42-51). After loading its precious cargo, the fleet set sail eastward, beating into the wind 300 miles to the better-protected port of Cartagena for a respite and refurbishing in December. Then in January the fleet made sail from Cartagena and, with the trade winds to starboard, sailed northwestward along the Central American coast past Jamaica and the tip of the Yucatan, around Cape San Antonio at the western end of Cuba, and along the Cuban coast to Havana.

Meanwhile the Mexican fleet waited in Veracruz or in nearby San Juan de Ulúa until February, and then sailed full-bellied with gold, silver and other valuable products of Spanish Mexico. Heading stubbornly into the trade winds, tacking endlessly back and forth, the fleet made its arduous way to Havana, and there the two bearers of Spanish wealth rendezvoused for the dangerous journey home.

The combined fleet could number as many as 100 vessels of every sort. The King's treasure was usually carried on board escorting warships, under heavy guard and official seals. The rest of the loot from the New World belonged to colonial aristocrats who had been given royal grants to exploit great plantations or to mine gold and silver. Much of this bullion remained in the New World, where it was hoarded in secrecy or lost to professional gamblers; but most made its way back to the Old World to pay investors and to support families left behind in Spain. These private treasure-troves were carried to Spain aboard merchant ships of every conceivable shape, size and quality—many with no means of self-protection whatever. They were often of doubtful seaworthiness after years in tropical waters, and their captains frequently were neither as trustworthy as they seemed nor as skilled on the reefbound passages of the Spanish Main as they claimed to be. And so the treasure shipments many times came to grief.

In late spring and early summer the assembled fleets departed and

Stealing ashore at dawn, French privateers fall upon the inhabitants of Cartagena and set ablaze the city's thatch-roofed dwellings during the sack of the rich coastal port in 1544. The invaders robbed the Spaniards of more than 150,000 ducats, a fantastic sum.

threaded their way through the narrow passage between Cuba and Florida, with the prevailing winds against them and coral reefs or shoals increasing as they approached the equally narrow channel between Florida and the Bahamas. But once the ungainly clutter of sail managed to beat its way into the trades around the tip of the Florida peninsula, it could turn north along the coast, taking the trades on its starboard beam and making good use of the added thrust of the Gulf Stream on every encrusted bottom. Reaching the latitude of Bermuda, the treasure fleet at last could turn eastward and ride the westerlies that prevail at that latitude across the Atlantic to Seville.

Such were the perils of passage that every year many vessels from each fleet failed to reach Spain. The shallow and treacherous Bahama waters were studded with the rotting ribs of Spanish ships that had run aground; sudden tropical squalls and Atlantic storms scattered the fleets and exacted a heavy penalty. And then, of course, there were the continuing attentions of the predators, who were still managing to take a goodly number of ships in spite of the convoys.

Some of the more daring of these sea rovers no longer waited for the treasure galleons to cross the Atlantic, but began raising sail to the northeasterly trades and running before the wind in a bold search for plunder on the Spanish Main itself. The work of the privateers operating in the Caribbean was made easy for a number of reasons. The Spaniards had organized their treasure fleets primarily to guard against predators prowling the eastern Atlantic, on the approaches to Spain. In their arrogance, the Spanish had great difficulty accepting the fact that their supremacy on the Spanish Main itself might be under challenge. Apart from the ships that guarded the treasure fleets, only an occasional warship was sent to patrol the Caribbean and the Gulf of Mexico. These were often clumsy, poorly armed and badly manned, and in any case they were too few and too scattered to police a body of water half again as big as the Mediterranean.

Thus many merchantmen sailed alone while on the Spanish Main. They were extremely vulnerable. According to royal regulations, every vessel employed in the New World trade was supposed to carry at least two large brass cannon, six iron guns and a certain number of smaller weapons. But owners or charterers were reluctant to burden a ship with so much ordnance; the tonnage of guns, cannon balls and powder casks would reduce the amount of treasure or cargo she could carry. Many a large vessel sailed for the New World armed with nothing but two rusty iron guns mounted on the port and starboard rails, a dozen or so shot in the bilge for ballast, and a keg of spoiled powder.

Spanish captains, moreover, were notorious, even in a cruel age, for maltreating their crews. And the seamen took their revenge when they could. One Spanish sailor, flogged unmercifully for some trivial offense in Cartagena, found his way back to Spain, crossed the Pyrenees to France and signed on with the French corsair Robert Baal. The Spaniard led Baal to a cove near Cartagena where they could anchor without being detected; then he guided the Frenchman overland to approach Cartagena's fortifications from the unguarded rear, after which the sailor reveled in the sight of the port in flames. ✦

The treasure galleon: war horse and beast of burden

The great Spanish treasure galleons that traversed the Atlantic in the 16th and 17th Centuries were among the most advanced oceangoing vessels of the age. If their mission was to succeed, they had to perform as men-of-war as well as heavy-duty transports, and they were designed with both of these functions in mind.

The most striking feature of the galleon was a hull that sloped sharply inward as it rose, tapering to a top deck that was considerably narrower than the ship's beam at the water line. This served to concentrate the enormous weight of her ordnance—as many as 60 bronze and iron guns—near the ship's center line, improving stability.

Nevertheless, with her high sides and towering sterncastle, the Spanish galleon was easily rocked and, because of the short length of her keel in proportion to her hull length, she also pitched heavily in stormy conditions. The galleon was an extremely uncomfortable ship at sea.

But she was eminently seaworthy. Her length-to-width ratio of 3½ to 1—125 feet to 35 feet in this reconstruction of a typical vessel—made her sleeker and therefore faster than the broader-beamed ships that preceded her. In addition, she incorporated a brilliant advance in the design of her bow. In traditional designs the fo'c's'le was a looming triangular superstructure almost as high as the poop, but on the galleon it was reduced to a relative-ly low square structure set back from the stem, where it was less apt to catch the wind and force the ship's bow to leeward. As a result, the galleon could sail as close as six points to the wind.

Aloft, two and three billowing banks of square sails rode on the foremast and mainmast. The mizzenmast and the sternmost mast, known as the bonaventure mast, had lateen sails, which enhanced the maneuverability of the ship, particularly into the wind.

So as not to imperil her precious cargo, the treasure galleon as a rule shunned any contact with other ships. If challenged, she would invariably run rather than fight. Large crescent-shaped blades fixed to her yardarms would slash the sails and rigging of an enemy that closed to within boarding distance. These blades were arranged so that they would easily disengage to allow the galleon to escape.

Should hand-to-hand combat prove to be unavoidable, archers stationed in two fighting tops above the main yards of the foremast and mainmast could shower the enemy's decks with arrows and iron bolts. Firearms were forbidden in the fighting tops, where a spark could easily set the ship's sails aflame.

All told, the galleon could carry nine sails, which in a fair following wind could push her 500-ton bulk forward at a respectable eight knots, though only half that speed was the norm when she was heavily laden on her return to Seville.

SPANISH TREASURE GALLEON, 1600

Spied from a passing vessel, a treasure galleon appeared to be all menacing guns, but viewed from within she betrayed her role as a cargo ship.

A sealed compartment on her orlop deck was packed with small chests of silver and gold. On the same deck and in the hold below were barrels of fresh water and provisions, stacks of exotic hardwood, casks of sugar, liquid amber and tobacco, and sacks of prized llama wool, all guarded by soldiers.

These fighting men and the ship's crew—nearly 200 of them—slept on the gun deck, sometimes swinging in hammocks, a mode of berthing they had borrowed from the New World Indians. The captain, sailing master and as many as 40 paying passengers occupied cabins in the sterncastle.

The helmsman stood aft on the gun deck and peered out through a wooden hood in the deck above. To steer the ship, he manipulated a device known as the whipstaff, an upright pole that was joined to the end of the tiller and pivoted in the deck floor—although, like any sailing vessel of her size, the galleon was held on her course as much by the set of her sails as by the position of her rudder.

To sustain the enormous force of the wind in her top-hamper, each of her masts was anchored into one of her main hull timbers. The mizzenmast and bonaventure mast were stepped to deck beams, and the foremast and the mainmast descended through each deck to mast steps on the keel. The bowsprit, lashed to the beakhead with heavy gammoning and mortised at its afterend into the riding bitts, had to be skewed slightly off the center line to get around the foremast.

Below the water line the galleon's planks were smeared with a viscous mix of tallow, sulfur, white lead and crushed glass intended to prevent toredo worms—wood-eating marine organisms—from destroying the hull.

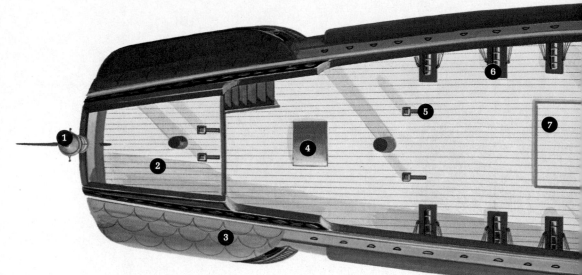

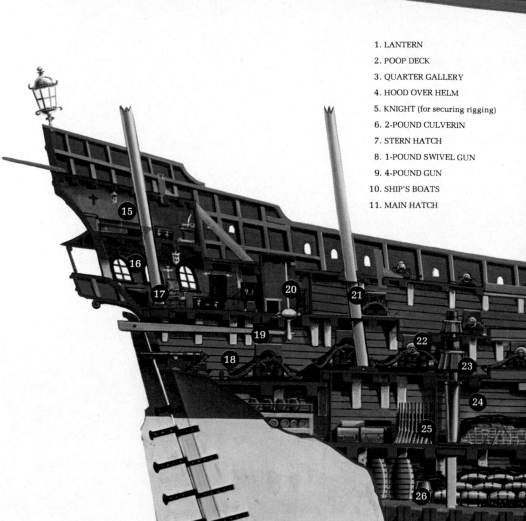

1. LANTERN
2. POOP DECK
3. QUARTER GALLERY
4. HOOD OVER HELM
5. KNIGHT (for securing rigging)
6. 2-POUND CULVERIN
7. STERN HATCH
8. 1-POUND SWIVEL GUN
9. 4-POUND GUN
10. SHIP'S BOATS
11. MAIN HATCH

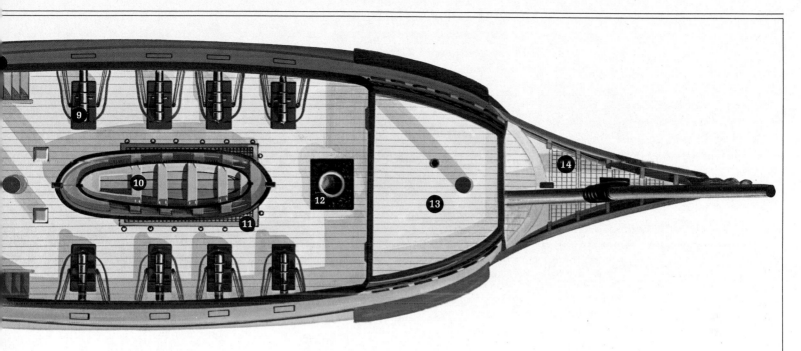

12. FIREBOX AND KETTLE
13. FORECASTLE DECK
14. BEAKHEAD
15. SAILING MASTER'S CABIN
16. GREAT CABIN (for captain)
17. BONAVENTURE MAST
18. GUN DECK
19. TILLER
20. WHIPSTAFF
21. MIZZENMAST
22. BRONZE 9-POUND GUN

23. CAPSTAN
24. TREASURE ROOM
25. SMALL ARMS
26. WATER CASKS
27. KEEL
28. MAINMAST STEP
29. HOLD
30. MAINMAST
31. HANGING KNEE
32. BILGE PUMP
33. ORLOP DECK

34. LOWER MAIN HATCH
35. ANCHOR CABLES
36. FRAME
37. DECK BEAM
38. LUMBER
39. RIDING BITTS
40. FOREMAST
41. HAWSEPIPE
42. STEM
43. GAMMON LASHING
44. BOWSPRIT

y the year 1553 the privateers were becoming so bold that they were a source of dread to every Spanish settlement in the Caribbean. The most feared of the corsairs at the time was François Le Clerc, a privateer with a wooden leg, who became known from one end of the Spanish Main to the other as Pie de Palo, or Pegleg. He led a squadron of 10 French warships to the Spanish Main and pillaged small port towns on the coast of Hispaniola and Puerto Rico; in 1554 he sacked Santiago de Cuba, relieving its inhabitants of 80,000 pesos' worth of booty. Worse was to occur two years later, when a Frenchman named Jacques de Sores destroyed the city of Havana, leaving the port so desolated that, when another French corsair squadron sailed into the harbor three months after the raid, nothing worth looting remained.

By then the Spaniards were thoroughly alarmed and at last decided on powerful action. The man chosen to command the treasure fleets in 1555 was Admiral Pedro Menéndez de Avilés, a Spaniard true to the age of conquest: bold, restless, energetic and brutal. Born to landed gentry in the Asturian city of Avilés, Menéndez ran away to sea at the age of 14. Sixteen years later, in 1549, after establishing a reputation as a fearless and clever fighting captain, he was commissioned by King Carlos to drive the French privateers away from the Spanish coast. This he did with great success, giving the King reason to hope that he might be able to improve matters on the Spanish Main.

For years the annual fleets had been escorted and supervised in careless fashion, with many ships straggling or wandering away from the convoy even in the most benign weather. Menéndez was ruthlessly impatient of lesser men, and he quickly moved to straighten out his command. Escorting warships were given strict orders to herd merchantmen into proper convoy, and Menéndez scalded the ears of overgreedy captains who attempted to sail without the required armaments. The admiral paid particular attention to the condition of the galleons. These were the largest and stoutest vessels in the fleet, serving both as convoy protectors and as treasure transports (pages 32-35). Properly sailed and manned, they were enough to intimidate any enemy who was not in command of an equivalent man-of-war. Menéndez was a stern disciplinarian and saw to it that his galleons not only were individually fit for combat but took position in clusters upwind of the merchantmen in order to have the weather gauge over any attackers.

Under Menéndez the convoy system began to work efficiently for the first time, and the number of ships in convoy lost to predators dropped to virtually none. His success earned Menéndez the confidence of both King Carlos and his son, Philip II, who assumed the throne of Spain in 1556 on his father's abdication.

Over the next half-dozen years Menéndez worked out a plan for the general defense of the Spanish Main. In 1562 he sailed from Spain as the commander of a vast Armada de la Carrera de Indias: 49 sail including six war galleons. During this voyage he visited the key harbors and existing forts, probably in the company of a team of Spanish architects, and settled on his final proposals for King Philip's approval. His plan was threefold: all passages to and from the Indies would be made in

Pedro Menéndez de Avilés, dispatched by Philip II to crush the French Huguenot settlement in Florida, led his mission with fierce religious fervor. He announced that he had "come hither to hang all Lutherans, according to my King's orders, which are so precise that I can pardon no one. If I find any Catholic, he shall be well treated, but every heretic shall die."

convoys of the quality he had evolved, except for urgent sailings of fast, well-armed ships with special licenses; formidable cruiser squadrons would be based permanently in the Caribbean to patrol the seas and hunt down corsairs; and certain selected harbors would be strongly fortified and heavily garrisoned with troops so as to preclude attack by enemies.

The harbors Menéndez chose were Cartagena, which guarded the Isthmus of Panama and sheltered a wintering treasure fleet; Santo Domingo, the administrative and cultural center of the Antilles; Santiago de Cuba, which guarded the Windward Passage between Hispaniola and Cuba; San Juan de Puerto Rico, because it was farthest to windward; and most vital of all, Havana, where the two annual fleets assembled for the homeward voyage. Both Cartagena and Havana would get major new forts. To complement Havana in the control of the Florida channel, Menéndez suggested that another base be built somewhere in Florida.

He chose for the moment not to fortify Veracruz, the major Mexican port. Because it was an open roadstead exposed to violent north winds prevalent in that area, ships put into Veracruz to load or unload but not to stay, and as soon as the vessels departed the population of the port quickly retired to the nearby mountain town of Jalapa, which had a more salubrious climate. Ships in need of haven on the Veracruz route made for San Juan de Ulúa, an island 15 miles down the coast that provided shelter against the northers. The harbor was protected by several batteries of cannon but did not boast an actual fort. This seems to have satisfied Menéndez, probably because both Veracruz and San Juan de Ulúa were so deep within his defenses that attacks there appeared unlikely.

As for Panama's great treasure port of Nombre de Dios, its minor fortifications appeared adequate for those brief periods when the treasure ships dropped anchor in the harbor. The escorting war galleons would protect the port from attack until the flotilla moved on to sanctuary in Cartagena. And in Nombre de Dios, as in Veracruz, the local population regarded the coast as unhealthy and withdrew to the interior between treasure loadings, leaving little to guard.

Menéndez was not the kind of man to carry out such an ambitious program without making enemies. Some of these foes were powerful, and they conspired to bring about his imprisonment in 1563 on charges of smuggling. Menéndez spent two years in prison pending trial. But the evidence was not good enough to stand up in formal court, and he was finally freed and allowed to resume his work. Fortifications were begun at each of the vital ports on the Spanish Main, with special emphasis on Cartagena and Havana.

Meanwhile Philip II was increasingly disturbed by the threat to the Spanish Main posed by French efforts to found settlements in North America. Forty years before, France had sponsored the voyage of the Italian explorer Giovanni Verrazzano up the North American coast to the mouth of the Hudson River, Narragansett Bay and the great islands at the mouth of the St. Lawrence River. Ever since the French under Francis I and later under Charles IX had been attempting to establish their own empire in the New World—imagining that rich Indian civilizations such as the Aztec and the Inca might well await plundering in the great forests of Canada. But all these efforts had so far come to nought, in part because the French were preoccupied by their incessant wars with Spain and by religious strife that pitted French Catholics against Protestant Huguenots. Indeed, it was the Huguenots who established the first viable French settlements in North America, and it was they who now appeared to threaten the dominions of Spain's King Philip II.

Seeking a place in the New World where they could practice their religion without oppression, the French Protestants planned to settle north of Spanish territory in Florida. In 1562 Admiral Gaspard de Coligny, the Huguenot leader, dispatched two ships of colonists under the command of a resourceful French captain named Jean Ribault. Captain Ribault put 25 colonists ashore on the South Carolina coast, saw to it that they built a sturdy log hut surrounded by a high parapet, and then sailed away, promising to return with more settlers. But the colonists found life in the New World much harsher than they had imagined; after a difficult winter they revolted, murdered their leader and put out to sea in a battered sloop, intending to return to France. They all surely would have perished had they not been rescued by a passing English vessel.

Meanwhile Admiral Coligny sent off a second group of 300 colonists, this one led by René de Laudonnière, a young aristocrat who had accompanied Ribault on his early voyages, and in 1564 they established Fort Caroline on the St. John's River in Florida. At the mouth of the river they built a stockade shaped like an arrowhead. But as their first year passed with no sign of support from home, the settlement was restive and desperately in need of supplies.

When word reached Spain that French heretics had settled in the midst of Spanish Florida, Philip II immediately ordered his redoubtable Admiral Menéndez to proceed at full speed with his long-planned establishment of a Spanish fort and colony in Florida.

Menéndez was directed to "explore and colonize Florida and, if there be settlers or corsairs of other nations, drive them out." Jean Ribault, who sailed from France in May 1565 with fresh supplies and settlers for the colony at Fort Caroline, received orders from Admiral Coligny that were equally explicit: "Do not let Menéndez encroach on you."

Menéndez set sail from Cadiz in June, just weeks after Ribault's departure. His force of 30 ships and 2,600 people—of whom 2,000 were soldiers or marines and the rest settlers and seamen—vastly outnumbered Ribault's seven ships and 300 fighting men. Determined to catch the French, Menéndez raised all possible sail, doing nothing to avoid a storm that lashed his fleet in mid-Atlantic. Some of the smaller vessels could not keep up and were scattered by the storm. The Spaniard did not wait for all of them to regroup at the intended rendezvous at Puerto Rico. He pressed on with only five ships and barely 600 men, taking a direct course through the shoals of the Bahamas. One night his flagship grounded three times, but a heavy quartering sea carried her clear.

Menéndez reached the mouth of the St. John's River on the morning of September 4, six days after Ribault had anchored beneath the guns of Fort Caroline. Outnumbered only slightly, but outgunned by the advantage of the fort, Menéndez withdrew and sailed quickly southward 50 miles along the palmettos, sandbars and shallow inlets of the coast to a lovely bay he had selected as the site for his Florida colony. It was, he

Admiral Gaspard de Coligny, who organized and helped finance two efforts to found a Huguenot settlement on the east coast of Florida, harbored few illusions about the caliber of his colonists: "There were no tillers of soil—only adventurous gentlemen, reckless soldiers, discontented tradesmen, all keen for novelty and heated by dreams of wealth."

A Florida Indian chieftain invites Huguenot leader René de Laudonnière in June 1564 to pay homage to a stone column erected to King Charles IX by an earlier Huguenot expedition. "These Indians were worshipping this stone as an idol," said one Frenchman. "There were offerings of fruits, and a bow and arrows, and it was wreathed with boughs of trees esteemed choicest."

Defended on two sides by ditches and sod walls and on the third by a high wooden barricade, Fort Caroline was established on the south bank of Florida's St. John's River by the Huguenots in 1564. But within 15 months the fort was taken in an overland surprise attack by the jealous Spaniards, who slaughtered most of the compound's inhabitants.

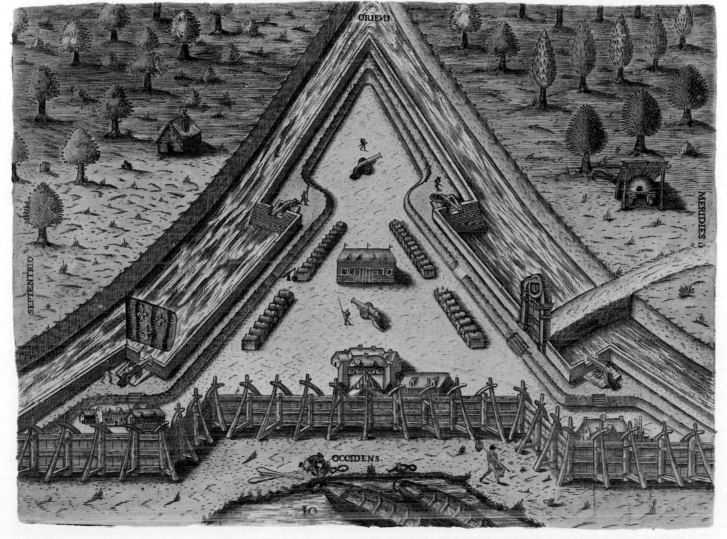

said, "a good harbor with a good beach." Since his ships had first sighted Florida on August 18, the feast day of St. Augustine, Menéndez named his new settlement after the saint. But this tranquil haven was soon to provide Menéndez with the most perilous moment of his career.

Only three of the Spanish ships were small enough to enter the bay; Menéndez' flagship and another galleon were so large and heavily laden with armament and supplies that they were unable to negotiate a sandbar at the harbor's entrance. Menéndez had them unloaded and sent them off to Havana with skeleton crews to bring back reinforcements and the rest of his original storm-scattered fleet. He waited aboard his flagship until the two big galleons were ready to sail and then bode their crews farewell and climbed down into his longboat to proceed ashore. In order to pack this last ship's boat as full as possible, Menéndez had ordered the boat's oars left aboard the flagship, assuming that the brisk onshore breeze would enable him to sail smartly into the harbor. But the breeze suddenly vanished as the tide began running out, and Menéndez found himself with a few crewmen and officers and a heavy load of stores becalmed outside the sandbar.

The Spaniards spent a miserable night of it, sleeping restlessly on the piles of cargo, rocking in the offshore swells. And with the light of dawn, they faced disaster. Two French warships stood forth clearly on the northeast horizon.

Captain Ribault had followed after Menéndez, taking with him 200 fighting men. Fort Caroline was left with only a small force, but Ribault could not resist the chance to teach the Spaniards a crushing lesson.

Like Menéndez, Ribault had been becalmed at nightfall, but he was far enough out to sea to pick up the morning winds before they stirred close inshore, and now he was bearing down on the greatest admiral of the Spanish Main. He spied the boats with their Spanish occupants at the entrance to the harbor. Soon, if the wind remained in his favor, he would be in position to capture them. But at the last moment the water rippled and the breeze from the east reached Menéndez' longboat. The sail filled, and she gathered way and surged over the bar into the harbor, followed by the other Spanish vessel. Backing his sails furiously to avoid the green water above the bar, Ribault turned and headed south, frustrated.

The last Menéndez saw of the French ships was their topsails as they disappeared over the horizon. That night a norther struck and it was Menéndez' turn to seize the initiative. Calculating that the wind direction would keep Ribault far to the south, unable to beat his way easily back up the Florida coast, Menéndez set out overland on foot to attack Fort Caroline with 500 men. For four days they slogged north, pushing through swamps and crossing inlet after inlet. The stinging, biting, burrowing insects were maddening, and the men cursed the heat and the tropical squalls that deluged them. But at last, after 50 harrowing miles, the Spaniards reached Fort Caroline, to find it—as Menéndez had guessed—comparatively defenseless.

The Spaniards made short work of the assault. Some 52 Frenchmen escaped to the interior, where they probably died, but Menéndez killed 200 others, sparing only the women and children. Then, leaving most of his force to hold the fort against the expected return of Ribault, he took

his 35 best men and marched three days through clearing weather back to St. Augustine. There he learned from local Indians that the storm had served him in an unexpected way. Because their sails had not been reefed properly before the storm's fury struck, the Huguenot ships had been driven ashore and their crews and soldiers were at that moment struggling back up the coast in sad disarray.

Menéndez hurried south on foot to meet them. He and his men found the first contingent of Frenchmen at the south end of Anastasia Island, and confronted them across a deep inlet. The castaways numbered nearly 200, but they were starving and suffering from exposure. Captain Ribault was not among them, and even if he had been the outcome would likely have been the same. When they realized that Fort Caroline had been captured, the Frenchmen felt they had no recourse but to surrender. The Spanish admiral promised them nothing more than to deal with them "as God directs me."

Ten at a time the Frenchmen were ferried across the inlet in a dugout. Ten at a time they were fed and their hands bound behind their backs. When they were all across the inlet, fed and bound, Menéndez gave the order to execute them.

Thirteen days later Menéndez intercepted a second party of French castaways, this time including Captain Ribault, at the same inlet—and with the same outcome. The beach where the French Protestants died was forever more known as Matanzas, the Place of Slaughter. On a marker among the live oaks festooned with Spanish moss, Menéndez left an inscription: "I do this not to Frenchmen but to heretics."

Thus was the French menace to the Spanish Main settled by Admiral Menéndez—at least for the moment. But now there were other challengers for the spoils of the Main. This became clear in a report made to King Philip II in October 1566 describing a meeting in London between the Spanish Ambassador and Sir William Cecil, Chief Counselor to England's Queen Elizabeth.

Before Elizabeth's accession something of a pact had existed between England and Spain. The two ardently Catholic monarchs, Philip II of Spain and England's Queen Mary, had even married each other for reasons of state (page 59). But Elizabeth had no such ties to Catholicism; one of her first acts upon assuming the throne in 1558 had been to declare England a Protestant state, and repressions against Catholics had grown in severity over the decade. Though Elizabeth for years danced a diplomatic minuet with Philip II to avoid an open break, England increasingly emerged as Spain's rival for supremacy in Europe.

Small wonder, then, that Elizabeth's advisers, among them Sir William Cecil, sought slyly to sound out the Spanish throne on the matter of the Main for the benefit of the Queen's council.

"Secretary Cecil," wrote the Spanish Ambassador from London to Madrid, "sent to ask me to furnish them with a memorandum of the places where it is forbidden to trade without Your Majesty's license. I sent it to him, saying that the places were all the West Indies, continent and islands." The Spanish Ambassador then added a note of foreboding: "He sent to say that the council do not agree."

With huge casks of gunpowder stored in the central magazine and harquebuses and heavy cannon bristling from all sides, the Spanish fort at St. Augustine appears in this 16th Century watercolor to be impregnable against interlopers. Established in 1565, St. Augustine served as a base from which to drive the French from Florida and later as a reprovisioning stop for treasure fleets.

Carrying the King's wealth to the coffers of Seville

For 11 months a year the squalid little Panamanian port of Nombre de Dios lay asleep in the tropical heat. But each December a cloud of sails on the horizon heralded the arrival of the great treasure fleet to transport the riches of the New World back to Seville. And suddenly Nombre de Dios was the most important city on the Spanish Main, alive with traders and colonists, gamblers and whores, soldiers and officials, all drawn there by the glittering cargo.

The treasure was brought in by mule train after a passage of many weeks from the mines of Peru. "The spectator would remain thunderstruck at the streets crammed with chests of gold and silver," wrote one awed Spaniard. The gold was in small bars weighing a few pounds, while the silver was cast in both small bars and 70-pound loaves. Royal silvermasters carefully examined the king's portion to make sure nothing had been pilfered, and private owners hovered no less anxiously over their fortunes, weighing, repacking and marking their fabulous bundles.

It took up to six weeks for the galleons to off-load their Old World goods and take on board the treasure coming across the jungled hills. Always pestilential in the sweltering heat, Nombre de Dios suffered fierce epidemics while jam packed for the treasure loading and the accompanying fiestas. "When the fleet is here," wrote a traveling English prelate named Thomas Gage, "it is an open grave." So the treasure galleons sailed as soon as the holds were filled.

The journey, first to Cuba to join with other galleons and thence across the Atlantic, often took three months or more. The passengers and crews relieved the tedium by fishing for dolphins or celebrating saints' days, feasting on turtle and suckling pig, and firing cannon. "The cannon ceased not from sounding, nor the Spaniards from singing all night," wrote Gage of a voyage in 1625.

Meanwhile in Seville anxiety mounted whenever the fleet was overdue. In 1667 the Venetian Ambassador reported that Genoese bankers had warned King Philip: "Unless the fleet arrived soon, they would be unable to negotiate more loans for him; Philip fell into such a state of shock that he had to be confined to bed." The King drained his purse to pay for masses throughout his realm—and at last the ships appeared. "There is great rejoicing," wrote the Ambassador, "not only in the royal court but all over the land."

After a trek across the Isthmus, a well-guarded mule train loaded with silver pauses on a jungled ridge before descending to Nombre de Dios on Panama's Caribbean coast. Each of the mules is burdened with as much as 300 pounds of bullion. At right, the chief muleteer looks for stragglers. Half-naked slaves drive the surly and exhausted beasts as the Spanish muleteers tighten packs for the last weary miles into port, where the annual flotilla of treasure galleons is waiting impatiently at anchor.

In a ruffled collar as befits his high station, the royal silvermaster (above, right) hefts a cake of silver as a clerk records the contents of each case of silver ingots after the journey from the mines. When the cases are tallied and repacked, an assistant and his apprentice affix seals that must not be broken before the hoard reaches Seville. One copy of the tally was shipped with the bullion, two others went on sister ships, and a fourth was held by officials in the New World.

Port workers carry out the treasure in small but sturdy lighters to the deep-draft galleons anchored in the harbor at Nombre de Dios. There, crewmen haul on blocks and tackle to hoist the heavy cases of silver aboard. At the stern of one galleon (right foreground) four men struggle to heave bales of indigo, cochineal and other valuable goods through an afterport. Meanwhile vendors (left foreground) have put out from shore in bumboats with juicy guavas, papayas, bananas and other tropical fruits, which they will peddle both to the ships' crews and to the port workers as they labor in the stifling heat.

Straining a hemp loading net, cases of silver descend through openings in two decks into the dark treasure hold of a galleon. An armed guard (lower right) keeps watch from the main deck while a boatswain's mate in the hold stands ready to whip laggard workers. The bullion later was fastened down with heavy canvas covers and crisscrossed ropes to keep it from shifting in a storm.

Climbing out of the hold to the gun deck, the boatswain, streaming sweat from his exertions, passes his royal register to the captain and the silvermaster as a signal that the king's portion has been loaded. Crewmen wait for him to leave the stacked bullion before nailing down massive planks over the hatch, and a ship's boy (rear) stands watch near the hold with water buckets in case of fire.

The portly galleon captain shows off a huge emerald from his private chest of New World treasure to the silvermaster, who is holding a solid gold chain. Officers of the treasure fleet acquired personal hoards through private trading on the Main. Another one of the captain's prizes, a scarlet macaw from the Panamanian jungles, struts on his perch while two gunners clear the tackle on the stern chaser. If the gun was used, it would be fired from a port in the captain's cabin.

48

Off Havana, where a convoy is forming for the journey home, passengers crowd the poop deck to welcome a boatload of visitors from another vessel nearby. Amidships, a cook's helper (center foreground) shoulders a roast suckling pig on its way to the officers' mess table, where the guests will dine. In the shelter of the ship's boats are a caged howler monkey (center) and two caged puma cubs, one of which is pawing at a soldier's sword (left). Along the port rail, gun crews go through practice drills for the dangerous passage ahead, while one man straddles a cannon (right foreground) to ream out the touchhole.

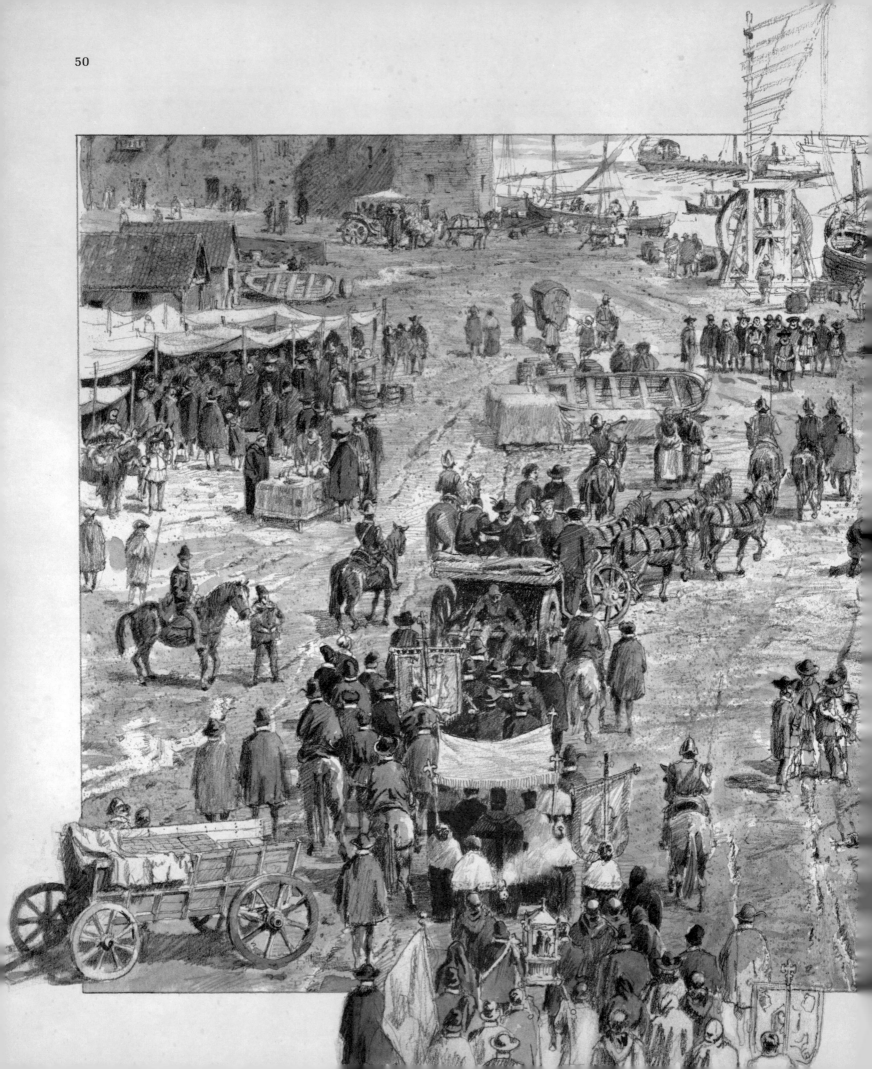

Safe at last in Seville's Guadalquivir River after weeks at sea, the treasure fleet and its assembled captains are welcomed by a procession of government and religious dignitaries. The great galleons have been forced to anchor in deep water downriver and have loaded their cargoes onto smaller craft, which now crowd the quay, while more arrive every minute. Some heavy crates are unloaded by a treadmill-powered derrick (top center), and stevedores carry smaller items. In the fiesta atmosphere, vendors in dockside stalls are doing a fine business selling wine and dishes of meat, fish and saffron rice.

RICHARD SCHLECHT

Chapter 2

The merchant who enflamed Spain's New World

hen England's Sir William Cecil asked the Spanish Ambassador to supply Queen Elizabeth's council with a list of those places where Englishmen might trade freely on the Spanish Main in 1566, he was not actually making a request at all. His query was more in the nature of a demand; indeed, as the Ambassador undoubtedly understood, Sir William was making a declaration of national intent—and giving the Spanish crown fair warning.

For decades the English, no less than the French, had been envious of the Spanish and casting covetous eyes on the wealth of her New World empire. English freebooters were assuredly among the buccaneers of many nationalities who bedeviled the Spaniards in the early years of the 16th Century. Plunder on the Main would continue to be a choice attraction throughout the 17th Century. But for a maritime nation trade was essential, and England was determined to have her full share of commerce across the Atlantic.

A royal official by the name of Richard Eden had already stated as much long before Lord Cecil's confrontation with the Spanish Ambassador. In 1553 Eden had published a slim volume, entitled *A Treatise of the New India*, that enjoyed a wide audience among London merchants. In his book Eden had described in glowing terms the abundance of the new Spanish domain in the Caribbean, and had challenged the Spaniards' claim "to be Lordes of halfe the world." The English, continued Eden, had every right "to make attempts in the New World to the glory of God and the commodity of our country." If only his countrymen had been alive to the opportunities before the Spaniards tightened their hold, he concluded, "that Rich Treasury in Seville might long since have been in the Tower of London."

The English had already had a taste of trade in the New World that awakened them to its remarkable potential for profit. In 1530 William Hawkins, an enterprising captain sailing from Plymouth, had ventured across the Atlantic to the coast of Brazil. There he took on a cargo of dyewood, which was much prized by wool merchants, and brought it back to England, where it was sold at enormous profit. However, other Englishmen did not quickly follow his lead. King Carlos I of Spain had explicitly forbidden English seafarers to trade in the Caribbean, and he had warned that the Spanish warships and soldiers would not hesitate to enforce his decision—a policy that would be continued by his successor on the Spanish throne, Philip II. It remained for Hawkins' son John to follow in his father's footsteps, and take the next bold strides into the New World.

In all, the younger Hawkins would make three voyages to the Spanish Main between the years 1562 and 1569. He would begin his career as a trader with entirely peaceful intentions, having no thought for anything except fair exchange and fair profit. However, through one circumstance or another, he would find that he was adopting increasingly aggressive tactics, until ultimately his relations with the Spaniards in the New World exploded into open conflict. Indeed, the history of his conduct during his six years of commerce in the Caribbean might be termed the evolution of a freebooter.

John Hawkins, an English merchant and slave trader, set himself to test the Spanish monopoly on the Main and twice brought home glory and profits. Among his prominent backers was Queen Elizabeth, who, though nominally at peace with Spain, was not averse to a profit exceeding 50 per cent on a private investment of little more than £2,000.

The Ihesus of Lubeke tunnes vijc

Gond
Marr
Gonni

John Hawkins was scarcely 21 when his father died, leaving the family shipping business to John and another son. Little is known of his early years in Plymouth. While growing up, of course, he had been surrounded by sailors and merchants and had heard tales told by his father and older brother, William, of the Guinea coast, the Canaries and Brazil. In the years following his father's death he probably sailed as a privateer against the French in the English Channel and no doubt began to develop the toughness, shrewdness and ambition that were to characterize his career as a trader-mariner. At about this time he also made several voyages to the Spanish-owned Canary Islands, a way station for galleons going to the Caribbean. There he heard all the breathless stories about the Spanish Main's abundance of gold and silver, and met Spanish merchants who handled a thriving trade in the New World's more mundane but nevertheless valuable products: tobacco, sugar, hides and cacao.

Hawkins' merchant acquaintances convinced him that handsome profits could be made on a trading voyage to the Spanish Main. The biggest ports would probably be closed to him. But in smaller, less carefully controlled settlements, they said, plantation owners were willing to pay well in silver, pearls and cattlehides for European manufactured goods, the sale of which was monopolized, at artificially high prices, by the Spanish government's Casa de Contratación in Seville.

Ponderous castles fore and aft, designed to repel boarders, tower over the deck of John Hawkins' flagship, the Jesus of Lubeck, in this 16th Century watercolor. The cumbersome but capacious vessel belonging to Queen Elizabeth was already 20 years old in 1564 and was about to be scrapped when she was refurbished and loaned to Hawkins for his slave-trading ventures.

The item that was in greatest demand in the Spanish colonies, however, was neither European nor manufactured but was easily obtainable: African slaves, upon whose labor the plantations were by now almost entirely dependent. Only Spanish merchants and a few favored Portuguese traders were licensed to engage in slaving, yet because of Casa strictures, including a special head tax of 30 ducats for each slave sold, they had not found the trade profitable and were neglecting their monopoly. As a result, unlicensed Portuguese traders were smuggling and selling thousands of slaves each year, while local Spanish officials—most of them planters themselves—looked the other way.

The opportunities were too great for a man like Hawkins to resist, and in 1562 he made his first move into the Main. With his father-in-law, Benjamin Gonson, he organized a slave-trading expedition. He sailed for the Guinea coast, with three small ships, and there he managed to obtain about 300 slaves, as he later related, "partly by the sword and partly by other means." The voyage across the Atlantic was without incident, and Hawkins had no trouble selling his human cargo to plantation owners on the island of Hispaniola. So eager were the Hispaniolans to buy slaves that one local official charged with combating smugglers actually granted Hawkins a license to conduct business in his bailiwick.

The Englishman returned home in September 1564, convinced that the Main offered no end of promise. He had scarcely finished counting up his handsome profits when he began to plan a second voyage to the Caribbean. The news of his first success made the formation of an investors' syndicate an easy matter. Merchants and middle-class speculators were joined by a number of high-ranking noblemen, including the Earls of Leicester and Pembroke, and Lord Clinton, the Lord Admiral of the Queen's Navy. In addition to these contributors, a number of venturesome but impecunious young gentlemen signed on in exchange for a share of the profits. And there was yet another participant. A new Queen, the Protestant Elizabeth, had ascended the throne in 1558, and she viewed Hawkins' enterprise as a way of tweaking the papist Spaniards while making herself some money. After interviewing Hawkins, she offered to lend the syndicate a royal ship.

Hawkins immediately accepted—he could do no other—and then may have wondered what he was letting himself in for. The vessel Elizabeth chose, the *Jesus of Lubeck*, was a massive 700-ton, heavily armed ship with a towering poop and forecastle. But she was slow, elderly—Elizabeth's father, Henry VIII, had bought the vessel from the German Hanseatic League in 1545—and in great need of repair. Nevertheless, she was one of England's largest ships, and would make a formidable flagship for Hawkins' fleet once she was put in shape.

While the *Jesus* was being refurbished in the royal dockyards in the Medway River near London, Hawkins fitted out and victualed three additional ships down the coast at Plymouth. One of them was the *Salomon*, his vessel on his first voyage. The other two were the *Swallow* and the *Tiger*, small Hawkins family ships of 30 and 50 tons. The ships were stockpiled with provisions (mostly beans) for 500 slaves, and trinkets, woolen cloth and linens. A crew of 150 men was signed on to work the four ships, and on October 18, 1564, the tiny squadron cleared Ports

Following Hawkins' second slaving voyage, Queen Elizabeth awarded him this coat of arms in gratitude for the profits she realized. The grant specified, "for a crest, a demi-Moor proper bound in a cord," obviously denoting Hawkins' occupation. The three bezants at the top of the shield, resembling coins, connect the bearer to wealth, while the "point wavy" at the base of the shield identifies him with maritime pursuits

mouth Harbor bound for the Guinea coast. Hawkins' shipboard regulations were short and to the point. Let every man, he told the sailors, "serve God daily, love one another, preserve your victuals, beware of fire, and keep good company."

Almost exactly a year was to pass before Hawkins saw home again. And in that time he would learn a great deal more about the geography of the Spanish Main and the ambivalent nature of the Spanish settlers there, who, though they were anxious to trade with foreigners, feared the wrath of the authorities in Seville.

For several months the English ships cruised along the hot and humid coast of Guinea, bartering for slaves with Portuguese traders and African chieftains. At times the crew went on slave raids themselves. During one attack Hawkins and his men were ambushed by 200 Africans and barely escaped to their ships, leaving behind seven dead comrades. Yet by one means or another Hawkins had secured more than 400 slaves by January 29, 1565, and he stood out to sea, anxious to get on with his business.

As they set sail for the Americas, Hawkins and his fleet were plagued by periods of flat calm—including one worrisome stretch of 18 days during which water supplies had to be rationed and the men's spirits fell while their tempers rose. Eventually the ships entered the belt of the easterly trades—known to 16th Century seamen as the "ordinary breezes"—and, with the wind on their quarters, scudded across the Atlantic to the Caribbean. Still, it was March before Hawkins dropped anchor at the island of Margarita, off the coast of Venezuela, where the Spanish maintained a pearl fishery.

At first it all seemed like a repeat of his cordial welcome by the Hispaniolans. The mayor of the island's small town was effusive in his greetings. According to a journal kept by John Sparke, one of the gentlemen-adventurers aboard the *Jesus*, the Spaniard "had both beeves and sheepe given us, for the refreshing of our men." But when the island's Governor was informed of Hawkins' desire for trade he proved a testy, officious and definitely uncooperative fellow. He absolutely refused to sanction the sale of Hawkins' slaves, citing King Philip's royal injunction against dealing with foreigners. Further, to make any trading as difficult as possible for the Englishmen, he denied them the services of a local pilot they had hired. Neither Hawkins nor any member of his crew had ever seen this coast, and navigating without benefit of expert help would cost them precious time and trade. Finally, as soon as Hawkins had departed, the Governor made haste to inform the authorities at Santo Domingo, capital of Spanish America, that an Englishman was attempting to trade on the Main. The response was an edict forbidding all Spaniards to have any truck with the impudent interloper.

Hawkins sailed south to the mainland of South America, where he and his men traded a few pewter whistles, knives, glasses and other trinkets to friendly Indians for New World foods. Tasting sweet potatoes for the first time, young Sparke declared them to be "the most delicate roots that may be eaten, and do far exceed our parsnips or carrots." The pineapple looked like a pine cone, he related, but "of the bigness of two fists, and more delicious than any sweet apple sugared." The Indians were prob-

*In a harbor among Spanish ships,
Indian pearl divers work the Venezuelan
oyster beds in this late-16th Century
engraving by the Belgian artist Theodore
de Bry. The Indians were willing to
trade pearls for mere trinkets (as they are
doing on the island at upper right),
but not the Spanish Governor: he refused
to part with a single pearl when
Hawkins came to the area to trade in 1565.*

ably Chibcha, remnants of the once-populous tribe that had spread
throughout the Caribbean before the white men came. And these survivors of Spanish slaughter, Sparke learned, were now assailing the hated
conquerors. They were excellent hunters, he wrote, and skilled with
bow and arrow. "The Spaniards for fear thereof arm themselves and their
horses with quilted canvas of two inches thick, and leave no place of
their body open to their enemies, saving their eyes, which they may not
hide, and yet oftentimes are they hit in that so small a scantling."

Hawkins had now been under way from Africa for two months. His
slaves, chained in the ship's holds under inhuman conditions, were
weakening and dying in considerable numbers. His supplies of beans
were getting low. Anxiously he pressed on west along South America's
northern coast until, on April 3, he came to the settlement of Borburata,

near present-day Caracas. There at last he found buyers for his slaves.

The Spaniards at first cited the various decrees forbidding them to traffic with foreigners, to which Hawkins responded that he was a peaceful and honest trader. English merchants freely called at Spanish Flanders, the Canaries and Spain itself, he argued. What difference was there between one part of the Spanish Empire and another? Finally the Spaniards allowed Hawkins to bring 30 slaves ashore. But then they haggled so vigorously over the price that Hawkins became angry. According to Sparke, Hawkins told the Spaniards in exasperation that "it was not only a license he sought, but profit, which he perceived was not there to be had, and therefore would seek further."

At this point the local Governor arrived and commenced an elaborate charade that only annoyed the impatient Hawkins more. First, to provide himself with an alibi for dealing with the Englishman, the Governor required Hawkins to petition that "he was come thither in a ship of the Queen's Majesty's of England, being bound to Guinea, and thither driven by wind and weather, so that being come thither, he had need of sundry necessaries for the reparation of the said navy, and also great need of money for the payment of his soldiers."

That accomplished, the Governor granted the Englishman a license to sell the slaves. But then greed got the better of the Spaniard, and he demanded a special seven and a half per cent excise tax, plus a 30-ducat customs fee on every slave sold. In a fury, Hawkins marched 100 of his men, armed with bows, arrows, harquebuses and pikes, into the town square and, by one Spaniard's account, threatened that he "would not leave a thing standing" unless the levies were dropped.

The Governor quickly backed down, and Hawkins sold 30 slaves. But force had settled the issue for Hawkins, and as his voyage continued he came to use force or threat of force as a standard tool of his trade. At the next large Spanish settlement, Rio de la Hacha, 350 miles west along the coast, the timid Spanish authorities again demanded that Hawkins engage in pretense. They suggested, according to later testimony at a Spanish court of inquiry, that Hawkins "threaten and feign to intend to burn the houses of the town in order that the residents might prove that they were forced to trade with him."

Hawkins acted out the charade. But then, just as at Borburata, complications developed. The Spaniards announced that they would pay half price for slaves. Hawkins, knowing that once again he was being tested, landed 100 men and some artillery; the Spanish rallied 180 soldiers to face the invasion. But one blast from Hawkins' cannon sent them diving for cover, and seconds later, before a man was injured on either side, they called for a truce. Soon trade began in earnest; the English remained in Rio de la Hacha for more than a fortnight, selling quantities of wine, flour, cloth, linens and clothing, as well as 300 slaves. In payment the English received gold, silver and pearls worth perhaps £6,600.

Hawkins had now disposed of all his cargo for a sum exceeding £10,000, and on May 31, 1565, the *Jesus of Lubeck* and her small squadron set a northerly course toward Hispaniola, and then sailed west, following the winds and currents until they could round Cuba and head east again, riding the Gulf Stream through the Straits of Florida.

Old World roots for New World rivalries

The fierce enmity that developed between Englishmen and Spaniards in the New World had more to it than greed for gold. The conflict was rooted in personalities and events 4,000 miles away, and was nourished by the terrible religious hatreds of the day.

The drama centered around England's Tudor King Henry VIII and his quarrelsome offspring (shown in the painting below). In 1533 Henry scandalized and infuriated Catholic Europe by divorcing Catherine of Aragon, daughter of King Ferdinand of Spain. Henry then added injury to insult by establishing in England a Protestant state independent of Rome.

There followed a quarter century of political and religious instability in England, while Europe looked on with fascination and increasing dismay. Henry's son, Edward VI, vigorously pushed the nation even further into Protestantism. But when he died in 1553, the throne passed to his half sister Mary, most Catholic daughter of the divorced Catherine and wife of Philip, heir to the Spanish crown. Together Mary and Philip supported a bitter and bloody resurgence of Catholicism in England that lasted until 1558, when the final contest of religions was played out.

On Mary's death that year, her half sister, Elizabeth, ascended the throne. Elizabeth was as firmly Protestant as Mary had been Catholic. Once and for all, Elizabeth rejected Catholicism as England's state religion, thereby earning the distrust and eventual hatred of Philip, now Spain's King. As relations worsened, Elizabeth encouraged such bold Englishmen as John Hawkins to embark on forbidden voyages to the Spanish Main—an act that eventually escalated into full-fledged assaults on Spain's overseas empire.

In this Protestant allegory of the Tudor succession, Henry VIII passes the kingship to his kneeling son, Edward VI. The Catholic Bloody Mary and her consort, Philip II of Spain, stand to the left, joined by the god of war. Waiting patiently on the right is Elizabeth, preparing to admit the goddesses of peace and plenty.

On his way home Hawkins stopped at the French Huguenot settlement of Fort Caroline, established the year before along the North American coast. Queen Elizabeth had supported the French attempt to establish a base in the New World, and had instructed Hawkins to check on how the settlers were faring. He found them in desperate condition, notwithstanding the natural abundance of the surrounding land. "The country was marvelously sweet and the ground doth yield victuals sufficient, if they would have taken pains to get the same," reported Sparke. "But they being soldiers, desired to live by the sweat of other men's brows." The "other men" Sparke mentioned were the Indians, who, after welcoming the French, had turned hostile when the Huguenots demanded more and more from them. They had practically laid siege to the fort, often ambushing colonists who ventured into the countryside.

By the time Hawkins arrived the Frenchmen were reduced to surviving on acorns, and only 40 of the original 300 settlers were in reasonably good health. René de Laudonnière, the French leader, told Hawkins that he planned to leave unless help came soon from home. Hawkins sold Laudonnière one of his empty ships, the *Tiger*, and all the provisions he could spare. Then Hawkins sailed for home, fully expecting the French to follow. The date was July 28, 1565. It was only a month later that Jean Ribault arrived at Fort Caroline with the long-awaited reinforcements, and in his wake came the merciless Pedro Menéndez de Avilés, the Spanish admiral who slaughtered Ribault's men and most of Fort Caroline's male settlers in "God's service" (pages 38-41).

The *Jesus of Lubeck* arrived back in England on September 20, 1565, with her two small companions trailing along like ducklings in the wake of a mother mallard. Hawkins and his backers had every reason to be pleased. After expenses the voyage netted a profit estimated at between 45 and 60 per cent. The hope of much greater profits was implicit in a letter from Hawkins to Elizabeth, in which he wrote that he had "always been a help to all Spaniards and Portugals that have come in my way, although many times in this track they have been under my power." He was obviously feeling on top of the world, and in November when he was invited to dine in London with the Spanish Ambassador, Don Guzmán de Silva, Hawkins was only too happy to oblige.

At the meeting de Silva probably learned little that he had not already known. But Hawkins' self-assurance and obvious abilities were enough to alarm the Ambassador, and he wrote King Philip urging decisive action—but not yet. "It may be best," he wrote, "to dissemble so as to capture and castigate him on the next voyage." In a second meeting with Hawkins, the Ambassador was blandly assured by the Englishman that he would not return to the Indies without the Spanish King's permission. De Silva did not believe it, and again reflected his concern in a dispatch to Philip. "It seems advisable to get this man out of the country, so that he may not teach others, for they have good ships and are greedy folk with more liberty than is good for them."

Whether he was dissembling or not, de Silva protested vigorously in the spring of 1567 when he learned that Hawkins was planning yet another voyage. This time, as de Silva's spies reported, Queen Elizabeth

John Hawkins' home port of Plymouth, seen here on a 16th Century English coastal chart, was a deep and well-protected natural harbor and the starting point for many expeditions to the Spanish Main. Hawkins and his 407 men sailed in six ships from here in 1567, as church bells pealed and townsfolk shouted their farewells from shore.

was placing two of her warships at Hawkins' disposal: the *Jesus of Lubeck* again and the smaller *Minion,* an armed vessel of 300 tons. Hawkins said publicly that he was only going to Africa in search of gold, but the Ambassador demanded assurances from the Queen herself that the expedition would steer clear of the Caribbean. Elizabeth coolly told the Spanish Ambassador half the truth: Hawkins, she said, was headed for Africa. A little later de Silva learned that Hawkins' ships were lading beans, standard provender of slaves, and rich silks, much admired by New World colonial planters.

A few weeks later the Ambassador filed a second formal protest. This time Elizabeth explicitly and stoutly denied that Hawkins was bound for the West Indies. If in fact the Spanish were dissembling in hopes of getting Hawkins in their clutches, Elizabeth and Hawkins were masters at the same game of falsehood.

All during the summer of 1567 Hawkins continued to assemble and fit out his fleet at Portsmouth. To accompany the *Jesus* and the *Minion,* he himself furnished four smaller ships totaling 333 tons: the *Willam and John,* the *Swallow,* the *Angel* and the *Judith.* The expedition's crew numbered 408 men. And among them was Hawkins' cousin, a tough-minded and experienced young seafarer named Francis Drake.

By the end of August preparations were nearly complete. And now came a Spanish reaction somewhat more ominous than Ambassador de Silva's cries of diplomatic protest. On a fine summer day a squadron of seven Spanish warships appeared in Plymouth Sound. The Spaniards failed to strike their colors and topsails—as was customary when entering a foreign port—and pressed on toward the inner harbor, where Hawkins' fleet lay. As soon as Hawkins saw the Spaniards he opened a furious warning fire, and continued the cannonade until they bore off and made the required salute.

Anchoring in a cove near Plymouth, the Spanish commander complained to officials of his treatment, insisting that he bore no malice. The Spaniards then sailed away, but the Spanish Ambassador took his countryman's protest to Queen Elizabeth. Again he demanded to know what Hawkins was up to, and now the Queen dutifully asked Hawkins to state the purpose of his expedition. All patience and pretense at an end, Hawkins wrote Elizabeth: "My sovereign good Lady and Mistress, The voyage I pretend is to lade Negroes in Guinea and sell them in the West Indies in truck of gold, pearls and emeralds." The Queen, by one contemporary account, "gave new commandments," approving of Hawkins' plans and supporting his efforts to trade "as he had heretofore done in other voyages." Thus, on October 2, 1567, John Hawkins took his six ships out of Plymouth and down the Channel into the Atlantic.

The voyage to Africa was beset by storms. The *Jesus* took a battering and sprang numerous leaks; "in the stern," a seaman later reported, "the leak was so great that into one place was thrust 15 pieces of baize cloth." Hawkins made repairs at Tenerife in the Canaries and pushed on to the Guinea coast of Africa. But this time it was no easy matter for the Englishmen to collect a cargo of slaves.

Since Hawkins' last voyage to the Guinea coast, Portugal had seri-

Death and profits in an abominable trade

No one knows for certain how many African slaves were transported across the Atlantic to a short life of terrible toil in the mines and plantations of the Spanish Main. But estimates set the figure at one million during the 16th and 17th Centuries. Almost all of these came from West Africa.

The trading companies of the colonial powers—Portugal, France, Holland and England—stationed agents all along the West African coast to barter for slaves. The vendors were local chiefs who were only too pleased to be rid of their criminals, or to profit doubly from war by trading away enemy prisoners.

The strongest and healthiest young men might bring as much as £9 worth of trade goods: weapons, iron bars and textiles. The women and the very young could be purchased for as little as 24 shillings, or a piece of woolen cloth. Once bought, the slaves were branded like cattle, with a company trademark on the breast or buttock, and then imprisoned until the slave ships arrived.

Up to 600 slaves were jammed into a 120-foot ship for the five- to 10-week voyage to the Caribbean. They were chained hand and foot, lying below-decks and on tiers of narrow shelves in the dark, dank hold. They were brought up on deck twice daily for food, which was mainly beans. There were no sanitary facilities whatsoever, and sailors told of being able to "smell a slaver five miles downwind." Such was the stench of vomit, excrement and disease that "no European," said an observer, could "dare put his face to the hatch without being nauseated."

Perhaps 20 per cent of the slave trad-er's cargo might perish on the voyage. Many of the survivors were covered with sores (which the sellers attempted to mask with gunpowder), or were afflicted with dysentery (concealed by oakum forced into the anuses of the victims). But so desperate for labor were the Spanish—and later the British and French—that they would willingly pay from £16 to £22 for a slave who was moderately fit.

After deducting expenses, a slaver could count on a minimum profit of £2,500 from each trip, and some voyages returned as much as three times that amount. Noted a contemporary English economist by the name of Malachy Postlethwait: "The Negro trade and the natural consequences resulting from it may be justly esteemed an inexhaustible fund of wealth and naval power to this nation."

Small forts marking the locations of major slaving factories dot this early-17th Century English map of the slave coast from Guinea in the west to Benin. The factories were sources of wealth, trade and prestige for coastal chiefs, and Europeans had little difficulty leasing the land on which to build them.

White traders proffer copper arm bracelets to a Benin chief in this African bronze relief dating from 1600. Such bracelets, called manillas, could be bartered freely for slaves, gold or ivory.

Armed Portuguese slave hunters use trained dogs to chase down Africans for transport to the colonies. Though sometimes slavers rounded up isolated individuals this way, or raided small villages, more often they traded with local chiefs for whole batches of human stock.

With a wailing farewell from those on shore, a boatload of slaves is rowed out through the surf to a ship anchored off the African coast. Given half a chance, many slaves would hurl themselves from the longboats, preferring death in the shark-infested waters to shipment to a faraway land they believed inhabited by a race of giant, red-faced cannibals.

ously begun to enforce its monopoly of the African trade. No local slavers would sell to him, so Hawkins was forced to chase down his own chattels. At the end of November a number of his men were wounded during an attack on an African village, and eight died in agony, their jaws locked shut, from poisoned arrows. Hawkins himself was wounded but quickly recovered. At one point the frustrated Englishmen took a Portuguese caravel that had been abandoned by its owners when French corsairs attacked and burned a coastal town. Hawkins hoped that the small vessel could be used to sail up shallow rivers where slaves might be bought or captured. Over the next few weeks, he acquired three more ships: a small bark purchased from the Portuguese and a pair of small armed French ships whose captains decided to join his enterprise.

Now 10 ships strong, Hawkins' squadron cruised southeast to Sierra Leone. There his slaving parties pushed farther inland in search of their quarry, and two seamen drowned in a swampy river when their small pinnace foundered and sank after colliding with a hippopotamus. By January 12, 1568, Hawkins had taken scarcely 150 slaves, and by his own count he had "nothing wherewith to seek the coast of the West Indies."

The expedition might have ended then and there, except for a sudden and dramatic reversal of fortune. A local African king in Sierra Leone, laying siege to an enemy town, negotiated for help with the well-armed Englishmen, promising in return that they could take the prisoners. Hawkins quickly agreed. When the town was subdued Hawkins loaded his ships with 260 more slaves and set a course west to the Caribbean.

It took more than seven weeks to cross the Atlantic, and a discouraged Hawkins noted in his log that the passage was "more hard than before hath been accustomed." There was more frustration in store when the visitors reached the settlements on the Spanish Main and discovered that local officials were even less eager to wink at trade than they had been previously. "We coasted from place to place," wrote Hawkins later, "making our traffic with the Spaniards as we might, somewhat hardly, because the king had straitly commanded all his governors in those parts by no means to suffer any trade with us."

By the time they reached Borburata, where trade had been relatively easy before, Hawkins had decided to take matters in his own hands. When the new Governor showed reluctance to give him a license, Hawkins simply declared that he needed none and, without further ado, set up booths on the shore and traded for more than a month, while his powerfully armed fleet rode at anchor in the bay behind him.

The Englishmen faced harder resistance when they reached Rio de la Hacha, where a local official assembled a troop of armed men to defend the town, as they had during Hawkins' previous visit. Francis Drake, now in command of the *Judith*, entered the harbor first and demanded leave to fill his water casks. The Spanish opened fire and Drake, in quick response, sent two shot flying into the colonial treasurer's house and then anchored out of range until the rest of the fleet arrived. Hawkins landed with 200 men, routed the ragtag defenders, captured the port and set fire to several houses. The colonists indicated their fervent desire for peace, and Hawkins in turn promised to pay for the damages his men had done. "Thus," wrote Hawkins, "we obtained a secret trade, where-

An English seaman on shore leave
wears the baggy pants and shaggy felt hat
of his trade, in this woodcut from a
16th Century Italian volume on costumes
of the world. On board ship such finery
gave way to workaday garb: plain leather
jerkin and less cumbersome trousers.

upon that the Spaniards bought of us to the number of 200 Negroes.''

Word of Hawkins' firmness may have preceded him to the next settlement, at Santa Marta. For there, after a chat with the local Spanish officials, Hawkins feigned a conquest, putting ashore 150 men and "shooting out of the ships half a score shot over the town for a color." The "defeated" Spaniards gladly bought 110 slaves from Hawkins, and the Englishman departed with good wishes all around after just a few days.

But neither confrontation nor negotiation worked any magic at the next port, Cartagena, the most important city on the South American mainland. Behind their massive fortifications, the Cartagenans coldly rebuffed the English traders. "We could by no means obtain to deal with any Spaniard, the governor was so strait," noted Hawkins. To show his determination to trade, he sent the *Minion* to bombard the town. But the Cartagenan shore batteries answered shot for shot, and Hawkins soon called off the fruitless exchange.

There was now nothing left but to sail for home, though Hawkins still had about 50 healthy slaves chained in his holds. On July 24, outside Cartagena, he paid off and said farewell to one of the French captains who had joined him, and he sank a second vessel, now unneeded, that he had acquired in Africa. Then, with his remaining eight ships, Hawkins set sail for the Straits of Florida, hoping "to have escaped the time of storms which then soon after began to reign."

He hoped in vain. On August 12, as the fleet approached the Florida coast, a terrible gale roared out of the east. For four days it tore at the ships, and "so beat the *Jesus*," recalled Hawkins, "that we cut down all her higher buildings. Her rudder also was sore shaken, and withal was in so extreme a leak that we were rather upon the point to leave her than to keep her any longer." Hawkins signaled his squadron to "put roomer"—turn and run before the wind. One vessel, the tiny *William and John*, apparently missed the signal, struggled on and eventually made a miraculous passage back to England with about 50 men. The rest were swept along like spindrift by the howling winds and awful seas until they found themselves in the shallows off Florida's west coast.

For two days Hawkins poked along the coast, searching for a place where he could careen and repair the *Jesus*. But the inshore waters all shelved too gradually for the 700-ton flagship to reach a beach. In desperation, Hawkins turned seaward—only to encounter a second frightful gale. This one was from the north and battered the ships for three days, and when it mercifully abated the fleet had been blown across to the Triangles, a group of islets off Mexico's Yucatan Peninsula.

Hawkins was now in waters where no English ship had ever ventured, and the *Jesus* was more in need of repair than ever. On September 11, in the Bay of Campeche, Hawkins stopped a Spanish merchant ship, not for loot but simply for information. Her captain informed him that the only nearby harbor that was well protected from the season's northerly gales was at the small island of San Juan de Ulúa, 15 miles south of Veracruz. But Hawkins also learned that the heavily armed Spanish flota, the treasure fleet, would make its annual call at San Juan at the end of September. At best the English could count on only 10 to 12 days in which to make their repairs and be gone.

Hawkins turned southwest, and late in the evening on September 15 raised the rocky island. The following morning his seven ships approached San Juan in single file, with the stricken but still-imposing *Jesus* in the lead. Nearing the harbor, Hawkins passed orders to fly the English royal standard on the main-topmast of the *Jesus*, and on the foretopmast of the second-in-line *Minion*.

Ashore, seeing the ships but not the flags, Francisco de Bustamante, the lieutenant treasurer of Veracruz, scrambled into a pinnace with a crew and set out for the approaching vessels. Bustamante was rehearsing an effusive speech of welcome, for he thought, as did every other Spaniard on the island, that the ships were the long-awaited flota.

The Spaniards did not realize their mistake until the last minute. "The Queen's arms," explained an officer of the *Jesus*, "were so dim with their colors through wearing in foul weather that they never perceived the lions and flowers de luces till they were hard aboard." Bustamante and his crew found themselves staring into English pistols, and Hawkins ordered them aboard the *Jesus* before any alarm could be given.

On San Juan de Ulúa, the commander of the Spanish garrison, one Antonio Delgadillo, also mistook Hawkins' ships for the flota and ordered a welcoming salute of five unshotted cannon. Hawkins carefully replied and ranged his ships around the harbor, preparing to anchor. Only then did Delgadillo realize his error. But it was too late; the English were in position to wipe out the town with their cannon. Delgadillo tried to rally his forces, ordering them to load their cannon and fire, but in panic they piled into small boats and fled to the mainland. Thus Hawkins had gained command of the port that Admiral Pedro Menéndez de Avilés, when surveying the Main's defenses only a few years before, had confidently regarded as beyond the reach of any foreign sail.

But Hawkins, at this stage, still did not think of himself as an enemy. He sent a messenger to find Delgadillo, to assure him that the English intentions were peaceful and to make arrangements to repair and reprovision the *Jesus*. Hawkins even managed to suppress his trader's instincts in the interest of maintaining peace: all this while he had been carrying the surviving slaves in his hold, but he apparently did not attempt to sell them at San Juan de Ulúa. He also sent word to the authorities in Mexico City, the capitol of the Viceroyalty of New Spain (present-day Mexico) that he had come only "by force of weather," and he hoped "that at the arrival of the Spanish fleet, which was daily looked for, there might no cause of quarrel rise between us and them."

Hawkins hoped in vain. At that very moment the 13 ships of the Spanish flota were less than a day's sail from the Mexican coast. On the flagship was Don Martín Enríquez de Almansa, son of the Marquis de Alcañizes, and the newly appointed Viceroy of New Spain. Enríquez

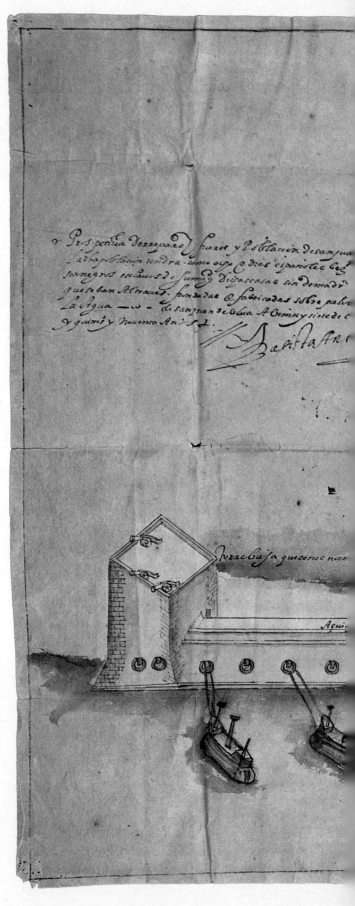

Moored to heavy rings, a flotilla of Spanish ships rides at quayside in this 1590 sketch of the fortified island of San Juan de Ulúa, site of Hawkins' defeat by the Spaniards two decades earlier. The legend at upper left in this drawing by a military engineer named Juan Antonelli explains that the houses of the inhabitants "are made from the wood of stranded ships."

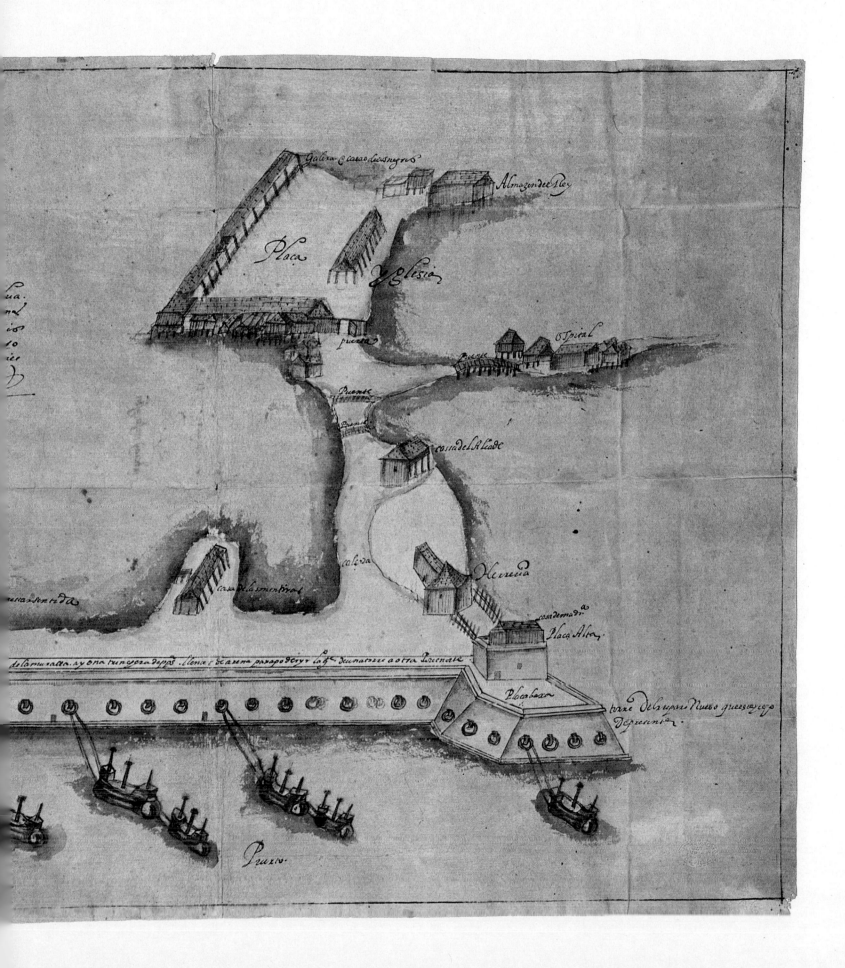

undoubtedly knew Hawkins was in the Caribbean but, like Menéndez, did not dream of an interloper so far west, so deep in the Spanish New World empire. His thoughts were on the voyage, now nearly over.

Enríquez was sailing as the honored passenger of Francisco de Luxan, captain general of the flota. Luxan's flagship led a convoy of 11 merchantmen, heavily laden with wine, cloth and manufactured goods for New Spain, and meant to freight the year's accumulation of treasure back to Europe. Bringing up the rear was a second Spanish man-of-war, under the command of Admiral Juan de Ubilla. The Viceroy-designate, Enríquez, held no official appointment at sea, only the privileges of an honored passenger, but among his papers he carried a royal commission vesting in him supreme command should he find cause to exercise it.

That cause came at San Juan de Ulúa the next day, September 17, when port commander Delgadillo clambered aboard Luxan's flagship, breathlessly bearing the news of Hawkins' arrival.

The Englishman, Delgadillo said, had declared his peaceful intentions, and promised to clear the port as soon as his ships were seaworthy. Hawkins had also informed the Spanish that "I would suffer them to enter the port," provided "some order of conditions pass between us for our safe being there and maintenance of peace." Hawkins proposed that while the *Jesus* was being repaired each side should put up 12 gentlemen "as hostages for the maintenance of peace, and that the island, for our better safety, might be in our own possession." Finally, intent as always on selling his cargo, Hawkins requested a license "to sell as much wares as might furnish our wants."

Upon receiving Hawkins' messages, Enríquez assumed immediate command and issued a call to council. Luxan, Ubilla and the other captains of the Spanish fleet gathered on the flagship. Enríquez was enraged at Hawkins' effrontery. He proposed to the Spanish commanders that they instantly attack the Englishmen. Unlike the provincial officials on the Main, whom Hawkins had so easily bent to his will, Enríquez, as Viceroy of New Spain, had no intention of compromising with the hated English. But the naval commanders pointed out to the Viceroy that the flota could not enter by force so long as the invaders held the island battery at the harbor's entrance. Yet it was true that to remain outside of the harbor was to risk shipwreck in the event of a storm. The council of captains persuaded Enríquez to go along with Hawkins' truce, at least initially, and to exchange hostages, only reducing the number from 12 to 10. Afterward, the commanders pledged, "they would do as his illustrious lordship might advise."

The next morning, September 18, the nobleman Enríquez wrote to the merchant Hawkins and agreed "to accept the proposal that your honor makes, asking me to deliver hostages and to enter the port in peace." But he had plans to destroy this infuriating English interloper.

No sooner had the council of war adjourned the night before than Enríquez dispatched an appeal to the nearby city of Veracruz, requesting as many troops as were available. The city had responded with 150 soldiers, who arrived that same night, raising the Spaniards' fighting strength to more than 1,000 men. And now, as he prepared for the exchange of gentlemen hostages, Enríquez even contemplated dressing up

Riding high on light seas, vessels of a Spanish fleet in the Caribbean travel in tight protective formation in this 17th Century engraving. So concerned were the Spanish about enemy privateers that, by royal decree, "no ship may leave the convoy for any reason, not even to pursue an enemy sail. If ever a ship breaks this rule, her captain and navigator will each be fined 50,000 pesos and forbidden to sail to America for two years."

"certain seamen and certain soldiers attired like their betters." But he was dissuaded by Admiral Ubilla, who pointed out that common soldiers, knowing their lives were likely to be a forfeit, might give the attack plans away. From his own ship, Ubilla grandly offered his color bearer, two squad masters and his own nephew. He would go himself, he said, but he realized that his services would be of more value with the flota.

Meanwhile, on San Juan, Hawkins prudently gave orders to man the small fortress guarding the harbor. His men took a number of cannon from the smaller ships in his squadron and mounted them alongside the 16 Spanish pieces already in position. Then, according to a prisoner on board the *Jesus*, the English "removed most of their men from their smaller ships and transferred them to the flagship, which vessel, anchored at the harbor mouth, they prepared and cleared for action."

For three days following Enríquez' arrival, a southeast wind kept the flota anchored in the roadstead. But on September 21 the winds backed to the east and the Spanish entered the harbor. By Hawkins' account, the sailors from both fleets "labored two days placing the English ships by themselves and the Spanish by themselves, the captains of each part promising great amity on all sides." The two fleets, totaling 20 ships, were now anchored side by side, close under the lee of the small island, their bowsprits actually overhanging the land. The guns in the fort, each manned by a crew of Englishmen, had been trundled around until they now covered the Spaniards at point-blank range.

It was time for Enríquez to call a second council of his commanders. The Viceroy proposed that in the night Admirals Luxan and Ubilla, with 150 hand-picked men, secretly board a large Spanish merchantman that was moored in the harbor extremely close to the *Minion* and the *Jesus*. At a trumpet signal from the flota's flagship, the Spanish would haul the vessel alongside the *Minion* and board the Englishman. To capture the island guns, Enríquez directed that the 150 soldiers from Veracruz be hidden belowdecks on a number of Spanish ships anchored close to shore; at the signal they would scramble out along the overhanging bowsprit, drop to the ground and race to assault the fort. The remaining Spaniards would attack the English ships once the battle had begun.

The time of the assault was set for noon the next day, September 23. Early that morning Hawkins noted that the Spaniards were busily engaged in "shifting of weapon from ship to ship, and many other ill likelihoods which caused us vehement suspicion." Hawkins sent Robert Barrett, master of the *Jesus*, who was fluent in Spanish, to question the Viceroy. Barrett returned with word from Enríquez that no "villanies" would occur. But the Spanish preparations went on, and Hawkins sent Barrett a second time to seek further reassurances.

The time was 10 o'clock, and as Hawkins sat down for a hasty meal one of the Spanish hostages drew a dagger from his sleeve and tried to stab the English captain. An aide overpowered the assailant and, all appetite lost, Hawkins returned to the deck. Looking across the cargo hulk, he now recognized Admiral Ubilla standing on the vessel, and shouted across, accusing the officer of treachery. When the Spaniard cried back that he was doing his duty, Hawkins picked up a bow and shot an arrow at Ubilla. He missed, and at that instant Ubilla signaled Enríquez.

Aboard the flota's flagship, the Spanish Viceroy was assuring Barrett of his innocence. But he now dropped the mask, had Barrett clapped in irons and ordered the trumpet signal for the attack to begin.

Screaming "Santiago," Ubilla and his men boarded the *Minion*. But before the Spanish could gain control of the ship, Hawkins and some men from the nearby *Jesus* leaped aboard the *Minion* to counterattack. One English sailor recalled that Hawkins "with a loud and fierce voice called unto us, saying 'God and St. George! Upon those traitorous villains, and rescue the *Minion!* I trust in God the day shall be ours.'"

Firing their pistols, slashing and thrusting with their cutlasses and pikes, Hawkins and his men swept the Spaniards from the *Minion*. Then three other Spanish ships slipped up to grapple with the *Jesus* in a second attack, which Hawkins also beat back. But it was obvious, with other Spaniards in the harbor joining the fray, that the English were outnumbered and in real danger. Hawkins ordered the moorings of the *Minion* and the *Jesus* cut, in an attempt to clear away from the melee.

While the battle raged on board the ships, the Spanish land assault, led by Delgadillo, overwhelmed the Englishmen defending the island battery. At the sound of the Viceroy's trumpet, Spanish soldiers came out of hiding and charged the guns. "Our men ashore," Hawkins lamented bitterly, "being stricken with sudden fear, gave place, fled and sought to recover succor of the ships." Only three of the island's defenders survived; the rest, Hawkins reported, were massacred "without mercy."

With the island fort in their possession, the Spaniards commenced a fierce bombardment of the drifting *Jesus* and *Minion*. But by now the two English ships had been carried to within point-blank range of the anchored Spanish flota. Ignoring the damaging fire from the fort, they blasted the Spanish vessels with broadside after broadside, sinking the Viceroy's flagship—which came to rest upright in the harbor mud—and setting another ship on fire.

The English vessels also had been badly cut up. One Englishman saw that the *Jesus* "had five shot through her main mast, her foremast was struck asunder with chain shot, and her hull was wonderfully pierced with shot." The *Minion* was battered but serviceable. However, the other English ships had fared terribly. The *Angel* was sunk, the *Swallow* and the Portuguese caravel were captured, and the remaining French ship was abandoned in flames by her crew. Only the *Judith*, originally moored farthest from the melee, got clear undamaged and anchored at a distance, where her captain, Drake, was helpless to affect the outcome.

Hawkins, at last convinced that "there was no hope to carry the *Jesus* away," positioned his doomed flagship as a shield between the island battery and the *Minion* so as to transfer "such relief of victual and other necessaries from the *Jesus* as time would suffer us and to leave her."

The stratagem appeared to work, until Ubilla rigged two fire ships to float down on the English, which, wrote Hawkins, "bred among our men a marvelous fear, so that some said, let us depart with the *Minion*." Hawkins, who had been directing the loading of goods and provisions from the *Jesus*, was one of the last to leap off that ship before the *Minion* drew clear. She had 200 men on board; the only other English survivors were some 30 men on the *Judith*. The other 100 men in Hawkins' force

The fate of Hawkins' castaways

They were all volunteers, the 100 seamen who scrambled ashore on the east coast of Mexico when John Hawkins fled the Spaniards in the fall of 1568. The men reasoned that they stood a better chance in enemy territory than on the high seas in Hawkins' overcrowded and scantily provisioned *Minion*. And indeed, when the *Minion* limped into an English harbor three months later, only about 15 of the 100 crewmen who had stayed aboard were still alive. But the fate of the castaways was equally grim.

Soon after landing, 30 of the men, led by David Ingram, turned northward and set out to follow the Gulf Coast clear around to a rumored French settlement in faraway Florida. The rest headed south to Tampico, where they surrendered to the Spaniards—and were immediately jailed.

After four days the captives were ordered outside, where men with nooses awaited them. Miles Philips, a 14-year-old who had been Hawkins' page boy, later recalled the anguish that engulfed his countrymen. "Crying and calling to God for mercie and forgivenesse of our sinnes," he wrote, "we prepared our selves, making us ready to die."

The men were not hanged, but were roped together with the nooses and herded to Mexico City 200 miles away. Eventually most of the captives were parceled out as servants to well-to-do Spaniards, who accorded them moderately good care. But in 1571 the Spanish Inquisition was established in Mexico, and life became a hell for the Englishmen.

As suspected heretics, Philips and his fellows were again clapped into prison. Many were tortured; all were questioned rigorously about their religious beliefs and kept for month upon month in dark and fetid cells. Then in early 1574 the hapless seamen were informed of their punishment. Philips and a handful of other youths were sentenced to lengthy penance in monasteries, but their older comrades were not so fortunate. One was strangled and burned; the others were given as many as 300 lashes and sent to the galleys as slaves, where they labored until they died.

Miles Philips was released from the monastery after three years, and finally made his way home along a tortuous route that took him to Guatemala, Venezuela, Cuba, the Azores and Spain. In England he learned that David Ingram and two of his hardy companions had not only survived the trek to Florida, but had continued on up the Atlantic Coast for another 1,500 miles to Nova Scotia, where they encountered a French fishing vessel that gave them passage home.

Ingram was vague about the 27 others who had set out with him on his epic walk. He knew of only three who had died; the rest, he suggested, had given up the journey and stayed behind with the Indians. "Verely I doe thinke," wrote Philips, "that there are of them yet alive, and married in the said countrey."

Two heretics, condemned by the Inquisition in the 16th Century, are about to be burned at the stake in a public ceremony in Spain. The Inquisition's first mission was to root out heresy among Spanish Catholics, but it was also used to punish captured English Protestants like those from Hawkins' luckless crew.

were either dead or Spanish prisoners doomed to years in the dungeons; some, including Robert Barrett, were put to death by their captors.

The battle had raged for more than six hours. At dusk the *Minion* and the *Judith* anchored just beyond the harbor for the night, out of range of the shore guns, and precisely where the Spanish flota had lain six days before. That night, to Hawkins' utter surprise, Drake made good his escape, heading for England. Hawkins, bitter that Drake "forsook us in our misery," remained at anchor and took stock of his predicament. Naturally, he had left his remaining slaves on board the abandoned *Jesus* (some of them had been there for nine months) as well as the Spanish hostages. He had managed to transfer the bulk of his gold and silver— about £13,000 worth—to the *Minion*. But the Englishmen had taken little else. In the rush to escape, Hawkins' men had managed to bring few provisions from the *Jesus*.

All the next day, September 24, the *Minion* was pinned down on the Mexican coast by a heavy north wind, in grave danger of dragging her anchor and being driven aground. But the following day, to Hawkins' vast relief, "the weather waxed reasonable and we set sail" although, "having a great number of men and little victuals, our hope of life waxed less and less." As the battered *Minion* beat eastward, the English were reduced to stewing oxhides from the ship's cargo. This diet was hardly enough to sustain the labor of keeping the leaking vessel afloat, and on October 8 the *Minion* put in to the Mexican coast, where 100 men elected to remain ashore rather than starve on the *Minion*. Some of those left behind would survive years of hardships imposed by Spaniards, Indians, and the hostile land, but most would succumb to the rigors that faced them ashore (pages 70-71).

The *Minion* staggered on across the Atlantic. The majority of her 100 or so men died long before Hawkins reached the coast of Cornwall on January 25, 1569. Those who managed to survive were so weak that, according to Hawkins, "We were scantly able to manage our ship." Hawkins did not record exactly how many men made it home on board the *Minion*, but a Spanish agent in England reported to Madrid that the number was no more than 15.

Considering all the vessels lost, the profit from the voyage was negligible. The Spanish agent informed his monarch that "Hawkins has come from the Indies with four horseloads of gold and silver, which, however, I believe will not pay the costs."

The consequences of the expedition, however, were considerably greater than the profits. For the first time Spaniards and Englishmen had fought a pitched battle on the Main. The Spaniards had won this initial encounter, but the voyage, and Hawkins' earlier ones, had exposed the Spanish Main in all its vulnerability; the Spaniards could not control their widespread empire effectively enough to keep it closed to an aggressive foreigner in search of wealth. That lesson did not escape Francis Drake, Hawkins' young cousin. And if Drake needed a reason, other than his keenly whetted appetite for gold, to justify his returning to the Main to plunder and wreak some havoc of his own making, he now had a ready excuse that he would offer freely to all who inquired in the years to come: his burning hatred of the Spanish for their treachery at San Juan de Ulúa.

Chapter 3

The fire and fury of El Dragón

CIVITAS CARTHAGENA in Indiæ occidentalis continente sita, portu commodissimo, ad mercaturam inter Hispaniam et Peru exercendam.

CARTAGENA

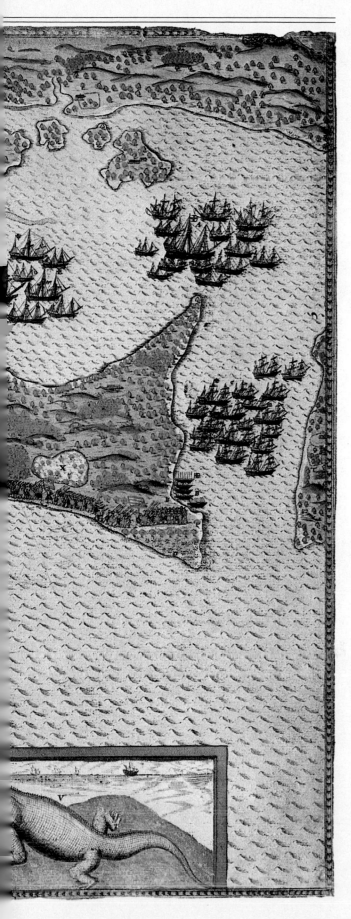

ohn Hawkins and Francis Drake arrived back in Plymouth within days of each other in January 1569, having fought their way separately through the Caribbean easterlies and then across 6,000 miles of stormy Atlantic. No record exists of what was said at their reunion, nor of whether Hawkins ever reproached his brash young cousin for sailing away from the debacle at San Juan de Ulúa without orders—and without ascertaining whether the older man had survived. In any case, the two men worked together now and again throughout the rest of their lives. And both dedicated themselves to wreaking terrible vengeance on the Spaniards for having cheated and bludgeoned them out of the profits of trade.

In Drake the fury flamed so fiercely—and his desire for Spanish treasure was so great—that he made no fewer than six return voyages to the Spanish Main over the next three decades. Of these, four forays were epochal, not so much for the gold they returned—indeed only two were very successful in that respect—but rather for their fantastic adventures, and for their triumphs of human spirit over every adversity.

Repeatedly, Drake's expeditions were beset by false starts and calamitous setbacks. The captain was forever engaged in some trial of wits—against the Spaniards, against the elements and on occasion even against his own men. Again and again, by the most minute accident of timing, captured cities would yield no treasure, cornered quarries would elude his grasp, even bagged treasures would slip through his fingers. Yet again and again Drake rebounded from disappointment. He was never at a loss for ideas to amend his plans, to cheer his weary men onward, to leave the Spaniards quaking in fear of where he might spring his next attack.

It was for these traits, perhaps more than for his actual swag, that Francis Drake earned the adulation of his countrymen and the awe of the Spaniards, who came to call him El Dragón—the Sea Serpent. At one point Philip II of Spain offered a reward of 20,000 ducats for Drake's life. Many a 16th Century city was ransomed for less.

This man who rose to be one of the monumental figures of his age came from humble origins. According to contemporary accounts, Francis Drake was born around 1540, the eldest of 12 sons of Edmund Drake, who was a tenant farmer living in the village of Tavistock near Plymouth. Edmund was apparently an outspoken champion of Puritanism, at a time when the Reformation was scarcely two decades old and passion blazed between Catholics and Protestants.

In 1549, relate the accounts, a Catholic uprising in Tavistock impelled

Francis Drake's raiders storm along the beach toward the city of Cartagena in this bird's-eye view of the battle, published two years after Drake's 1586 victory. The English fleet is shown in the three successive anchorages it occupied during the action (indicated by the letters S, A and N). The reptile shown in the inset is an iguana, prized, said an English account, for its "very dilicate meate."

the Drakes to flee to the safely Protestant stronghold of Kent, where the impecunious Edmund lodged his brood in an abandoned hulk hard by the King's dockyards on the Medway River. There, while the father preached the fire and brimstone of the new religion to His Majesty's sailors, the child Francis played among spars and rigging, and began imbibing the lore of the sea. Both the religious fires and the promise of the ships were to leave indelible marks on him—and to drive him throughout his life's work.

Young Francis Drake was not long in putting his learning to practical use. He shipped to sea at 14 as apprentice to the master of a tiny coastal vessel that piloted French and Dutch merchant ships into the Channel and frequently smuggled refugees from the Spanish Inquisition into England. From the outset he seems to have made a strong and favorable impression on his captain and fellow seamen. When the master died, Drake, who was not yet 20, inherited the ship. Before long he sold it, and with the proceeds traveled down to Devon to find service with his cousins the Hawkinses—the family whose scion John, some 10 years Drake's senior, would soon be peddling smuggled slaves on the Spanish Main.

After sending Drake along as a junior officer on a few of the family's slave-trading ventures to the Guinea coast, John Hawkins evidently deemed the young man ready for command and in October 1567 put him in charge of the *Judith* on the voyage that led to the San Juan episode.

If the disaster at San Juan de Ulúa taught Drake nothing else, it taught him the necessity for thorough planning, and now as he prepared to attack his enemies he made two voyages of reconnaissance to the Spanish Main. Of the first, in 1570, just a year after his return to England, scarcely anything is known save that it spanned about six months and was financed by Hawkins. The second venture took place in 1571, and a few details exist.

Drake's ship was the *Swan*, a little vessel of scarcely 25 tons and only a few guns. But Drake had chosen her for this very reason: inconspicuous and harmless, she could go virtually where she pleased, triggering no alarms among those who chanced to see her. Drake left Plymouth in March and within weeks he was easing through the Caribbean, intent on scouting the coastal contours of the Spanish Main, and the ways and means by which the Spaniards drew their wealth from the area.

Somewhere on the Gulf of Darien, which laps the east coast of the Isthmus of Panama, Drake put in at a secluded bay hidden by a jungle that descended to the water's edge. There was good fishing in the bay, as well as fresh-water springs and an abundance of fruit and game ashore. (Drake named the site Port Pheasant for the flocks of wild fowl to be found in the forest.)

From that comfortable hideaway, Drake scouted the 500-mile scalloped coastline between Cartagena, the capital of the Spanish Main, and Nombre de Dios, the Isthmus port from which the annual treasure fleet embarked for Spain. What he did not learn from his own stealthy prowling in the *Swan* he acquired by the shrewd tactic of befriending the Cimaroons—runaway African slaves who shared his hatred of the Spaniards and willingly gave him help.

England's indefatigable privateer, Sir Francis Drake, shown in a 1581 portrait by court miniaturist Nicholas Hilliard, was the scourge of Spain's dominion over the West Indies during the late 16th Century. "Anyone who goes adventuring with me," boasted Drake, "will have his money back six or seven times!"

Drake returned from his reconnaissance trip around the new year, and immediately began planning the expedition that in some respects was the greatest of his life, for it summoned forth his full talents for organization, forethought, unflagging stamina, stunning surprise and brilliant recovery from misfortune. A detailed account of the voyage, edited in 1592 by Drake's nephew and namesake, son of his youngest brother, Thomas, was published in 1626 under the title *Sir Francis Drake Revived*. The great seafarer himself contributed to the narrative, and in a preface to it his nephew states that Drake made the voyage to right the wrongs he had endured at the hands of the Spanish at San Juan de Ulúa.

This time he did not slip away from England quietly, as he had in the past. The Hawkins family and other wealthy Plymouth merchants were on hand to wish him Godspeed as he left Plymouth on Whitsunday Eve, May 24, 1572, with 73 men in two ships: the *Pasha*, a 70-ton vessel that he commanded himself, and the little *Swan*, now captained by his brother John. Another brother, Joseph, went along as a member of the company. They were provisioned for a full year and armed to the teeth with cutlasses, pikes, pistols, muskets, even bows and arrows. Their most precious cargo, according to the nephew's narrative, consisted of "three dainty pinnaces made in Plymouth, taken asunder all in pieces and stowed aboard, to be set up as occasion served." These handy prefabricated craft were versatile boats of 20 tons that could slip in and out of waters too shallow for the oceangoing *Swan* and *Pasha*. They carried sails but could be rowed if the wind failed.

With a brisk northeast wind off his quarter, Drake laid straight for his mark. Twelve days out he sighted the Canary Islands, where transatlantic vessels usually put in for water and provisions. But Drake's little fleet, related the account, "never struck sail nor came to anchor, nor made any stay for any cause, neither there nor elsewhere, until twenty-five days after," when it reached the New World.

Arriving at Port Pheasant, where Drake had left supplies the year before, the expedition found that someone had been there in the interim and had dug up all the stores. Undaunted, Drake settled in and set his men to assembling the pinnaces. When the vessels were ready, he moved camp from Port Pheasant to an island about 75 miles from Nombre de Dios. He named it the Isle of Pines for its dense forestation. There he hid the *Pasha* and *Swan* in a sheltered cove and, leaving a small detachment to mind them, set out near the end of July with most of his men in the pinnaces for Nombre de Dios. The great adventure was about to begin, and in mounting excitement the English raiders rowed in rhythm to the songs of their native Devon.

Five days later, on a dark night with only the stars for light, the tiny fleet crept stealthily toward the bay beneath the town, and anchored out of sight behind a promontory. Drake intended to wait until dawn and pounce on the town just before it awakened for the day. But the men were tense with anticipation, and at 3 a.m., as a late-rising moon brought a glow to the eastern sky, Drake declared it to be dawn.

They came ashore on a beach outside Nombre de Dios. A lone Spanish sentry guarding a nearby shore battery spotted them, and fled to arouse the town. Drake paused long enough to topple the battery's guns, then rushed on—as the clanging church bell sounded the alarm and drew the suddenly wakened population into the marketplace.

But Drake had a plan too sly for the sleepy citizens to counter. At the edge of Nombre de Dios he split his force into two groups, sending half of the men under his brother John around the outside of the town to enter the marketplace from the far side, while he and the remaining raiders marched up from the harbor with a flourish of trumpets and drums and a shower of flaming arrows. The Spaniards pulled themselves together long enough to retort with what Drake's nephew's account called "a jolly hot volley of shot." A musket ball killed one of the trumpeters and another struck Drake in the leg.

For the rest of his life he was to carry that musket ball in his flesh. But for the present he bore his wound in silence, cheering on his unsuspecting men. Meanwhile a new burst of trumpets and drums and a fiery rain of arrows announced the arrival of Drake's brother John and the other detachment from the far side of the town. The Spaniards were now confused and terrified. They fled by the hundreds down the side streets and out into the countryside—while the English made their way to the Governor's house, flung open the cellar door and there by the light of torches beheld an incredible cache of silver bars stacked like cordwood in a pile 70 feet long, 10 feet wide and 12 feet high.

But Drake was after greater booty still, and he stayed his men from falling upon the silver, telling them that the King's Treasure House down by the waterfront was likely to have more gold and jewels than their pinnaces could carry away. He was about to order them to it when suddenly his wound overcame him. With a groan he stumbled forward and fell. Only then, noticing his bloody trousers and footprints, did the men realize that their commander had been shot.

Drake ordered his brother and the men to proceed to the Treasure House. But John would hear none of it. Nor, to their credit, would the men; there would always be treasure, provided there was Drake. Instead they bound their captain's wound with a scarf, gave him a nip of spirits and carried him back to the pinnaces—abandoning the shining booty.

For several days the raiders camped on an island beyond gunshot of the harbor while Drake nursed his wound. They found plenty of fowl and fruit to eat, and looted a Spanish ship in the harbor of a cargo of fine Canary wine. Presently an envoy appeared from the town, bearing a white flag of truce. Drake, with an extravagant show of hospitality that would become his hallmark, plied his visitor with food and drink, then demanded gold and silver as his price for leaving the town in peace. The envoy departed to confer with his fellow townsmen—at which point Drake reconsidered his precarious situation.

His wound still troubled him and placed a burden on his force. The envoy would undoubtedly report this—as well as the meager size of Drake's band. If the more numerous and better-armed Spaniards chose not to pay, Drake could scarcely mount another attack now that all surprise was gone. Even worse, the Spaniards might invade the island and doom his entire enterprise. Drake decided on a tactical retreat. He and his men vanished from Nombre de Dios and reclaimed the ships they had secluded at the Isle of Pines.

A Spanish galleon fires a salute as it enters the Panamanian harbor of Nombre de Dios, the original Caribbean terminus of the treasure trail from the rich mines of Peru. Although Drake failed to get any treasure from the town during his 1572 raid, the ease with which he and a few men took Nombre de Dios led the Spaniards to abandon it in favor of more defensible Portobelo to the north.

But Drake was never the man to linger over ill fortune. As soon as his leg had healed sufficiently, he took his little force across the Gulf of Darien to see what mischief he could stir up at Cartagena. Drake could not dream of assaulting so well-defended a city, of course. But finding a ship from Seville lying at anchor in the adjoining bay, he seized her at night while her crew slept belowdecks, then in the morning flaunted his triumph by hoisting English colors and sailing her past Cartagena harbor—out of gunshot but in full view of the Cartagenans. Cartagena rang its church bells in alarm and fired its cannon in helpless rage. Drake sailed the prize back to the Isle of Pines, after first depositing the Spanish crew unharmed on another island.

In taking on the additional ship, which, at 240 tons, dwarfed his other vessels, Drake was faced with a new problem: he did not have sufficient hands to man her in addition to the *Swan*, the *Pasha* and the three pinnaces. Clearly, something would have to go. He could not spare the pinnaces; they were indispensable for the surprise raids and swift getaways that were central to his plans. The *Pasha* was essential as his flagship. Reluctantly he decided to sacrifice the *Swan*—the ship for which both he and his men had the warmest affection.

Sensing that his men would balk, Drake resorted to a leader's license and engaged in an artful piece of deception. He summoned the ship's carpenter, Thomas Moone, and directed him to go down into the *Swan* secretly and bore three holes alongside the keel, then to lay something on top of the holes—enough to obscure them from view but not enough to prevent slow leakage. Moone unhappily did as his captain bade him. Next morning Drake set out to go fishing, taking his brother John with him. As they rowed past the *Swan*, Drake arched his eyebrows in mock surprise. Was not the *Swan* riding rather low in the water? John hurried to investigate and discovered that the hold was half full of water, obviously from sprung planking somewhere.

All day the men sweated and cursed over the pumps—while Francis Drake himself lent a hand from time to time. But it was no use. By late afternoon the men were exhausted and in a mood to agree when Drake suggested that the *Swan* was doomed. Sadly the men stripped the gallant little vessel of everything of value. Then they put her to the torch, and no one save Moone and Drake was any the wiser as to the real reason for the *Swan*'s demise.

Next in Drake's ever-fertile imagination was a plan for a daring assault on a mule train that fetched the magnificent Peruvian treasures across the Isthmus from Panama to Nombre de Dios. But as Drake knew from the friendly Cimaroons, the mule trains would not be moving till January, when the rainy season ended. It was now only September 1572, and for the next four months Drake left his men by turns at a hideaway along the Gulf of Darien to clear a site in the jungle for a new base while he took others off on miscellaneous shipping raids. The raids themselves reaped nothing more interesting than cargoes of hens, hogs, maize and honey; but they did provide food, and they kept everyone honed to a keen fighting edge. But in late November the misfortune that was beginning to cling to him like a leech made itself felt again.

Returning from a foray, Drake discovered that during his absence some of the men had spotted a small Spanish sloop passing offshore and they could not resist having a go at her. His brother John, who had been left in command, had tried to dissuade them, sensibly pointing out that they had neither the men nor the weapons for such an undertaking. But lacking his brother's firmness of command, John had succumbed to the men's urgings. "It shall never be said I will be hindermost, neither shall you report to my brother that you lost your voyage by any cowardice you found in me," he said. And so—armed, incredibly, with nothing but a broken rapier, an old harpoon and one rusty musket—John and a few of the boys raced their pinnace out to assail the sloop. In the boarding attempt, John Drake was immediately shot. His stunned companions broke off the attack and took him back to his ship, where he soon died.

Francis Drake returned to that sad news and shortly faced worse: an epidemic of yellow fever. In a scant few days 30 of the crew perished, among them his other brother, Joseph, and the ship's doctor, who escaped the disease only to die while sampling a potion he concocted in the hope of curing his patients. By the time the plague subsided, Drake's original force of 73 was reduced to 41.

Then, however, came the news he had been waiting for all these months. The Cimaroons reported that the Spanish fleet had arrived at Nombre de Dios to await the treasure coming overland from the city of Panama. Instantly Drake sprang back into action. Replacing his lost men with recruits from the Cimaroons, and leaving the ships and the pinnaces in the care of those recuperating from the disease, Drake set out overland in the first week of February to make his strike against the mule train that would soon be coming across the spine of the Isthmus. With him were 30 Cimaroons and 18 Englishmen.

Once the band left the fetid coast and climbed into the highlands, reported Drake's nephew, they found the way through the rain forest "very cool and pleasant by reason of those goodly and high trees, that grow there so thick." They climbed cheerfully upward along the same path the mules would travel, marching in the early morning, resting in the midday heat, resuming the march in the late afternoon, then halting again for the night. During their halts a guard stood watch at the edge of the encampment to listen for the tinkling bells that would announce the approach of the mule train. The rest of the company engaged in some impromptu acculturation: the Cimaroons taught the English how to make palmetto huts for shelter, and Drake taught the Cimaroons to say the Lord's Prayer.

After six days they reached the summit of the ridge that bisects the Isthmus. Here the Cimaroon chief led Drake to a great tree that had footholds cut into its trunk and a wide platform high in its branches. Reaching the platform, Drake beheld a sight that was to dazzle his inward eye for the rest of his life. Some 25 miles to the south the broad Pacific rolled off to one horizon; in the opposite direction the Atlantic reached to the limit of vision. Overcome with that combination of patriotism and religious fervor that so constantly drove him, Drake fell to his knees and, looking at the Pacific, beseeched the Almighty for "leave to sail once in an English ship in that sea." He would do so one day—but he had a more immediate job at hand.

Two days' march brought the band down the forested mountainside onto an open plain; another two days brought them within the environs of Panama. When they were close enough to count the ships in the harbor from a hilltop, Drake halted his men and sent a Cimaroon dressed like a Spanish slave into town. The man returned with the welcome news that a treasure train of mules would be setting out from Panama that very night for Nombre de Dios. Accompanying the train was to be no less a personage than the Treasurer of Lima, traveling with his daughter. Eight of the mules were to be laden with gold, one with jewels and five with silver.

Drake swiftly turned his men about-face and marched them 12 miles back into the jungle. His orders for the night assigned the men to positions strung out in the underbrush on either side of the trail. Any southbound travelers were to be allowed to pass unmolested toward Panama. Utmost quiet must be observed until Drake should blow his whistle; on that signal they were to leap out of hiding and fall upon the mule train.

Drake called for supper and a dram of brandy all around. Then the men took up their stations, and a hush fell over them all.

Darkness came, and for a long hour in the stillness nothing could be heard but the trill of treetoads and the calls of night birds. At last Drake's men heard the faint tinkle of mule bells. Then suddenly came the sound of hoofbeats—but they were those of a single horse, and they came from Nombre de Dios, the wrong direction. Drake's men crouched low in silence—all except one Englishman, Robert Pike, who lost his wits and leaped up out of his hiding place without waiting for Drake's whistle. A Cimaroon instantly pulled him down by his shirttails. The traveler continued on his way—spurring his horse to a canter.

After what seemed an interminable wait, the sound of the mule bells grew louder and louder. At long last the mule train entered the stretch where the ambush was set, and Drake patiently waited for it to align itself between his two strings of men. Then he whistled. Out they jumped to fall upon their quarry—and were greeted with yet another shattering disappointment.

The mule baskets proved to hold nothing but food, and neither the Treasurer of Lima nor his daughter nor an ounce of gold was anywhere to be found. A muleteer explained to the crestfallen Englishmen what had happened. The horseman, alas, had caught sight of the impatient Pike. And when he had encountered the treasure train a few miles down the trail, he had alerted its leaders that something was amiss. The Treasurer of Lima had immediately turned back to Panama with his daughter and the wealth, sending only the victuals on.

The Englishmen could scarcely believe their foul luck. But in adversity Drake always showed quicksilver resilience, and tonight was no exception. Rapidly grouping the men, giving them no time to mope, he hurried his raiders back along the path toward Nombre de Dios. Along the route they paused at Venta de Cruces, an inland settlement that served the Spaniards as a way station. Drake and his men had bypassed the village on their way across the Isthmus; now they raged straight through it, pillaging as they went, and then resumed their race to the shore and the pinnaces. Once again Drake had failed to gain any plunder worth recording. But his raid befuddled and upset the Spaniards. In a single night this infuriating Englishman had sprung out of nowhere, captured a mule train, pillaged a town and then vanished as inexplicably as he had appeared. He was as mystifying and elusive as he was terrifying. To minds just emerging from medievalism, with its rich literature of fabulous creatures, Drake's sudden strikes and equally sudden disappearances conjured up visions of the mythical dragon; hence the origin of the epithet El Dragón.

For the next five weeks Drake occupied himself with Spanish shipping. Dividing his men into three groups, he assigned some to guard the ships at the anchorage, while he sent a second group in a pinnace down the coast to the east. "Get along with you, Johnnie," he exhorted the friend he put in charge, "and bring back turkeys and fat hogs to fill the larder." Drake himself took another pinnace west with the remaining men. In a few days Johnnie's group had seized a Spanish sloop laden with livestock meant for the coastal settlements; the raiders set the Spanish crew ashore and took the sloop with the provisions to the anchorage.

Drake's group, meanwhile, seized another ship, this one carrying some gold. He and his men now had a small haul of treasure, and food for several weeks. More important, the warning was going from one Spanish ship to another along the coast that Drake was at sea again—which was exactly what he wanted. He had not abandoned the quest for the treasure-laden mule trains; he was only biding his time.

One day during this period, while cruising far from land, Drake came upon an 80-ton French privateer that had run out of water while searching for Spanish ships to plunder. Her captain, one Guillaume Le Testu, was a French Huguenot—and thus a fellow Protestant and enemy of the popish Spaniards. Drake took pity on him, and conveyed him to the secret anchorage to refresh his men. When Testu and his 70 crewmen asked to join Drake's party, Drake immediately accepted; having by this time lost close to half his English crew, he was willing enough to have extra hands.

By the end of March Drake concluded that the Spaniards on land had relaxed their guard. And now he put into motion one of the most outrageous exploits of his career. The target once again was the mule train from Panama. But this time Drake planned to intercept it at the northern end of the trail, just outside Nombre de Dios, where the Spaniards, having negotiated the mountains and jungles, would think they had nothing left to fear. It was a bold idea.

Leaving his ships under guard at the Isle of Pines anchorage, Drake transported 55 men—35 Englishmen and Frenchmen and 20 Cimaroons—in two pinnaces to the mouth of the Rio Francisco, about 20 miles west of Nombre de Dios. From there he marched his force overland to station them on the very threshold of the town, so close to the harbor that they could hear the ships' carpenters hammering through the sultry night, readying the Spanish fleet for the season's cargo of gold and silver.

And what a cargo it promised to be. From his Cimaroon scouts Drake

A warrior society of runaway slaves

The 30 escaped African slaves who led Francis Drake and his men through the jungles of Panama in 1573 were not merely an isolated group of runaways. They were known as Cimaroons from the Spanish *cimarrones* (cattle that run wild), and there were multitudes of them in bands throughout the Caribbean.

The first Cimaroon (later shortened to "maroon" by the English) was an African slave who arrived at Hispaniola in 1502 with the colonizing expedition of Nicolás de Ovando, and who fled to the mountainous interior within days of setting foot in the New World. Others soon followed, setting up villages in the forests that surrounded Santo Domingo's plantations. By 1570 the Spaniards estimated that more than 7,000 Cimaroons roamed the mountains of Hispaniola, with another 3,000 in the jungles of Panama and still thousands more in the brush of Cuba and the cavern-pocked limestone hills of Jamaica. Other communities spread along the northern littoral of South America, and later they sprang up in Surinam and Brazil.

The Spaniards harassed them unmercifully, destroying their communities and killing or reenslaving the inhabitants. But the Cimaroons endured and even prospered, cultivating a variety of crops and using improvised traps to hunt game. Visiting a Cimaroon stronghold, one of Drake's men proclaimed it "so cleane and sweet that not only the houses but the very streets were pleasant to behold."

Because they were in a constant state of war against their erstwhile masters, the Cimaroons evolved a strictly disciplined society that vested leaders with great authority. Desertion was commonly punished by death, and missionaries reported that the "choicest tortures" penalized murder, robbery and adultery. Religious beliefs, wrote one observer, were "attached to the superstitions of Africa with reverential ardour." In Haiti and Jamaica warriors sported amulets that they believed rendered them bulletproof.

As time went on, bolder Cimaroons attacked the Spaniards. In Hispaniola, Cuba and Jamaica, Cimaroons raided Spanish plantations from their wilderness villages, burning buildings, killing Spaniards and Indians, and stealing women. In Panama Cimaroon depredations reached such a point that in 1570 a Spanish official somberly concluded that "the matter that most urgently demands remedial action is that of dispersing the *cimarrones*, who (such is their daring and audacity) come forth upon the roads to Nombre de Dios, kill travelers and steal what they have with

had learned that no fewer than 190 mules were needed to carry it all, and that a company of 45 heavily armed soldiers had been detailed to guard the train.

When the mules approached, Drake was waiting in perfect ambush, and this time his men made no mistakes. At his whistle, two lines of raiders closed on the treasure like a dragon's jaws snapping shut. The Spanish soldiers put up a brief fight, killing a Cimaroon and wounding the French captain, Testu, in the belly. But they soon broke and ran, and Drake called to his men to let them go.

The loot was worth all the waiting, all the previous frustration. Drake's men found themselves in possession of 100,000 pesos in gold (enough to man and equip 30 Elizabethan warships) and 15 tons of silver. It was far more than the men could carry away themselves, and the lumbering, balky mules would make a quick flight impossible. Drake decided to escape with the gold and hide the silver until his men could return for it. The bags of silver were cached under bushes, leaves and tree roots in the thick jungle off the path, and the wounded Testu was propped against a tree. Posting two Frenchmen to keep watch, Drake promised to send for Testu and the silver as soon as he could. Then he and his men struck out along the coast for the pinnaces, staggering under the weight of the gold.

In Nombre de Dios the fleeing guards raised the alarm, and the Spanish authorities correctly guessed where Drake meant to rendezvous with his pinnaces. They dispatched seven warships to intercept the raiders. But for once luck was on Drake's side. A storm blew out of the west, driving the Spanish warships back to Nombre de Dios. At length Drake regained his two pinnaces and loaded on the gold. True to his word, he sent a party back to rescue Testu and collect what silver it could carry.

But the Spaniards had found the unfortunate Frenchman with one of his guards and had killed them. The other guard had eluded the Spaniards—but the silver had not. The Spaniards had scoured the woods and retrieved most of it.

Even so, Drake had all the booty he had ever dreamed of, and he decided it was time to head home. Before leaving, Drake split the spoils with the slain Testu's crewmen, who immediately set sail for their homeland. He then offered the Cimaroons the choice of anything they wanted. Being practical men, they chose the ironwork from the pinnaces, which Drake had decided to scrap. To the Cimaroon chief he gave a magnificently gilded scimitar as a token of friendship. And then, in a farewell gesture of contempt for the Spanish, Drake sailed past Cartagena once more, flying the English flag, the red-on-white cross of St. George, from the flagship's maintop.

The voyage home was swift and direct. Drake crossed the Atlantic in a mere 23 days, and arrived at Plymouth on Sunday, August 9, 1573— just as the local vicar was delivering his Sunday sermon. The news of Drake's arrival emptied the church as the congregation rushed down to the dock to greet the returning heroes. Within days all England was abuzz with excited accounts of the great quantities of gleaming gold the adventurers had brought home, and of the dashing and invincible captain who had led them.

From obscurity, Drake was suddenly the nation's cynosure. He had

A Cimaroon warrior in Surinam brandishes a European musket as he goes into battle in this 18th Century engraving.

them." The Spaniards' revenge on captured Cimaroons ranged from castration to death by roasting.

The alliances of convenience with Drake and other privateers gave the Cimaroons a perfect opportunity, said one of Drake's men, "to revenge the wrongs and injuries which the Spanish nation had done them." For their part, the privateers could scarcely have asked for better allies. Not only were the Cimaroons uninterested in gold and silver, but, as one of Drake's men observed, they "did us very good service, being unto us guides to direct us; purveyors, to provide victuals for us; house-wrights to build our lodgings; and had able and strong bodies, to carry our necessaries. When need was, they shewed themselves no less valiant than industrious, and of good judgment."

performed feats no other raiders had accomplished in the 80 years the Spaniards had held possession of the New World. He had stormed Nombre de Dios, the vital transshipment point of Spain's fabled wealth; he had harassed Cartagena, the capital from which the Spanish colonial empire was administered; he had looked out upon the far-off Pacific Ocean and returned home with a haul of gold such as had never been seen in England before. No record survives of how the spoils were divided, but Drake and his more than 30 surviving English companions were made rich for life.

If Drake's achievement was thrilling to Englishmen everywhere, it was a political embarrassment to Queen Elizabeth; while happy enough to see Spain twitch, she had no wish to associate herself with deeds that could provoke the King of Spain to war. She therefore publicly ignored her presumptuous subject, which, considering Drake's sudden fame, amounted to an expression of official royal disfavor. Privately, she may have granted Drake an audience, and it is possible that on her urging he disappeared. Whatever the reason, Francis Drake vanished from public view as suddenly as he had appeared. Possibly he went to Ireland; the Queen's men under the Earl of Essex were putting down an uprising in that chronically troubled land, and according to local legend Drake was among the English officers in Ulster.

In 1575, with Ireland quiet for the moment, Drake resurfaced in Plymouth. By this time Queen Elizabeth was vacillating between two camps of her courtiers, and between the two irreconcilable policies they were espousing. One was for more insistent harassment of Spain; the other was for appeasement. Just as the argument was becoming more heated, Drake came before Elizabeth with a proposal for a new voyage to the Spanish Main. His objective this time was to round the tip of South America and sail north to attack the city of Panama, the Pacific coast port where the Peruvian gold was assembled before its overland haul to Nombre de Dios. Such a proposition was too tempting to decline, and Elizabeth resolved her diplomatic quandary with some royal sleight of hand. From her capacious private purse she gave Drake a large sum, probably about 1,000 crowns, while insisting that her ministers of state remain ignorant of the transaction. That way she stood to profit financially if the venture succeeded, while remaining officially innocent of any affront to the Spanish throne.

The preparations went forward with an odd combination of fanfare and secrecy. Drake had no difficulty raising about £4,000 from Plymouth and London investors for a venture that was publicly advertised as a Mediterranean trading expedition to Alexandria, where English merchants swapped leathers and woolens for Egyptian cotton and Indian spices. He sailed on November 15, 1577. Spanish annals record that an ominous comet was seen plunging through the skies over the Spanish Main that night.

Drake's fleet consisted of the *Pelican*, 100 tons and 18 guns, the *Elizabeth*, 80 tons and 16 guns, and the *Marygold*, 30 tons and 16 guns. Two other ships, laden with provisions and gunpowder, were to be scrapped along the way.

Sailing with Drake in the *Pelican* were his youngest brother, Thomas, and a 14-year-old cousin, John Drake. Altogether he had 164 men, among them a couple of painters who were to sketch the route, and about a dozen gentlemen-adventurers who had shipped aboard for the sport. These latter supernumeraries carried authority by virtue of their social rank, and they might acquit themselves well in a battle. But they knew next to nothing about ships and the sea, and they had no responsibili-ties to keep them busy on the voyage. During the long months of inacti-vity, their position became increasingly irksome both to themselves and to the hard-working mariners. They were to give Francis Drake an acid test of his leadership.

Among them was an incorrigible schemer named Thomas Doughty. He and Drake may have become acquainted in Ireland, for Doughty was among the Queen's officers there. In style the two men were complete opposites, one a well-bred courtier who delighted in intrigue, the other a blunt man of action who had risen from the lower classes. They made an unlikely pair, yet they enjoyed a warm friendship. As secretary to one of the Queen's ministers, Doughty seems to have had a hand in giving Drake entré to the court when he was seeking support for his present venture; and Drake, for his part, put Doughty in command of the other adventurers. But both were forceful characters and fiercely ambitious men, and bound to clash.

The first sign of trouble between them came before the fleet had even left European waters. Coming upon a Portuguese merchantman with a cargo of wine, canvas, and silk and velvet fabric, Drake ordered it seized. Shortly thereafter a crewman reported to him that Doughty had stolen some of the items from the prize—violating a time-honored code that required the division of spoils openly among all hands. Drake confront-ed Doughty with the charge; Doughty denied it, saying that Drake's young brother Thomas was the culprit. Swearing "great oaths," accord-ing to one account of the voyage, Drake angrily moved Doughty to another ship, and—showing his faith in his brother—put Thomas in charge of the captured prize.

The fleet proceeded westward, passing through a series of storms that were the worst that Drake had ever encountered. As the gales raged and subsided and raged again, Drake lost sight of one ship after another. With the time lost in searching for them, it took him 54 days just to cross from the Cape Verde Islands to the South American coast, then another three months to pass down its length. Meanwhile Doughty was sowing seeds of divisiveness among the company, bribing and cajoling officers and men in an effort to win their loyalty away from Drake. According to one account, he told Thomas Cuttill, master of the *Pelican*, that "he had a good liking for him" and promised Cuttill £100 if he would take Doughty's side in case of trouble. Doughty next attempted to foment a mutiny against the master of a storeship. And to anyone who would listen he continually asserted that his authority was equal to Drake's.

When he impertinently suggested the same in Drake's presence, Drake swiftly imprisoned him and considered what further action to take. Dra-matically, Drake made up his mind as the fleet reached Port St. Julian, on the southeast side of the tip of South America—the very site where

Magellan had hanged two of his crew for mutiny 58 years before. Drake anchored the vessels, gathered the full company ashore and summoned Doughty before him. "Thomas Doughty," he announced formally, "you have sought by divers means, inasmuch as you may, to discredit me to the great hindrance and overthrow of this voyage, besides other great matters which I have to charge you, the which, if you can clear yourself withal, you and I shall be very good friends, whereto the contrary, you have deserved death."

Doughty denied any wrongdoing. Drake impaneled a jury of 40 men to try him. Among them were a number of Doughty's friends, testimony to Drake's desire for justice. One after another witnesses came forth, and one after another they quoted Doughty's seditious talk.

"What this fellow hath done," thundered Drake, "God will have all his treachery known." He asked the jury whether they found Doughty guilty as charged. They did, and Drake sentenced him to death.

It was one of the most difficult decisions Drake was ever to make. Death was a penalty he seldom inflicted—even on his Spanish enemies. But if Doughty's importuning of the men had been allowed to continue, Drake foresaw the certain dissolution of the enterprise, and this he could not countenance.

By the tradition of the times, a condemned man was entitled to certain courtesies if he was a gentleman. Drake zealously honored the codes. After the trial he and Doughty took communion together as though they were the best of friends. Drake next gave him as sumptuous a meal as he could provide at his captain's table. When Doughty had finished, Drake escorted him ashore. Doughty now knelt and prayed for the Queen and for the success of the expedition. As the crew looked on in silence, the condemned man laid his head on the block. The drummer commenced a roll. Drake gave the signal, and an officer brought down the ax and thrust up Doughty's severed head for all to see. While the bloody object was held aloft, Drake intoned to the hushed audience: "This is the end of traitors."

Having rid the company of its chief troublemaker, Drake was at pains to make clear the import of what he had done, and why. Before moving on, he assembled the entire company once again. "I am a very bad orator, for my bringing up hath not been in learning," he began. Then, with an eloquence that belied his modest demurrer, Drake launched upon a speech in which some historians discern the genesis of the vaunted discipline that became the backbone of the British Navy.

Without directly naming Doughty, he made oblique reference to the recent execution. "We are not to make small reckoning of a man," he said, but then asserted that "we must have these mutinies and discords that are grown amongst us redressed. Let us show ourselves to be all of a company." If any among his listeners did not wish to cooperate, he offered them an escape. "If there be any here willing to return home let me understand of them, and here is the *Marygold*, a ship that I can very well spare," he said. "But let them take heed that they go homeward, for if I find them in my way I will surely sink them."

Voices in the audience murmured that no one wished to return. "Well,

Sir Christopher Hatton, shown clasping a miniature of Queen Elizabeth, used his influence at court to win favor for Francis Drake. Hatton not only helped persuade Elizabeth to back Drake's foray on the Spanish Main in 1577 and 1578, but contributed 1,000 crowns of his own. The golden hind atop Hatton's coat of arms, after which a grateful Drake named his flagship, can be seen at upper right.

then," Drake went on, "came you all forth with your good wills or no?" The men answered aloud that they had. "At whose hands look you to receive your wages?" Drake asked them. "At yours," they replied. Having elicited their admission that he provided their welfare, he went on to demonstrate that it was also he—and he alone—who dictated the terms under which they sailed. He commanded each of the ships' captains to step forward, naming them one by one, and then announced: "I do here discharge every officer of all offices whatsoever."

Having firmly disposed of any mutinous spirit, Drake now appealed to the company's patriotism. "If this voyage should not have good success," he said, "we should not only be a scorning or a reproachful scoffing stock unto our enemies, but also a great blot to our whole country forever." And then, to signify his confidence in his company's loyalty, he pledged that there would be no further executions, summarily restored all his officers to their ranks and, according to his nephew's account, "wishing all men to be friends, he will them to depart about their business."

The crisis was over. No one would cross him again. And the expedition was ready to move forward.

On August 17, 1578, the fleet set sail from Port St. Julian, and three days later stood at the gateway to the Strait of Magellan, through which no nation's ships save Spain's had ever sailed. Here Drake decided to cannibalize the Portuguese prize ship seized at the Cape Verde Islands, reducing his fleet to three (the storeships had already been scrapped as planned). Then, as if to underscore the newness of the undertaking ahead, he changed the name of the flagship from the *Pelican* to the *Golden Hind*, a designation he chose in honor of a major contributor to the voyage, Sir Christopher Hatton, who bore that animal on his coat of arms. Finally, as the fleet began its passage through the towering glacial cliffs and churning waters of the strait, Drake ordered the three ships to strike their topsails in honor of the Queen of England.

After a tortuous passage—during which Drake himself sometimes had to scout ahead in a small boat—the fleet was met by a punishing storm at the entrance to the Pacific. For two solid weeks the winds howled, and Drake lost sight of first one and then the other of his two companion ships. As soon as the storm abated, Drake commenced a search that was to occupy him for four months; through December 1578 he nosed in and out of the Chilean fjords in hopes of finding his missing ships. Not until the new year did he abandon the quest and decide to proceed north without them. It later developed that the *Elizabeth*'s captain had given up the *Golden Hind* for lost and, fearing to venture alone into unknown waters, had turned back for England. The *Marygold*, never found, must have perished in the storm.

With only one ship remaining, Drake decided he had to abandon his plans for an assault on Panama. But he could still make mischief with Spanish coastal shipping, and this he now set out to do. Nearing the port of Valparaiso, he encountered a Spanish ship about to set off for Panama; seizing her, he made a haul of gold worth £8,000, 1,770 jars of wine and a pilot to show him the way up the coast to the Peruvian capital of Lima. A number of smaller captures along the way fetched Drake and his crew

4,000 ducats' worth of silver, a chest of bullion, a crucifix studded with emeralds, and valuable silks and linens. But at Callao de Lima they got wind of something that made all the foregoing seem trifling. A captured Spanish sailor told them that a big vessel named *Nuestra Señora de la Concepción* had sailed two weeks before for Panama. Because she was one of the few merchantmen that bothered to carry arms in these sequestered waters, the Spanish seamen nicknamed her *Cacafuego*, loosely translatable as "Spitfire." And for good reason was she armed: her hold was packed brimful with silver and gold.

Here was a prize worth chasing. Drake immediately set a course for Panama, and promised a gold chain to whoever should sight the *Cacafuego* first. All eyes on the *Golden Hind* greedily scanned the horizon for two weeks as the ship beat north by west in swift pursuit of the Spaniard. At last, on March 1, 15-year-old John Drake called out from a perch in the topmast that he could see a large vessel three leagues ahead.

Aboard the *Cacafuego*, which was taking her ease in the journey north, Captain Juan de Anton was surprised to spy another ship on the horizon, and, not expecting an enemy, put about to greet the stranger. Drake craftily waited until the *Cacafuego* came alongside, then sent his boarders swarming to the attack while bellowing for the Spanish captain to yield in the name of Her Majesty the Queen of England. Under a rain of musket balls and arrows, the astonished Spanish crew surrendered. Captain Anton was taken prisoner and brought aboard the *Golden Hind*, where Drake treated his captive with his usual courtesy.

First he gave the defeated captain a tour of the *Golden Hind*, and then he sat down with him for a festive dinner, where the service was gilded silver, violins played madrigals and young John Drake stood like a dutiful page at attention behind his cousin's chair, wearing the gold chain he had earned.

Meanwhile Drake had led the captured *Cacafuego* a safe distance to sea, beyond sight of the Peruvian coast. There it took four days to relieve her of her dazzling cargo: 13 chests of silver coins, 26 tons of silver ingots, 80 pounds of gold, and uncounted boxes of jewels and pearls. When the job was done, Drake wrote a formal receipt for Captain Anton to present to his own government and, before returning the prisoner to the now-lightened *Cacafuego*, wrote a note commanding the officers of the *Elizabeth* and the *Marygold* to grant the Spaniard safe conduct, should he fall in with either of them.

Drake himself must now be on his way. But which way should he go? The *Golden Hind* was bulging with spoils, and upon Captain Anton's return to Spanish territory Drake could expect Spanish warships to be on the prowl for him. To go back the way he had come would guarantee a fight. No mention is made in any of the accounts of the voyage that Drake, when he left Plymouth, ever intended to go beyond Spanish America. But now, to make good his escape, Drake proceeded to circumnavigate the world—a stunning feat of seamanship that no mariners had attempted since Magellan's forlorn survivors had straggled tattered and sick into Seville 57 years before.

In Drake's case it was a voyage marked by careful planning, excellent navigation and, consequently, a relative lack of incident. From South

Broadside to broadside amid clouds of gun smoke, Francis Drake's Golden Hind (foreground) and the Spanish treasure ship known as the Cacafuego grapple off the coast of Peru in this contemporary engraving. After plundering the vessel, Drake let her continue on her way, still flying her royal ensign.

America Drake sailed the *Golden Hind* north, putting ashore along the Mexican coast to commandeer provisions and repair some rotting timbers. He secured enough water to last 50 days at sea and then, at the end of July 1579, set off to conquer the Pacific.

For the next two months a benign following wind pushed the *Golden Hind* southwest across the seemingly endless ocean. Almost daily, rain showers replenished the water casks, and the men supplemented their diet by catching fish. At last, on September 30, Drake sighted one of the Caroline Islands about 6,000 miles from his departure point, and soon found himself surrounded by a horde of Carolinians in canoes. Drake exchanged a few gifts with the islanders, but when he refused to give more presents they grew angry and commenced pelting the ship with rocks. Drake sailed on, but he was harassed by the islanders for four days, escaping them after his men fired a harquebus barrage into the crowd of canoes, killing about 20 of the attackers. From the Carolines he continued west to the Moluccas, or Spice Islands, where he was greeted cordially by the Sultan of Ternate. Though the Sultan already had trade agreements with the Portuguese, he seemed anxious to expand his commerce with Europe and earnestly made a pact with Drake establishing England as an ally. To seal the friendship, he allowed the *Golden Hind* to depart on November 9 loaded with a hugely valuable six-ton cargo of cloves.

And now came Drake's most worrisome moment of the voyage. Sailing southwest, he ran aground on the night of January 9, 1580, on a coral reef east of Celebes. Hastily, he jettisoned some heavy cannon and backed the sails; within 18 hours he had worked his way free. Miraculously, the *Golden Hind* was still sound, and Drake coursed swiftly southwest, coming ashore at Java for provisions and more impromptu diplomacy, this time with the local rajah. Then came the news that Portuguese ships were approaching, and Drake set sail again on March 26, heading across the Indian Ocean.

Aided by fair southwest winds, the *Golden Hind* sped across the ocean in 56 days, twice as fast as Magellan's crew had sailed the 3,500 miles. It took Drake nearly a month to round the Cape of Good Hope, fighting contrary winds and landing frequently in search of water. But once past the Cape, Drake sailed rapidly north, turning the bulge of Africa, speeding past the Cape Verde Islands and the Canaries and finally arriving triumphantly at Plymouth on September 26, 1580.

All told, Drake had traveled 34,000 miles in 35 months since leaving England and had returned with about half of his 164-man crew still alive. It was a personal triumph of the highest magnitude, and his contacts with the island potentates of the East would one day expand into an empire for Britain.

But for all immediate purposes, the climax of the voyage had come in the seizing of the *Cacafuego*, and with her all the spoils the *Golden Hind* could carry. Even though he had given up his original idea of storming Panama, Drake had won his major objective; he had shown the vaunted Spanish Empire to be ill protected and vulnerable. Other powers took heed. From now on, the Main was to be a scene of international turmoil.

Drake's arrival in England occasioned an even greater outpouring of public joy and admiration than had his successful return from the Caribbean in 1573. He was mobbed everywhere he went, and pamphlets glorifying his exploits appeared all over the country. The backers of the voyage all profited magnificently, and none more so than Queen Elizabeth. For her secret investment of nearly 1,000 crowns, she received a dividend of no less than 47,000 crowns.

At the risk of further affronting the already enraged Spaniards, the Queen finally decided to make public her admiration and support for the heroic captain. She went so far as to board the *Golden Hind* at Greenwich to confer knighthood upon Drake in a gala ceremony. The event—which seized the nation's rapt attention—proved to be a hectic affair. While the Queen and the diplomatic corps were being given a tour of the flag-draped ship and a look at some of the chestfuls of gleaming silver the voyage had fetched, so many uninvited townsmen tried to push past the

During his round-the-world voyage, Drake genuflects before Babu, the wealthy Sultan of the Moluccan spice island of Ternate. Babu's people greeted the Englishmen with dishes of rice, chicken, sugar cane, plantains and coconuts. In return, Drake ordered his musicians on the Golden Hind to strike up a lively tune, which delighted the islanders and set the tone for a peaceful and profitable five-day sojourn.

royal guards that the gangplank collapsed, dropping 100 or so would-be party-crashers into the waters below.

After the guests had their fill from casks of wine and cauldrons of steaming food and were made the merrier by a troop of strumming musicians, Elizabeth commanded Drake to kneel before her. Then, with that love of wordplay in which Elizabethans delighted, she said: "Master Drake, the King of Spain has asked for your head, and we have a weapon here with which to remove it." Handing a gilded sword to the French Ambassador, she had Drake lightly tapped on the head and proclaimed a knight. The crowd cheered and threw their caps in the air.

With his wealth Drake bought an estate in Devon. Above the fireplace in its great hall he hung the coat of arms given to him by Elizabeth, bearing the Latin motto *Sic Parvis Magna*—"Greatness from Small Beginnings." The small boy who had had his first sniff of salt air from a humble home in an abandoned hulk in the Medway had traveled a great distance indeed.

Thus far Drake had been operating essentially on his own. He was to spend the next five years trying to persuade the Queen and her counselors to exploit for the nation's wealth and glory the path that he had opened. If Spanish ships plying the trade route from the Main to Seville were cut off at their point of origin, he reasoned, the fearsome might of Spain would collapse for want of gold. But he was putting forward an idea in advance of its time, and he had no luck until 1585. By that time Spain was building a massive armada and threatening to send it against the English coast, and Drake's strategy suddenly made sense. Now when he came before Queen Elizabeth with a new proposal, she listened.

Drake's plan was the most ambitious he had yet concocted. This time he meant to seize the cities of Santo Domingo and Cartagena, which would make him a threat to all the lesser ports in between. Continuing west, he would send a land expedition across the Isthmus to Panama, and then he would go northwest to Honduras, the site of some of the silver mines. In addition to silver, he expected to collect in ransom from the cities, he said, nothing less than two and a half million gold ducats—an amount nearly 12 times Elizabeth's budget for annual government expenses. Torn between the irresistible lure of such a fortune and fear of Spanish reprisals, Elizabeth dissembled and temporized. But at last she consented to England's first national assault against the Spanish Main.

She authorized the use of two ships from the Royal Navy—the 600-ton, 30-gun *Elizabeth Bonaventure,* which would serve as the flagship, and a 250-ton vessel named the *Aid.* Private merchants from England's seaport cities put up another 19 ships and several pinnaces, and a land force of 2,300 soldiers was raised.

The expedition was finally ready to leave Plymouth on September 14, 1585. After some stops along the Spanish coast and in the Cape Verde Islands, where he undertook minor raids against Spanish shipping to let King Philip know that he was "mightily at sea again," Drake turned west to cross the Atlantic and launch his grand design. It was late December by the time he reached the first of his objectives, Santo Domingo on the island of Hispaniola.

Santo Domingo was the oldest city in the Americas. It had been found-

In commemoration of Drake's epic circumnavigation, a grateful Queen Elizabeth I presented her knight with this rich gilt-on-silver trophy as a New Year's gift in 1582. The map engraved on the globe is by Gerardus Mercator, the Flemish cartographer and mathematician.

THE. Famouse West Indian voyadge made
by the Englishe fleete of 23 shippes and Barkes
wherin weare gotten the Townes of S·IAGO:
:S:DOMINGO, CARTAGENA and
:S·AVGVSTINES the same beinge begon
from Plimmouth in the Moneth of September
1585 and ended at Portesmouth in Iulie
1586 the whole coarse of the saide Viadge
beinge plainlie described by the pricked line
Newlie come forth by Baptista B

Norum bega

Virginia

The waye Homewarde

Ilandes of
Acores

Scale of 300 Leagues

Baye of Mexico

Jamaica   Hispaniola   S·Iohns Ilande

Ilandes of Capo
Verde

The waye Outwarde

WEST   INDIA

Equinoctiall

The Occean commonlie called
the South Sea

Brasill

Lima   The Cuntrye of Peru

North

East

Sea Connyes

Seuen or 18 Degres to the Southwarde of Rio de
Plata lye the Straites of Magellanos

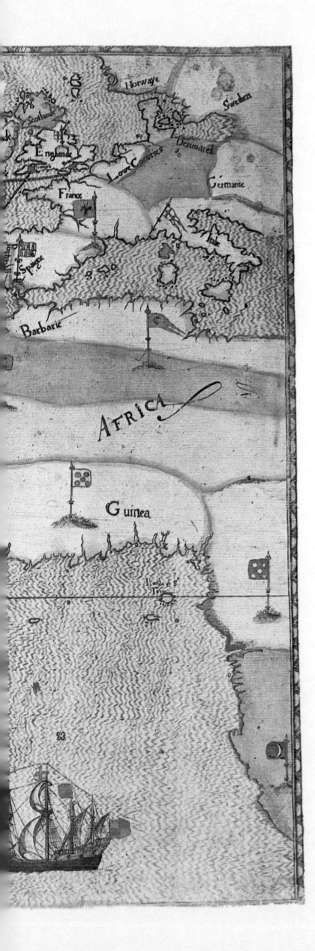

ed by Bartholomew Columbus, brother of Christopher, in 1496 and had served as the capital of the Spaniards' New World empire for the next five decades. At the middle of the 16th Century the Spanish colonial government, lured by the gold and precious stones on the mainland, had moved the capital to Cartagena. But the hidalgos who had remained at Santo Domingo were beginning to cultivate sugar and tobacco and were not short of wealth. Their mansions, standing on broad avenues fringed with stately palms, were among the most majestic in the Caribbean, and their city was the first in the New World to found a university, which lent it a cultural aura lacking in the rough-and-tumble outposts of the empire. For all these reasons Santo Domingo was the most prestigious of New World cities. And for all these reasons it seemed to Drake a promising hunting ground for gold.

His stratagem was a grander version of the one he had used when leading his first raids more than a decade before: some diversionary feints at sea followed by a surprise attack from landward. Just after daylight on New Year's Day of 1586, Drake wakened sleeping Santo Domingo with a deafening naval bombardment of the main fort guarding the harbor. While the astonished Santo Domingans rushed pell-mell to repulse this seaward threat, 1,000 troops who had been secretly landed in the night rushed in from the rear of the city. With volleys of musket fire and flashing cutlasses, they drove the citizens into the countryside. Then the English barricaded the marketplace and hoisted the flag of England on the castle tower. That done, Drake casually seized the lone Spanish vessel that rode in the harbor, and appropriately christened her the *New Year's Gift*.

Then began a time of mounting frustration and anger for Drake. When a quick search of the town turned up little or no gold, Drake sent an emissary to the Governor, who was hiding in the hills, and demanded a ransom of 500,000 ducats. The Governor declared that he could pay no such sum—to which Drake retorted by threatening to burn a block of the handsome city for every day he had to wait. For 30 days the Governor held fast; for 30 days Drake's men rummaged through deserted households and cellars and, finding no loot, left flames behind them. At the end of a month the Governor finally produced an offer of 25,000 ducats and Drake decided to call off the siege. The ransom was considerably less than he had counted on, but clearly the town would yield no more.

Hoping for better luck elsewhere, Drake turned southwest and headed across the Caribbean for Cartagena, which lay nestled on the Colombian shore inside a double harbor *(pages 72-73)*. Arriving in the afternoon, he

Drake's voyage of 1585 to 1586 is traced on this contemporary map, which shows how the marauders sailed in 23 ships to the Cape Verde Islands and sacked Santiago before crossing the Atlantic to plunder Santo Domingo, Cartagena and St. Augustine. The stop at Virginia on the passage home was to check on some English colonists put ashore 10 months before (pages 92-93).

brought the fleet to the mouth of the outer harbor and anchored, a diversionary tactic designed to keep the Spaniards' attention fixed on the ships. When night fell Drake disembarked his troops to march across the narrow spit of land leading past the inner harbor to the city. They found the approach more heavily fortified than they expected: the path had been studded with poisoned barbs, two Spanish galleys lay in the inner harbor, ready to enfilade the troops as they marched across the spit, and four cannon and 750 Spaniards guarded the entrance to the town. Drake's men evaded the first hurdle, bypassing the poisoned barbs and eluding the enfilading galleys by wading through the breaking waves on the ocean side of the spit. Then, in hand-to-hand combat, they forced their way through the rest of the route into the city.

The scavenging soldiers had better pickings in the households here than in Santo Domingo. They found jewelry and precious stones in family strongboxes. They also seized the bronze bells from the church tower and 80 pieces of artillery from the fort. But 110,000 ducats—a fourth of his initial demand—was all that Drake could wrench in ransom from Cartagena's Governor.

Nevertheless, with Cartagena under his heel, Drake had conquered the capital city of the Spanish Main and thus held a key to the Caribbean coast. But his victory was a pyrrhic one. He had lost two thirds of his men, either to skirmishes or to disease, and was in a weak position for assaulting Panama. And so the bold Drake, the awesome El Dragón, who in his younger days had never quailed in the face of the most improbable odds, was stricken with a fit of middle-aged cautiousness. He decided to pocket his disappointing loot and scrap his plans for Panama.

To stay-at-home strategists it seemed an incredible turnabout, and in afteryears such folk were to censure him for losing his nerve. But times had changed since Drake's earlier visits to the Main. The Spaniards were better prepared than before. Moreover, the two Governors' refusals to meet ransom demands—though Drake never knew whether they actually had the money—indicated a certain stiffening of Spanish resolve. Drake now believed that, to hold Cartagena and simultaneously march on Panama, he would have to send to England for reinforcements. There was no guarantee that Elizabeth would oblige, for to do so would mean leaving Britain's own coasts undefended—inviting Philip to hurl the promised Armada upon them.

Believing all this, Drake released Cartagena after six weeks of occupation and set sail for home. He traveled north, stopping to raid the Spanish settlement of St. Augustine in Florida, where he seized a dozen brass cannon and a treasure chest worth about £2,000. He next came ashore on the coast of Virginia, where his countryman Sir Walter Raleigh had sponsored a colony the year before. The colonists, reduced by hunger, disease and Indian attacks, were ready to quit the venture, and Drake put them aboard his vessels and took them home to England. He reached Plymouth on July 28, 1586.

The backers of the voyage were bitterly disappointed. The combined ransoms of Santo Domingo and Cartagena fetched only 15 shillings on every pound invested, for a 25 per cent loss. Yet for all its failures, the voyage paid dividends of another kind. Rumors swept across Europe

The lost colony of Roanoke Island

To Sir Walter Raleigh, the Elizabethan poet, courtier and adventurer, the riches of the New World lay not only in the treasure to be taken from the Spaniards but also in the abundant natural resources of the American coasts. With the support of Francis Drake, who sought an advance base for privateering, Raleigh launched two attempts to establish English colonies on the shores of Virginia.

The first venture ended disastrously. When Drake returned from the Spanish Main in 1586, he found 104 starving and demoralized colonists at the settlement on Roanoke Island, where they had landed 10 months before. He rescued them. The second attempt, made a year later, resulted in a mystery that has puzzled historians ever since.

To lead the second colony, Raleigh chose John White, an accomplished naturalist and artist, who had visited the Virginia shores twice before, in 1584 and 1585. But White unfortunately lacked the ability to command. When he and his 112 followers reached the West Indies, he could not persuade the ship's captain to halt long enough to acquire livestock for the colony. The captain insisted on hurrying on to Roanoke Island, where the first colony had failed.

The colonists went ashore but they demanded that White return to England for adequate supplies. On August 28, 1587, White departed from Roanoke, leaving behind 85 men, 17 women and 11 children, among them his newborn granddaughter, Virginia Dare, the first English child born in the New World.

Unable to secure funds, White did not return to Roanoke Island for three years. When he finally waded ashore on August 17, 1591, as a member of a privateering expedition, he found the place deserted. Only one cryptic clue to the pioneers' whereabouts greeted his eye. On a log was carved the word Croatoan.

That there was no cross appended cheered White, for that was the sign agreed upon should the colonists be forced to flee the island. But where were the settlers? Had they set off voluntarily to seek food and shelter among the Indians on neighboring Croatoan Island? Had they then been massacred? Or could they be alive somewhere inland? White never found out—nor has anyone else.

John White's map of the Virginia coastline shows the area between the mouth of Chesapeake Bay to the north and what is now Cape Lookout, North Carolina. The chart highlights in crimson both Roanoke Island, site of the ill-fated Lost Colony, and Croatoan Island, some 50 miles to the south, where the settlers may have sought refuge.

that Drake had annexed Panama, taken the whole of Hispaniola, begun building fortifications at Santo Domingo, and scattered the entire Spanish fleet. Not a word of it was true. But for Spain the effect was devastating. The Bank of Seville went bankrupt; the Bank of Venice, to which King Philip was heavily in debt, appeared likely to do the same; and the Fugger Bank at Augsburg, which circulated a newsletter to financiers, spread fear among other European banking houses. All these alarums and excursions subsided in time. But the effect was to diminish greatly the specter of omnipotent Spain that loomed so menacingly over the states of continental Europe and the British Isles.

For the next 10 years the bold adventurer who had touched off all these international tremors was for the most part occupied in pursuits closer to home. Elizabeth gave him the title of Her Majesty's Admiral-at-the-Seas, and named him to a commission charged with overseeing the royal dockyards. Meanwhile he was elected mayor of the town of Plymouth, and served also as a Member of Parliament. Except for a swift foray out to battle the great Spanish Armada when it finally attacked in 1588, he remained ashore throughout most of the decade. But he never lost his dream of strangling the Spanish trade route in the New World, and he persisted in trying to induce the Queen and her counselors to allow him one more voyage.

Toward the middle of the 1590s his prospects brightened, thanks to troubles that beset the Spanish Empire. French privateers were moving in increasing numbers onto the islands fringing the northern edge of the Caribbean, and Dutch trading vessels were nibbling along the coast of Venezuela. With such predators theatening the base of her wealth, Spain had to declare a moratorium on all debts at home in 1595 while she awaited the annual shipment of Peruvian gold. Drake urgently pointed out to his sovereign that now was the time to strike at Panama. Elizabeth wavered; by the time she finally made up her mind, most of the Spanish treasure fleet had already reached Seville. One ship, however, had put into San Juan, Puerto Rico, for repairs. That single ship had an irresistible cargo of three million gold ducats. Besides, there remained the entrepôt of Panama. Thus Drake belatedly got approval for another expedition and sailed in August.

It was a formidable undertaking: 27 sail, led by the flagship *Defiance*, with 1,500 seamen and 1,000 troops. But for Drake this voyage, like so many others, was to prove a study in frustration. The Queen had no sooner given her tardy consent than she insisted that Drake share command of the expedition with his old cousin and sometime mentor, Sir John Hawkins. Like the Spaniards, who said of Hawkins and Drake that "God made them, and the devil brought them together," Elizabeth seems to have judged them an inevitable team. She judged wrong. Drake had exercised independent command too often and too boldly to share it now with anyone else; and Hawkins, who was now almost 70, was crotchety and slow moving. Thomas Maynarde, an Army captain who wrote an account of the voyage, noted that Hawkins "entered into matters with so laden a foote that the other's meat woulde be eaten before his spit could come to the fire," and he added that it was not long before "cholericke speeches" were passing between the two men.

But Drake was soon relieved of the burden of dual command. Hawkins took sick on the outbound passage, and died just as the fleet came in sight of San Juan. "Ah," Drake said as Hawkins expired, "I could grieve for thee, but now is no time for me to lay down my spirits." Pausing only for a quick burial, Drake pushed on the next morning toward his target.

But his attack was doomed from the start. Because the expedition had taken so long to get under way, the Spaniards had learned of it at least three weeks before the English had even left Plymouth. They had moved the three million gold ducats out of the crippled ship, stored the treasure safely in an impregnable San Juan fort and blocked the entrance to the harbor with a sunken hulk. Without even attempting his old tactic of attacking from the rear of the city, Drake called off the assault. The first phase of the expedition had come to nought.

Promising his dejected officers he would take them to 20 places "more wealthy and easier to be gotten," Drake set a course for Nombre de Dios. But he found the town deserted; the transshipment point had been moved to Portobelo, a newer settlement 20 miles up the coast. Now even the ebullient Drake was beginning to lose his old spark. He mourned to Captain Maynarde that he "wondred that since his cominge out of England he never sawe sayle worthye the givinge chace unto." All he could do was burn the deserted town—a spiteful gesture that netted him no treasure. Meanwhile soldiers he had sent across the Isthmus toward Panama came staggering back in defeat after encountering a Spanish force on the trail.

As a last resort Drake decided to try his luck along the Honduran and Nicaraguan coasts. But he had to stop first to get water. Going ashore at the fetid and insect-ridden island of Escudo de Veraguas, he met a new disaster. A crippling wave of dysentery swept through the company—striking even Drake himself, who on earlier voyages had seemed miraculously immune to such afflictions.

On January 23, 1596, he took to his cabin aboard ship, unable to give his customary cheer to his men. After a while he seemed a little better and roused himself sufficiently to order the ship to proceed to Portobelo. But on the 27th, while the fleet was still under way, he fell into a delirium and demanded pettishly to be dressed in his ceremonial armor. Early on the morning of the 28th his fever and his raving subsided—and before sunrise he was dead. He was about 55.

The next morning the fleet anchored offshore a league or two from Nombre de Dios, the site where 23 years before Drake had executed his first dazzling triumph. The Englishmen placed their leader's body in a lead coffin. Two expendable ships were brought alongside the *Defiance* and set blazing for a funeral pyre, and the coffin was slid into the sea.

The great admiral who had led Britain in its first offensive against the mighty Spanish Empire would plague the Main no more. Spanish church bells pealed joyfully with the news, and the poets Lope de Vega and Miguel Cervantes celebrated Drake's death in verse. But the Spanish celebration was premature. Before Drake had been dead a quarter of a century, the Main would be harassed by many another gadfly swarming in on the path that the legendary El Dragón had cut.

The death of Drake, following his unsuccessful attempt to sack Panama, is somberly noted along with landmarks and navigational instructions in the pilot's log of his ship, the Defiance. Though Drake succumbed to dysentery—called the "bludie flix" in the log—the Spanish gleefully reported that he died of grief at his failure. His death date in the log, January 28, 1595, is according to the old-style Julian calendar. Based on the modern calendar, the year was 1596.

Tera Firma.

E·N·E   E·B·N.   Eſt   E·B·S·

Farlion   Baſtimentos   S·E·B·E   S·E   ya de punto Bello.

The coaſte lieth E·N·E·   and △△   The entraunce in to Puerto Bello   w·s·w·   Iſla de Buena Ventura.
                    9 D·15 m.   Rock or ſmale ſlande or Farlion
                                     de punto Bello

This lande heare preſentid ſherwith the firme or runinge of parte of the neck and
from Nombre de Dios / or ſmeane from the weſte Cape of Nombre de Dios Cauld
Baſtimentes vntill you com to the weſtwarde vnto the ſlandes of Laies Kinar
vieſas de Diſcribinge the rocks and ſlandes betwene thes too placis alſo the entranc
in to the good harburo calid Puerto Bello note hou the corraunte ſetith heare to the
N·E· The variaſion of the Compas 2 pointes to the weſt and all what ſameuer
J. haue heare in this place notid J haue notid it plamelie with our engliſhe
Compas as it hathe ſhewid with reſpecte of the variaſion

This Morninge when the diſcription notid or taken of this lande beinge the
28· of Januarie 1595· beinge wedens daie in the morninge S.ʳ Francis Dracke
Died of the bludie flix ryghte of the ſlande de Buena Ventura ſom· 6·
Leagues at ſea whom nou reſteth with the Lorde

The heretics who humbled the might of Spain

Though they were fewer in numbers than the English and French, the Dutch also prowled the Spanish Main, and in some ways they were the most exasperating interlopers of all. For one thing, Spanish claims to suzerainty over the Netherlands were being bitterly and successfully resisted by the Dutch. Moreover, the Dutch were Protestants, and thus heretics as well as rebels in the eyes of Catholic Spain.

The first Dutch forays into the Main were in 1599 for the purpose of securing salt from the vast deposits at Araya on the coast of Venezuela. Since salt was vital as a preservative in their thriving herring fishery, the Dutch were soon sending as many as 10 ships to Araya each month. And to the gathering of salt the Dutch added trade in hides and tobacco—as well as an occasional raid on Spanish shipping.

The Dutch grew bolder as it became ever more clear that Spain could not police its vast domain; Dutch planners calculated that for an investment of 2.5 million florins in ships and men, they could acquire a colony—namely Bahia, in Brazil—that would yield eight million florins each year from sugar, tobacco, cotton and timber.

The Dutch expedition, numbering 26 vessels with 450 cannon and 3,300 men, surprised Bahia in May 1624. While Dutch troops stormed the shore batteries, the warships sank or captured every one of the vessels in the harbor. By nightfall the Dutch flag flew over Bahia.

The Spaniards recaptured Bahia within a year by attacking with the greatest fleet ever seen in the New World—52 ships armed with 1,185 cannon and carrying 12,566 men. But victory was soured by catastrophe when Spanish Admiral Don Fadrique de Toledo lost most of his ships in a ferocious storm while returning to Spain. The Dutch, meanwhile, persisted in harassing Spanish shipping. In 1628 Admiral Piet Hein made one of the biggest hauls of booty in history by capturing off Cuba four galleons from the Spanish treasure fleet with cargo worth 15 million guilders.

By 1650 the Dutch had not only won their independence from Spain but also were in the New World to stay. The islands of Curaçao, Saba, St. Martin and St. Eustatius were thriving Dutch colonies. And these possessions helped make the Dutch indisputably the greatest traders in the world. As the Dutch poet Joost van den Vondel put it, "Wherever profit leads us, to every sea and shore, for love of gain the wide world's harbors we explore."

As welcomers on shore wave greetings, the Hollandtschen Tuyn makes sail along a bight of the Zuider Zee to Amsterdam in 1605 with a cargo of specie and sugar, after making a successful raid on the Spanish Main. Here the 1,000-ton privateer flies a flag with the lion of Holland from her mainmast and the banners of the Prince of Orange and Amsterdam fore and aft.

Unmindful of shore batteries to the left, Dutch warships crowd the harbor at Bahia, Brazil, to bombard the city in 1624. Wrote a Jesuit priest who witnessed the humiliating capture: "The panic was so general that neither whites nor Indians were of any use, everyone seeking a safe place without attempting to fight."

The citizens of Bahia minister to a wounded soldier in this allegorical Spanish painting celebrating the recapture of the city from the Dutch on May 1, 1625. At right, Admiral Don Fadrique de Toledo presents a tapestry that shows King Philip IV being crowned with a laurel wreath as he stands astride the corpses of Heresy, Anger and War.

Chapter 4

The rise of a bloodthirsty brotherhood

ne afternoon sometime in the early 1630s, a Spanish treasure galleon was making its way past the west coast of Hispaniola when the crewmen spied a swiftly moving pinnace bearing down on them. They hurried to inform their captain, who took one look at the small, single-masted craft and turned away in annoyance. "What then?" he exclaimed, according to a narrative published years later. "Must I be afraid of such a pitiful thing?" On that disdainful note, he descended to his cabin and gave the matter no further thought.

The captain was due for a surprise, because the pinnace—dwarfed though she was by the mighty Spanish galleon—was bent upon an act of astonishing impertinence. At the head of the 28 men she carried was a French desperado named Pierre Le Grand, whose deed this day would long outlive his brief career. By dint of vigorous rowing to assist the drive of the sails, Le Grand's crew brought the pinnace alongside the Spanish ship by dusk. The men nimbly nosed her in under the bow, then grappled onto the galleon's fore chains.

Just as the pinnace's crewmen were about to board, Le Grand made them an amazing proposal. He suggested that a hole be drilled in the side of his own vessel to make her sink. There would then be no turning back; either he and his men would succeed in their daring design, or they would die. The men roared their agreement and then, swearing oaths of mutual fidelity, they swarmed aboard the Spanish treasure ship, brandishing pistols and cutlasses.

What the Spanish crewmen were doing all this time is not related in the account. Presumably, having been sharply set down by their arrogant captain for calling him on deck the first time, they were reluctant to raise a further alarm. In any case, it was getting dark, and the true intentions of the men in the pinnace might not have been clear until it was too late—and by then the Spaniards were paralyzed with fear.

Some of the men from the pinnace headed straight for the galleon's gun room, where they seized the ship's small arms and slaughtered the few Spaniards who stood in their way. Others raced for the captain's cabin, where they found that worthy playing cards with his officers. The invaders put a pistol to his heart and ordered him to surrender the ship—which he instantly did. "Jesus bless us!" cried one of the stunned Spaniards. "Are these devils, or what are they?"

The answer to the bewildered Spaniard's question was that this handful of ruffians were buccaneers—a new and violent generation of poachers on the Spanish Main. The audacious Pierre Le Grand and his cutthroats were not even particularly exceptional examples of the breed. From the treasure galleon, Le Grand realized a haul that the account described as "a magnificent prize"—and then he faded from the scene. Nothing more is known about him. But there were thousands of such marauders swarming the Main in the 17th Century. Like John Hawkins, they were men interested in trade. Like Francis Drake and the other privateers, they made a fine art of belaboring the Spaniards and relieving them of their wealth. But the buccaneers shared a common characteristic that set them apart from all the earlier predators: unlike Hawkins, Drake and the others, these men made their lives on the Main; they inhabited

In a light pinnace dwarfed by the sun-gilded Spanish galleon looming over it, buccaneers close with their prey in this 1905 reconstruction by the famed Howard Pyle. So maneuverable and swift were the marauders' small vessels that many times they could slip in under the guns of a galleon and achieve boarding position before the victim could fire an effective shot in defense.

the very islands the Spaniards claimed for themselves. And, living cheek by jowl with their enemies, they brought the Spanish crown a century of unrelieved woe.

The name buccaneer comes from the Arawak Indian word buccan, meaning a grill of green wood on which meat was smoked over a slow fire; the early buccaneers learned the technique from the Arawak of the Greater Antilles, and it became a lasting trademark. No one knows who the first buccaneers were, or exactly when they established themselves on the islands that became their chief haunts: Hispaniola, Cuba, Jamaica and Puerto Rico. It is likely that a few castaway privateers—French, Dutch, English, Portuguese—along with some Spanish renegades were living in the sparsely colonized islands from the mid-16th Century on. Yet the great influx of venturesome men who turned buccaneers and set upon the Spanish did not begin until the 17th Century. And that influx was indirectly triggered, interestingly enough, by an act of the Spanish King himself.

In the year 1606 Philip III of Spain sent down one of the most unfortunate royal fiats of his long and benighted reign. He ordered his colonial subjects in Caracas, Venezuela, and on the neighboring islands of Margarita and Cumaná to cease forthwith the planting and curing of tobacco. It was an order comprehensible only in the context of the times, and in the context of Spanish cupidity.

Smoking, unknown to Europeans only a few decades before, was suddenly becoming a popular custom. To partake of the marvelous New World weed was "a point of good fellowship," as King James I of England had noted two years before. "He that will refuse to take a pipe of Tobacco among his fellowes," wrote His Majesty, "is accounted peevish and no good company, even as they doe with tippeling in the cold Easterne Countries."

Of more concern to his rival King Philip was the fact that tobacco was on its way to becoming a major import in England and on the Continent. But instead of reaching Europe in Spanish ships by way of Seville's tax-levying Casa de Contratación, tobacco was being transported freely across the Atlantic by Dutch, French and English smugglers who bought it illegally from Spanish settlers. Philip believed that a ban on the growing of tobacco in the environs of Caracas would drive away the alien ships calling at that port to collect it. He was right. The foreign ships were driven away—to other tobacco-growing Spanish settlements.

On the island of Trinidad, off the northeast shoulder of Venezuela, the smugglers found colonists unaffected by the ban and eager to swap tobacco for cloth, tools and wheat, for which the colonial authorities charged exorbitant prices. One English captain trading at Trinidad noted that 20 foreign tobacco traders visited the island in 1607, immediately following the imposition of the ban. The year after that, he reported that the number had climbed to 30. By 1611 an estimated 100,000 pounds of tobacco was being consumed in England alone; another 100,000 was probably going up in smoke in France, the Netherlands and the German principalities. Yet no more than a trifling 6,000 pounds of the leaf passed through the port of Seville.

As an overseer directs the planting of tobacco shoots, slaves in sheds roll the dried leaves for export, in this depiction of a 17th Century Caribbean plantation. Wrote an Englishman in 1612, to extol the wonders of the profitable New World crop: "It is planted, gathered, seasoned and made up fit for the Merchant in short time, and with easie labour."

But the illicit tobacco trade had effects beyond depriving the Spanish Treasury of customs duties. While they hawked their merchandise among Spanish settlers, some of the smugglers inevitably found places to settle themselves. From Trinidad they moved south along the mainland coast to the vast delta of the Orinoco River, then down to the mighty Amazon. The first non-Spanish settlements in South America were for the most part temporary trading posts manned by transient adventurers, "some of them doing it one year and another lot the next," as one Spanish official put it in a report to the crown. Few records of such transitory settlements survive, and even fewer accounts of reprisals the Spaniards took against them. Among the men who tried settlement on the mainland and found it too dangerous to stay was an Englishman named Thomas Warner. After leaving the mainland, Warner was determined to find a place where he could plant tobacco without further interference from the Spaniards.

Sailing around the Caribbean in 1622, he came to the small island of St. Christopher's, one of the northerly Lesser Antilles. He found the place well watered and blessed with such fertile soil, related a 17th Century chronicler, that "he well viewing the Island thought it would be a very convenient place for ye planting of tobaccoes." Warner returned to London, found a group of merchants to back him and in January 1624 was back on St. Christopher's with 15 or 20 Englishmen ready to sow tobacco. The small number of his companions obscures the monumental significance of his undertaking. Warner's tiny company was to be the first permanent non-Spanish settlement on the Main. Equally important, it inaugurated a European march upon the Lesser Antilles—where the Spaniards themselves had never settled at all.

It is doubtful that the Spaniards were even aware of Warner's presence for the first few years. They kept little check on the unwanted islands of the Lesser Antilles, and in any case they believed that remnants of the fierce Carib Indians would drive away any interlopers. But Warner and his men stood off the Carib until reinforcements arrived. Within the year a French privateer under Captain Pierre Belain came limping into the harbor at St. Christopher's after a losing fight with a stronger-than-usual Spanish galleon. Warner and his cohorts gladly received the bedraggled Frenchmen ashore. Before another year ended they had jointly driven away the remaining Carib Indians, and had agreed to divide the island of St. Christopher's—abbreviated as Saint Kitts by the Englishmen—between them.

Throughout the next few years other settlers followed close behind, spilling out onto Barbados, Nevis and Montserrat, until by 1630 the whole string of islands of the Lesser Antilles, reaching nearly 1,000 miles from Puerto Rico almost to the Venezuelan coast, had been settled. Some 3,000 Englishmen lived on Barbados alone. Close to a thousand Frenchmen took over Martinique and Guadeloupe and a number of other small islands. The Dutch meanwhile were occupying Saba and St. Eustatius. All told, possibly 18,000 northern Europeans had ensconced themselves in the Lesser Antilles. They were husbanding flourishing crops that besides tobacco now included indigo, ginger, cotton and later sugar and cacao. And, of course, their colonies were thriving ports of entry for smugglers; ships would bring all manner of manufactured goods from Europe, which then would be smuggled to Spanish colonists in defiance of the Spanish customs and tax laws.

But among all these prospering planters and smugglers were many men who shared in no profits and were fiercely anxious to change their lot. English, Dutch or French, the entrepreneurs who arrived to make a fortune from the soil brought with them an entourage of indentured servants to do the hard labor of sowing and reaping that slaves usually performed on Spanish colonial plantations. The servants were as mixed in temperament and social standing as they were in national origin. Some were perfectly respectable folk, the younger sons of large families in search of a chance to rise on their own account. Many more were footloose ne'er-do-wells, along for a change of scene. And a considerable number were common criminals, surly fellows who were given a choice of jail or labor in the colonies. Whichever the case, indentured servants signed on for a specified period of time (four years, seven years, sometimes 10 years), with the promise of freedom and a lump sum of money at the end. The payment might range from £5 to £10—enough to set up the most energetic among them as planters on their own. As late as 1640, £4 would buy 10 acres on Barbados.

A few of the indentured servants won their freedom and did set up as small planters themselves. Others were cheated by unscrupulous masters who failed to give them their promised payment when their time was up, and with neither money nor work they had no recourse but to drift. And many simply fled, with or without giving the work a try. Sir Henry Colt, a planter who went to Barbados in 1631, wrote home to his son George that 13 days after his arrival 40 indentured servants "stole away in a Dutch pinnace." Sir Henry might have added that there went a boatload of probable recruits to become buccaneers.

Around the time he made that observation, some disparate but coincidental developments were casting thousands of other men adrift on the Caribbean and making them candidates for a life of buccaneering.

First, the Spaniards were belatedly trying to stamp out the foreign settlements eating away the edge of their empire. In 1629 the annual fleet under Don Fadrique de Toledo sailed from Spain bearing consignments of wheat, arms, clothing, tools and coinage for Cartagena and Veracruz. Accompanying the merchantmen were 35 heavily armed galleons and 7,500 soldiers with orders to wipe out the Saint Kitts settlement en route. Toledo arrived off the island late in the summer, landed his men and dealt the colony a shattering blow. The settlers put up a valiant fight, but were quickly overwhelmed.

Toledo seized 700 prisoners (not including Thomas Warner, who was back in London selling the year's crop), packed them all on board captured ships in the harbor and shipped them back to France and England. He then destroyed Saint Kitts's crops and burned its houses. But about 400 settlers—both English and French—managed to escape to the island's hilly interior. After Toledo departed, many of the discouraged survivors took stock of what remained of their ruined island and decided that they had seen enough of it. They drifted away, seeking a new life and yearning for revenge.

A few years later other circumstances lent a hand in driving still more men out of the Lesser Antillean colonies. By the mid-1630s the Virginia plantations on the mainland of North America were beginning to flourish and export quantities of tobacco to England. The Virginia leaf was deemed superior to that grown in the Antilles, and tobacco prices plummeted on Barbados and the other islands, forcing small planters to give up and look for some other livelihood. Big planters bought them out and switched to sugar, a crop less vulnerable to the vagaries of weather and market conditions. Yet to make a living from sugar required not only vast tracts of land but also large gangs of laborers to do the backbreaking work of cutting, binding and hauling the heavy cane. White men wilted under the burden. But black slaves from Africa stood up well in the fields of cane and, more important, were a relatively cheap and abundant labor supply. The planters imported them by the thousands and dismissed all their white indentured servants.

Facing hard times in the Lesser Antilles, men from each of these groups—defeated colonists, failed planters, discharged and runaway servants—gravitated north to the Spanish-owned but thinly populated islands of Hispaniola, Cuba, Jamaica and Puerto Rico. All any party of men in a boat had to do was follow the prevailing winds and currents. When they arrived at the large islands they found everything they would need for survival.

Indeed, to many of them the Greater Antilles seemed a tropical Garden of Eden. The islands had always had plenty of water, wood, fowl and fruit. By the late 1500s, thanks to the Spaniards, they also had abundant game. In colonizing Hispaniola and the other big islands, the Spaniards had introduced hoofed animals: cattle, pigs and horses. When the lure of bright metal in Mexico and Peru sent large numbers of Spanish settlers off in headlong pursuit of El Dorado in the 1530s and '40s, ranches and plantations were abandoned. The animals roamed wild and, finding no natural enemies—the islands were virtually free from large predators—underwent a population explosion of fantastic magnitude. Richard Hakluyt, the English geographer and naturalist, observed that there was "so great quantity of cattell, and such increase thereof, that notwithstanding the daily killing of them for their hides, it is not possible to reduce the number."

What is more, the animals and almost everything else on the islands were free for the taking. Though the large Spanish port cities—Santo Domingo on Hispaniola, Havana and Santiago on Cuba, San Juan on Puerto Rico—continued to grow and prosper, large stretches of coastline and most of the interior did not see a Spaniard from one year to the next. These were the haunts of the early buccaneers, and these were the places that naturally beckoned to the smugglers, adventurers and dispossessed settlers from the Lesser Antilles.

History does not record how many non-Spaniards inhabited the large islands of the Caribbean in the first half of the 17th Century. But the figure was undoubtedly in the thousands. Adapting to the life of buccaneers, they hunted for food and enjoyed a thriving trade in provisioning the ships of French, English and Dutch privateers who used the islands as watering places. More important, the hides of the animals found a

While a Dutch man-of-war waits offshore in this 17th Century drawing, crewmen shovel rock-hard lumps of salt into wheelbarrows on a beach of Venezuela's Araya peninsula. To get the salt for their herring industry, the Dutch risked Spanish reprisals: in 1605 a Spanish fleet destroyed no fewer than 19 salt ships loading at Araya.

waiting market among European purveyors of saddlery, vests, helmets, boots, bags, bookbindings and furniture.

As early as 1604, well before the great influx of men from the Lesser Antilles, Pedro de Valdés, Governor of Cuba, informed the Spanish crown that 40,000 hides a year were being smuggled out of the islands. In later years unauthorized trade may have reached five times that amount. In return, the hide smugglers brought the buccaneers canvas sails and linen shirts, axes and awls, wines and liquors and, above all, arms and gunpowder.

The Spaniards' reaction to all this was to pull back their remaining outlying settlements, to prevent them from trafficking with the enemy buccaneers and the smugglers. In one case, Antonio Osorio, Governor of Hispaniola, ordered the transfer of three Spanish settlements from the island's north coast to the south coast, where he could keep an eye on them from Santo Domingo. When the settlers resisted, Osorio marched north with a body of soldiers and forcibly evicted them. "I resolved to enter the settlements in person," he reported to Spain, "and make them take away their women and belongings, compelling them to move with them to the new settlements and setting fire to their houses to make it clear that this had to be done." All that accomplished, of course, was to leave three fine harbors unsupervised, and the buccaneers and smugglers went right on operating from them. Soon the buccaneers were not only trading in hides, they were sailing out in their small boats to attack Spanish shipping.

By the very nature of their illicit enterprise the buccaneers left a dearth of recorded evidence about themselves. But luckily there are a few rich mines of information. One is a 17th Century narrative by John Esquemeling, an adventurer who spent some time as a buccaneer himself (page 116). The others are accounts by occasional priests who went among the buccaneers. Together such narratives provide a fascinating and for the most part authentic picture of outlaw life and tactics on Hispaniola and elsewhere.

"In general they were without any habitation or fixed abode, but rendezvoused where the animals were to be found," wrote the Abbé Jean Baptiste Du Tertre, a French cleric who went to the Spanish Main in the 1670s to minister to plantation slaves, and encountered the buccaneers on his rounds. These freebooters hunted game in groups of six or eight, setting out at dawn. Curiously, some groups specialized in pigs and some went after cattle—but they hunted one species or the other, not both at the same time. They indulged in no breakfast until as many animals had been killed as there were men in the party; then, as they skinned the beasts and put the flesh to smoke, they took time out for a spare repast of marrow bones. By evening, when the meat had been smoking for several hours—acquiring a deep red color and a zesty flavor—the buccaneers had a dinner of roast flesh. They stored the extra meat and the hides in rude sheds of leaves, branches and skins. If it rained they might take shelter in similar lean-tos themselves. Otherwise they lay down to sleep beside their buccan fires, whose smoke might drive off the mosquitoes.

As his warships bombard a fort,
Spanish Admiral Don Fadrique de Toledo
(foreground) brings in boatloads of
foot soldiers to attack British and French
settlers in his 1629 raid on Saint Kitts.
Hero of the recapture of Bahia, Brazil,
from the Dutch four years earlier,
Toledo on this occasion laid waste to the
tobacco plantations on Saint Kitts and
then shipped 700 of the island colonists
back to their European homelands.

When the sails of a smuggler or privateer loomed on the horizon, the buccaneers took their products to the harbor where the vessel put in, going out by canoe or pinnace to barter their meat and hides with the ship's crew. After a successful trade, an occasional dandy among them might strut about in crimson trousers and purple serape, but most preferred the buccaneers' own distinctive—and distinctively unkempt—clothing. "You would say that these are the butcher's vilest servants who have been eight days in the slaughterhouse without washing themselves," observed the Abbé Du Tertre. The buccaneers usually wore rawhide breeches to shield themselves from the thorns of the island cacti, a coarse-linen tunic-like shirt, pigskin boots and a hat to keep off the tropical sun.

The buccaneers were conspicuous for the openhandedness with which they spent their profits. Their main vice, according to Esquemeling, was drunkenness, "which they exercise for the most part with brandy. This they drink as liberally as the Spaniards do clear fountain water. Sometimes they buy together a pipe of wine; this they stave at one end, and never cease drinking till they have made an end of it. Thus they celebrate the festivals of Bacchus so long as they have any money left."

The island of Hispaniola, shown on a 1723 French map, was a prime hunting ground for buccaneers who pursued the abundant wild cattle that roamed its savannas. In time, the Isle de la Tortue, or Tortuga, to the northwest, became a buccaneer stronghold from which to attack Spanish shipping and coastal towns.

Women were as scarce among the buccaneers as on shipboard, and in this all-male society each buccaneer had his partner. Partners traveled together, protected each other in combat and shared bonds of companionship that were often as strong as those of a marriage. In the case of the death of one buccaneer, his partner inherited his belongings. But their baggage was scant: a pair of long butcher knives, which a buccaneer wore thrust into his waistband, a double-edged sword secured to a baldric, a belt that ran diagonally across his chest, and—the most prized possession—a gun with a spade-shaped stock and a four-foot barrel. A good French matchlock musket smuggled in from Normandy might be worth 20 hides, and almost without exception the buccaneers learned to be crack shots. It took a keen eye and a sure hand to bring down a pig in the bush or a galloping cow without ruining the hide.

When a band of buccaneers got tired of chasing cattle, or simply felt the lure of the sea, they might send a messenger along the coast to let it be known they were planning a raid. For days buccaneers in groups of six or eight would congregate at a specified rendezvous, bringing along their own guns, powder and knives. They usually met jovially over a barrel of brandy and a meal of smoked meat and boiled yams, and decided by vote where to lie in wait for a passing Spanish merchantman.

For men who led such an otherwise casual life, they had surprisingly rigid rules. The leader provided a scroll and drew up a written agreement to be signed—or marked—by all those present. Fixed sums of money were allocated in advance for special purposes. One such was a salary for the group's carpenter, whose role was vital in keeping the ship

Arrayed before a tropical fig tree with trailing roots, the flora and fauna in this 17th Century engraving are examples of what buccaneer chronicler John Esquemeling described as the West Indies' "great variety of natural productions that infinitely applaud and captivate the senses." The beasts in the foreground—from left, an agouti, opossum, iguana, wild pig and armadillo —were all widely hunted for food.

seaworthy and properly rigged; he might also serve as the surgeon if there was no one else available. And a schedule of compensation for wounds suffered in action was drawn up. The loss of a right arm was generally worth 600 pieces of eight; an eye usually brought 100 pieces of eight; so did a finger (a buccaneer could, after all, aim his musket with only one eye, but he needed both arms to fire).

On the conclusion of a successful cruise, all debts were to be paid from the common prize before any division of the spoils was made. Then the remainder would be handed around before the mast. The captain would be entitled to five shares, the mate to two. One share each went to all the rest of the crew—save the cabin boy, who got only half a share for performing the most unenviable job of all: in the event that the vessel was abandoned, it fell to him to set it on fire and then be the last to leave. He had to be nimble to catch up with comrades scrambling aboard another ship; few 17th Century cabin boys could swim.

As he signed the articles of agreement, or made his mark, each man swore not to conceal from his mates, recounted Esquemeling, "the least thing they find among the prey." The usual punishment for anyone found guilty of stealing was marooning—a fate that even these island-wise men regarded with horror. The condemned man was put ashore on a small and isolated cay with nothing but a flask of water and his weapons. Almost invariably it was a sentence of death, and a lonely, lingering one at that.

In preying upon the Spaniards' shipping, the buccaneers typically used tactics like those employed by Pierre Le Grand when he unburdened the treasure galleon of its cargo off Hispaniola. Probably half the vessels from which they mounted their bold attacks on the Spaniards' 200- and 300-ton galleons were no bigger than 50-ton pinnaces. Because the buccaneers used small craft and because they made it a practice to strike their sails as they approached their targets, the vessels were usually not visible from a short distance away, and when they could be seen they looked deceptively innocent.

As the buccaneers' tiny pinnace came close to its prey, one of their superb marksmen, seated in the bow, would fire his musket first at the Spanish steersman and then at the men handling the sails, while the rest blasted at the portholes to keep the curious from looking out. If there were several boats in the raiding party, one would wedge itself against the Spaniard's rudder. Then, with both ship and helmsman disabled, and the rest of the Spanish crew thrown into confusion, the buccaneers would swarm aboard, uttering ferocious yells and slashing with their cutlasses as they beat a path for the captain and the treasure.

Crewmen of no account were summarily beheaded, or put adrift in a small boat; the captain and any officers able to pay a ransom were held until they did so. Counting ransoms, a successful raid could fetch even the lowliest seaman among the buccaneers a prize that ranged from £700 to £1,000.

As the buccaneers grew bolder and more numerous, they came to call themselves the "Brethren of the Coast," a term that seems to have come into use some time in the 1640s. The originator of the phrase is un-

Holding his long-barreled, supremely accurate musket, a pipe-smoking buccaneer pauses with his mastiffs as he returns from a hunt to his village on Hispaniola. The buccaneer's dogs— as important to his livelihood as his gun— flushed out wild pigs and cattle from the tropical underbrush, making them easy targets for the sharpshooting hunter.

known, but the words reflect the unity with which the buccaneers saw themselves as allied against the common enemy—the Spaniards—irrespective of their own national origins. The term also acknowledged a certain change in their ways. The roaming, isolated bands began to coalesce into larger and larger groups. They established more or less permanent encampments—notably on the north coast of Hispaniola and the south coast of Jamaica. And while they still hunted and did a lucrative business in hides, these hordes of brethren increasingly turned their energies to plundering the Spaniards wherever they were weak, at sea or on land.

A favorite haunt for large numbers of buccaneers was a humpbacked sliver of rock 25 miles long off the northwest coast of Hispaniola. Columbus, who discovered it on his first voyage, named it Tortuga, meaning "turtle," for its resemblance to that aquatic creature.

Tortuga was a buccaneer's dream. The island permitted planting on a small scale; it boasted an excellent harbor; it gave easy access to the hunting grounds on the larger islands; it lay athwart important Spanish shipping routes through the Windward Passage and along the coast of Cuba; and finally it was eminently defensible. There were only a few places on the island where an enemy could land in force. The north shore was pounded by the Atlantic surf, and most of the south shore, except for the harbor, consisted of shallow bays and flats covered with dense mangrove tangles.

The first recorded occupation of Tortuga was in the 1630s, when an Englishman named Anthony Hilton sailed over from Hispaniola with a band of buccaneers and built a base camp for raiders coming and going through the Windward Passage. Hilton seems to have lasted as chief of Tortuga for only a few years before he was succeeded by a more ambitious—and effective—buccaneer. The new leader was Jean Le Vasseur, a Huguenot who had been driven from his homeland and had gone to seek his fortune in the New World.

A military engineer by profession, Le Vasseur made Tortuga a proper stronghold, adding some man-made marvels of engineering to the blessings already bestowed by nature. On the island was a flat-topped mountain overlooking Basse-Terre, as the French called the harbor. The mountain itself was protected by almost impenetrable bush and crowned with a 30-foot outcropping of solid rock. Out of this rocky prominence, Le Vasseur carved the aptly named Fort de Rocher, the Rock Fort, and armed it with two dozen cannon. From the harbor side, the fort could be reached only by ladders. Nearby was a natural spring that made it possible, by Esquemeling's account, for 700 or 800 men to hold out there indefinitely.

For 12 years, while taking a percentage of all buccaneer loot that passed through the port, Le Vasseur reigned as a sort of buccaneer king, and a mean, greedy king he was. Not content with a share of the plunder, he also levied a special tax on all the hides brought into Tortuga from Hispaniola. When a Spanish prize ship yielded up a silver Madonna and the devoutly Catholic Frenchmen on Saint Kitts sent word asking if they might have it for their church, Le Vasseur insultingly gave them a wooden facsimile, saying that they were doubtless too spiritual to notice the difference. Finally, in 1652, he appropriated the mistress of one of his lieutenants, and that was going too far. One afternoon as Le Vasseur went to inspect the port's warehouse the lieutenant lay in wait and stabbed him to death.

Le Vasseur was followed as Tortuga's chief by the Chevalier de Fontenay, another hardcase Frenchman who could be just as merciless toward his own men as Le Vasseur had been—as he proved when the Spaniards arrived in January 1654 to assault the stronghold. The Spaniards sent five heavily armed ships and a number of smaller transports, which fought their way into the harbor and landed a force of several hundred men. While some of the soldiers kept the buccaneers atop the cliff occupied, other Spaniards set a gang of slaves to hacking a path through the bush and dragging cannon up the mountain at the rear of the fort. When a rain of cannon balls began to crash into the buccaneers' stronghold from behind, one of Fontenay's lieutenants suggested that they surrender. "Traitor!" cried Fontenay. "If I am forced to it, you will not be here as a witness!" And he shot his lieutenant dead.

Yet nothing could save the fort. The Spaniards managed to conquer it—for the only time in its history. Incredibly, they merely deported Fontenay back to France, and were content to let the rest of the buccaneers flee across the water to Hispaniola. Then the Spaniards withdrew their troops—and back like the tide came the buccaneers, in greater strength than ever before.

Tenacity was only one of the qualities the buccaneers brought to their unceasing conflict with the Spaniards. They were as ferocious and opportunistic as wolves and cruel to the point of barbarism. So hurtful were they to their victims that the Spaniards who fell into their hands sometimes promised to comply with any buccaneer demands even before the buccaneers had a chance to say what they wanted. And to all this the buccaneers added an unfailing guile that befuddled their enemies time and again. Esquemeling's tales of their exploits are farfetched. But they reflect the sense of fear and frustration the Spaniards were experiencing in the center of their New World empire.

Nothing delighted Esquemeling's storytelling heart more than to relate near-miraculous buccaneer escapes from Spanish clutches. According to the chronicler, a buccaneer nicknamed Bartholomew Portugues because of his birthplace was surely one of the slickest rogues ever to dupe a Spaniard. Prowling the coast of Cuba with a mere 30 men in a vessel mounting only four small guns, Bartholomew came upon a great galleon en route from Cartagena to Havana. The Spanish vessel carried 20 heavy guns and a crew of 70 men, but the dauntless Bartholomew attacked nonetheless. "After a long and dangerous fight," recounted Esquemeling, Bartholomew "became master of the great vessel." He lost 10 men killed and four wounded, but he inflicted double those losses on his adversaries and found that he had won 70,000 pieces of eight as well as 120,000 pounds of valuable cacao beans (the raw material of the chocolate trade).

Unable to return immediately to his lair on Jamaica because of contrary winds, Bartholomew headed for a secluded anchorage on Cuba's

A watercolor map of Tortuga, drawn by French explorer Samuel de Champlain during an expedition in 1600, depicts the fine harbor and its proximity to Hispaniola, which later made the 25-mile-long island a natural stopping place for buccaneers. The first such brigands arrived in 1638; at the peak of their activities Tortuga was host to thousands of raiders.

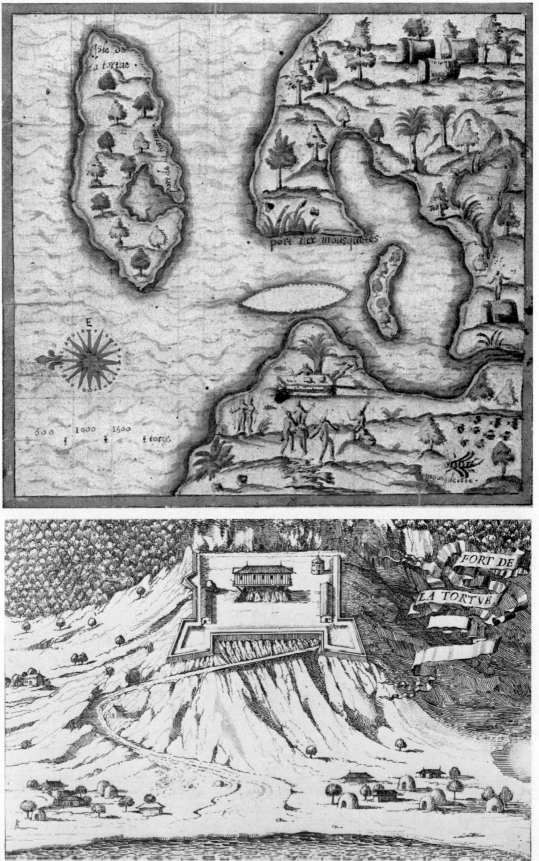

Bastion of buccaneer resistance to the Spaniards, Tortuga's mountaintop citadel was built in 1640 by a French engineer named Le Vasseur and proved well-nigh impregnable. In numerous attacks over the years, the Spaniards took it only once, in 1654, but soon retired, leaving the buccaneers to reoccupy their redoubt.

A man of letters among the marauders

This elaborately adorned frontispiece introduced the first edition of John Esquemeling's De Americaensche Zee-Roovers, or Buccaneers of America, which was produced in Dutch in 1678.

"I assure the reader that I shall give no stories taken on hearsay, but only those to which I was eyewitness." So wrote John Esquemeling in the Netherlands in 1678 as he began his chronicle of the buccaneers of the Spanish Main.

Whether Esquemeling was unswervingly faithful to his vow is open to some question, for his tales in the *Buccaneers of America* occasionally appear a trifle tall. But he unquestionably did accompany bands of freebooters, including Henry Morgan, throughout the Caribbean for nearly a decade before returning home to write the first—and still the most authentic—account of their exploits.

Esquemeling's origins remain as obscure as those of his buccaneer characters. Scholars are confident that he was a Frenchman born around 1645 at Honfleur on the Channel coast. He begins his account by stating that in his youth he was sent to the Caribbean as an indentured servant of the French West India Company. He apparently spent some time in Tortuga in the hands of a cruel master—described by Esquemeling as "the most perfidious man that ever was

born of woman"—who nearly starved him to death. Later he was purchased by a barber-surgeon who seems to have given him a thorough grounding in medical skills. After only a year Esquemeling was granted his freedom and decided to join the buccaneers. "Naked and destitute of all human necessaries," he wrote, "I determined to enter into the wicked order of the pirates, or robbers at sea."

Esquemeling served his apprenticeship in the buccaneer strongholds of Hispaniola, where he participated in raids and, in his leisure hours, studied the flora and fauna of the West Indies. ("Wild boars fatten to admiration here on apricots," he observed, and "dates are the food extremely coveted by the hedgehog.")

At some point he apparently moved to Jamaica, and he spent years roaming the Main from there in the company of English buccaneers. He acted as expedition surgeon on many raids and was paid handsomely for his services after each success. "A competent salary for the surgeon and his chest of medicaments," he noted, "is rated at 250 pieces of eight." Such generous compensation was merited, for the work of cauterizing wounds with red-hot irons and amputating limbs was an arduous business.

Esquemeling became disenchanted with buccaneer life during his return from Morgan's raid on Panama in 1671. The journey was harrowing and the men, said Esquemeling, were reduced to "foraging for a few crocodile eggs" to keep from starving. It all seemed to the chronicler "a sign of the reward that attends wickedness."

At last Esquemeling declared himself appalled at the atrocities and excesses of "these pirates who spend 3,000 pieces of eight without leaving themselves a shirt to wear in the morning." In 1674 he returned to Europe and made his home in Amsterdam, where he established a medical practice and penned his masterpiece.

In his wildest dreams Esquemeling could not have imagined the sensation his work would stir among armchair adventurers all across Europe. The first Dutch edition, illustrated with woodcuts by an anonymous artist, was sold out within three months, and a second printing was soon gobbled up as well. A German translation was put on sale in 1679, followed by a Spanish edition in 1681, two English translations in 1684 and a French version in 1686. "Nothing like this," said a London reviewer, "has ever been published in England."

In fact, the retired buccaneer had helped forge a literary tradition. For English novelists such as Daniel Defoe and Jonathan Swift recognized the broad appeal of Esquemeling's tales of adventure and were inspired by them to create a new genre of imaginative travel chronicles, including such classics as *Robinson Crusoe* and *Gulliver's Travels*.

Cape San Antonio, intending to take on water while he waited for a favorable breeze. But just as he and his prize rounded the cape, disaster overtook him. Three Spanish galleons bound from Havana to Mexico suddenly bore down on the buccaneers. "They were easily retaken, both ship and pirates," wrote Esquemeling laconically, "and stripped of all the riches they had pillaged so little before."

The galleons continued majestically on to Campeche, chief port of the Yucatan Peninsula, where the whole band of buccaneers was thrown in prison. All, that is, except Bartholomew, who was kept under close guard aboard ship while a special gibbet was built to hang him from. But Bartholomew was not finished yet.

During the night, when his jailer dropped off to sleep, Bartholomew eased the fellow's knife from his belt and stabbed him to death. Bartholomew was still trapped, for the ship was anchored far out in the roadstead, and he was no better able to swim than the average cabin boy. No matter. From the ship's stores the crafty buccaneer seized two earthen wine jars. Whether he drank the contents or poured them overboard is not recorded. In any event, he corked the wine jars, strapped them one on either side of his torso—and behold!—a life jacket. Without further ado he slipped into the water and bobbed his way to shore in the dark of the night. He was well on his way to freedom by the time the Spaniards discovered his absence the following morning.

All that day, search parties combed the countryside around Campeche, while the buccaneer gleefully watched from the safety of a hollow tree. When he saw that they had called off the search, he slipped away through the woods and two weeks later turned up at the Cape of Golfo Triste, some 120 miles from the scene of his capture. There Bartholomew Portugues found a buccaneer vessel filled with old comrades from Jamaica, and before very long, related Esquemeling, he who had been so lately "a poor miserable prisoner and condemned to the gallows" by "a second turn of fortune's wheel had become rich and powerful again."

In another instance, said Esquemeling, the Spaniards were cheated of vengeance against a buccaneer by their own greed. The hero of the tale was a clever fellow named Pierre François, who was cruising off the Venezuelan coast in a pinnace with 26 companions when he spied a dozen Spanish ships of the sort that carried slaves to dive for pearls. Pulling down his sails, Pierre ordered his crew to row nonchalantly along the shore as though theirs was just another fishing vessel. Reaching the pearl bank, he and his men suddenly sprang upon the Spaniards' flagship and captured it, together with a fine cargo of pearls worth 100,000 pieces of eight.

Alas for Pierre, his seamanship was not the equal of his guile. In trying to make his escape, he piled on too much sail—and down crashed the mainmast. The remaining Spanish vessels overtook him in a trice.

Finding himself trapped, Pierre called once again on his wits and won from the Spaniards the buccaneers' lives in exchange for the loot, which presumably Pierre threatened to send to the bottom. The Spaniards accepted the pearls and—true to their promise—put the buccaneers ashore safe and sound.

In the case of Rock Brasiliano, a Dutchman so named for a spell he had

spent in Brazil, terror was the lever that pried open the dungeon doors. Rock was known far and wide as a buccaneer of awful ferocity who tortured and murdered his captives. He undoubtedly expected like treatment when he was seized with a boatload of freebooters off Campeche and thrown into prison. However, Rock devised the stratagem of writing a letter to the Spanish Governor purporting to be from fellow buccaneers lurking off the coast. Esquemeling perversely neglects to explain where in a Mexican dungeon Rock found a quill and scroll, or how he managed to gull the Governor into thinking that the letter came from outside the prison. In any event, the letter advised the Governor that he "should have a care how he used those persons he had in his custody. For in case he caused them any harm, they did swear unto him they would never give quarter to any person of the Spanish nation that should fall into their hands."

Esquemeling goes on to say that the Governor (undoubtedly shuddering at the vision of himself on a buccan spit) "began to fear what mischief they might cause by means of their companions abroad," and thereupon released Rock and his friends—fatuously exacting an oath that they give up buccaneering. The buccaneers gladly gave their oath—and just as cheerfully went back on their word the moment they were loose. When last seen in Esquemeling's pages, they are setting forth again to raid out of Jamaica.

The buccaneer who most fascinated Esquemeling—in an awful sort of way—was Francis L'Ollonais, a Frenchman from Les Sables d'Ollone, or the Sands of Ollone, in Brittany. L'Ollonais had spent part of his youth as an indentured servant in some unspecified place that Esquemeling designates only as "the Caribbee Islands." No record survives of how he performed that role but, if the youth was father to the man, he must have been the surliest churl ever to plow a field. He was nevertheless a compelling leader. Once he had won his freedom and joined the buccaneers on Tortuga, he advanced from crewman to captain after only two or three expeditions against the Spaniards.

No more ferocious trio roamed the Spanish Main than the grim-faced predators above (left to right: Rock Brasiliano, Bartholomew Portugues and Francis L'Ollonais), who were immortalized in the chronicles of fellow buccaneer John Esquemeling. Rock Brasiliano was so vicious, according to Esquemeling, that "he commanded several Spaniards to be roasted on wooden spits for no other reason than that they would not show him the hog yards where he might steal a swine."

Having ripped the still-beating heart from a Spaniard tied to a tree in the jungle of Honduras, Francis L'Ollonais jams it into the mouth of a second captive, while his men murder yet another of their hapless victims. "It is a common thing among the privateers," reported an observer, "to cut a man in pieces, or tie a cord around his head and twist it with a stick until his eyes pop out."

He was not only a man of ambitions, but a man of large ambitions—
the first, by Esquemeling's reckoning, to advance from raids on shipping
to a large-scale assault on a major mainland city. He set his sights
on Maracaibo, a town of 4,000 inhabitants and the pearling center of
Venezuela. Setting out from Tortuga with no fewer than 660 men, he led
a fleet of eight ships. And, naturally, L'Ollonais sailed in the biggest
one, a vessel mounting 10 guns.

Luck was with the buccaneers from the start. Off Puerto Rico, L'Ollonais and his men intercepted a 16-gun ship bound for Mexico with 40,000
pieces of eight and chestfuls of jewels worth again as much. Proceeding
southwest past the Isle of Savona, he soon scored again, capturing
an eight-gun ship bound for Hispaniola with a hold full of muskets,
7,000 pounds of powder, and 12,000 pieces of eight meant to pay the
Spanish Hispaniolan garrison.

L'Ollonais had already won a reputation for atrocity by lopping off the
heads of the prisoners he took—or feeding them the raw flesh of mules
and starving to death those who could not stomach such fare. Now he
sailed leisurely south across the Caribbean. After a three-hour attack on
the Venezuelan fortress of De la Barra, L'Ollonais allowed just enough
survivors to escape to spread panic everywhere. By the time he reached
the outer defenses of Maracaibo, the Spaniards were sending frenzied
rumors ahead with exaggerated accounts of the host about to descend.
As Esquemeling narrated the story, a band of terrified soldiers ran
pell-mell into the city howling: "The pirates will presently be here with
2,000 men and more!" The citizens of Maracaibo fled with the soldiers.
L'Ollonais took possession of the city, seized a haul of food and wine,
and pursued the refugees into the forest, where they yielded up another
20,000 pieces of eight and a train of mules laden with household goods.

Thinking that so rich a town should have greater wealth than that, and
that the inhabitants had probably hidden their treasure at Gibraltar,
the next port up the coast, L'Ollonais marched his men in that direction. There the buccaneers found the Spaniards ready to fight: a battery
of eight guns was mounted above the town. But by feigning retreat,
L'Ollonais drew the unwary Spanish soldiers away from their own defenses—and then suddenly turned back and slashed through them, killing 200 and taking another 150 prisoners.

By the time the buccaneers entered Gibraltar, most of the inhabitants
had fled to the woods. While his men stormed through the town, looting
the monastery and the houses, L'Ollonais sent an emissary to the fugi-
tives in the woods, demanding a ransom of 10,000 pieces of eight and
threatening to burn down the town if he did not get it. The citizens
hesitated; L'Ollonais started burning at once. Frantically, the citizens
pleaded with him to put out the fire, and came up with the demanded
ransom. With the money securely stowed in his ship's hold, L'Ollonais
turned back to Maracaibo and, under the threat of punishing the town
with more of the same, extorted another 30,000 pieces of eight from
those unhappy citizens.

His objective won, L'Ollonais decided to bring his expedition to a
close. After an eight-day passage, he put in at a secluded anchorage on
Hispaniola. There he and his men unloaded the ships. When the treasure

ïfit, orto Feaft. P. 140.
Attendants.

Crowned with feathers and bedecked with necklaces of golden beads, a Darien Indian chief of Panama marches at the head of his entourage in this 1699 engraving from a volume of reminiscences by a British buccaneer. These fierce Panamanians sometimes assisted the marauders preying on Spaniards, but they were basically hostile to all interlopers.

was all amassed, each man repeated the oath that every buccaneer took on setting out, that he was concealing nothing from his fellows. Then they counted up their haul. Between the ransoms, the looting and some more ships' prizes that Esquemeling must have forgotten to detail, they found they had a total of 260,000 pieces of eight, quantities of silks and linens worth another 100,000 pieces of eight, and a quantity of silver plate. After dividing the loot, they made their way back to Tortuga. There, wrote Esquemeling, "they made shift to lose and spend the riches they had got in much less time than they were purchased by robbing. The taverns, according to the custom of pirates, got the greatest part thereof; insomuch that soon after they were constrained to seek more by the same unlawful means they had obtained the preceding."

So L'Ollonais was off again, this time on an expedition to Puerto Caballos, a silver-rich depot along the Nicaraguan coast. With a fleet of six ships and 700 men, he made the passage across the Caribbean without incident. At Puerto Caballos he roared through the town, seizing the contents of its two warehouses and sacking the citizens' homes; when several Spanish householders refused to divulge the whereabouts of their troves, L'Ollonais pulled out their tongues as an object lesson to other reluctant residents. Esquemeling does not recount the size of the buccaneers' haul, but L'Ollonais appears to have found it satisfactory, for he left the town standing.

Pushing his luck, he decided to move on inland—presumably to get closer to some silver mines—and so set out for the village of San Pedro. But that village could not be reached without a treacherous overland march, and on the way L'Ollonais committed an infamous atrocity for which he is remembered with horror.

Stumbling on an ambush, he eventually overran the position and learned from his captives that the Spaniards had stationed similar ambuscades all along the route to the city. L'Ollonais ordered the prisoners to show him another way to get there. They protested that there was none; off the beaten path the woods were impassable. At that, L'Ollonais went into such a fit of rage that he seized a prisoner and with his cutlass cut open the hapless man's chest, pulled out the still-beating heart with his hands and bit into it with his teeth, snarling: "I will serve you all alike, if you show me not another way." He then stuffed the heart in another prisoner's mouth. Quivering with fright, the prisoners took L'Ollonais into the woods—only to have him find for himself that they were right. As he turned back, he roared: "By God's death, the Spaniards shall pay me for this!"

But fortune at last forsook the buccaneers. At the mouth of the River Nicaragua, L'Ollonais and his men encountered a mob of Darien Indians—an untamable tribe that the Spaniards had learned to dread. Well they might. The Indians fell upon the 700 men and only a few buccaneers escaped. Most were killed; they were the lucky ones. A number were captured, including L'Ollonais. The Indians roasted all alive save L'Ollonais, on whom they had special designs. Seizing the buccaneer leader by his extremities, they tore him to pieces while he uttered bloodcurdling screams. They then threw his body limb by limb into a fire, and flung his ashes to the winds, "to the intent no trace nor memory might remain of such an infamous, inhuman creature," wrote Esquemeling. "Thus ends the history of the life and miserable death of that infernal wretch."

In Esquemeling's accounts the buccaneers, whether in small groups or in great concentrations, were entirely independent, bowing to no government and no laws except their own. But in the 1660s, though the chronicler does not write of it, great changes were in the wind. By then the buccanneers had been bedeviling the Spaniards for 30 years and more, with only occasional notice from the governments of Europe, which were otherwise preoccupied with concerns closer to home. However, now a new generation of rulers had come to power, ready to claim the territories that their smuggler-settlers had overrun.

None was more eager to do so than the King of France—the dashing and elegant Louis XIV. King in name since the age of five, Louis assumed power in his own right in 1661 at the age of 23. Among the innovations he fostered was the French West India Company—a syndicate of merchants backed by royal funds and royal authority—whose mission it was to secure French trading rights in the New World.

In 1665 the new company dispatched one Bertrand d'Ogeron, a captain who had already been trading all over the Spanish Main for perhaps a quarter of a century, to oversee the interests of France in Hispaniola, where the French-led buccaneers were virtually in control of the entire west end of the island.

D'Ogeron was hard put to fulfill his mission. The buccaneers were "scattered along the coasts of the island of Hispaniola in inaccessible places, surrounded by mountains or great rocks of the sea, by which alone they can pass from place to place in their little boats," he wrote home to his government. "They live like savages without recognizing anyone's authority and without any one chief, and they commit a thousand brigandages."

Clearly, it would take a certain imagination to assume command of these unruly fellows. But d'Ogeron was the man for the job. One day—according to a tale told not by Esquemeling but by some anonymous observer—d'Ogeron was seized with an inspiration. *"Corbleu!"* he exclaimed to a friend. "I shall order chains from France for these rascals!" The word spread throughout the island that d'Ogeron was planning something drastic. But what could he have in mind?

Several months went by before they had their answer. At length a ship arrived at Tortuga's harbor and, to the astonished eyes of a quayful of buccaneers drawn there out of curiosity, there came mincing and swaying down the gangplank 150 harlots plucked from the streets of Paris, where they had been given their choice of jail or Tortuga. *"Alors! Who wants a wife?"* cried d'Ogeron as the women sallied into the all-male preserve. "What will you bid for these fine ladies?" Before long, the entire cargo had been bought.

Nothing could better have symbolized the subtle changes that were stealing over the Spanish Main. Plundering and smuggling still had a long and happy life ahead. But the buccaneers themselves were beginning to be domesticated. Wives—and inevitably children—heralded

Carrying their worldly goods in neat bundles, a group of harlots from Paris— given a choice between emigration and imprisonment—depart for the New World in this 17th Century engraving entitled The Sad Embarkation. *The importation of prostitutes as brides for settlers became a common way to stabilize the rough-and-tumble colonies in America.*

the approach of yet another generation. It was one that would have vested interests in the land. And a royal representative meant that a certain percentage of the profits of trade (by any name) would redound to the crown that could keep a rein on its own subjects.

All through the 1660s and the next decades, the French consolidated their control over the western half of Hispaniola, calling the colony Saint Domingue and bringing in thousands of immigrants with their slaves to plant tobacco and sugar. The colony grew in relative peace until 1690, when France found herself at war with the rest of Europe and the French Governor led some 1,000 buccaneers and colonial militia to sack and burn the Spanish settlement at Santiago de los Caballeros in the north central part of the island. Later that year the Spaniards retaliated by invading and destroying the French town of Cap-Français on the north coast, thereby setting off a series of raids and counterraids that would inflame the island for almost a decade.

France was only one nation whose subjects were among the interlopers on the Main. In the three decades since the 1630s, the number of northern Europeans on the Main had risen from 18,000 to an estimated 100,000, and they occupied an estimated 2,500 square miles of supposedly Spanish territory. Most numerous were the English, 50,000 strong, who had spread far and wide through the Lesser Antilles into the Bahamas, and whose presence on another of the buccaneers' haunts, the nearby island of Jamaica, was causing tremors that were felt throughout the Spanish Main.

Chapter 5

A sea-roving devil named Henry Morgan

o the indigenous Arawak Indians the place was known as Haymaca—Island of Fountains—for the thermal springs that spouted from the limestone honeycombs of its interior plateau. To the Spaniards under whose flag Columbus had claimed it, the island was at first Santiago, and then Jamaica, in an approximate Spanish spelling of the Indian name. By any appellation it was a land largely avoided by Spanish colonists, who favored the richer mineral deposits and civilized cities of Cuba, Hispaniola, Puerto Rico, and the mainland of Central and South America.

Scorpions skulked in dark Jamaican corners, multitudes of land crabs made strange nighttime sounds as they scuttled from the forests to feed on the beaches, sandflies left bleeding welts, and clouds of malarial mosquitoes required that green-wood fires be built to windward at night. All these creatures occurred on the other large islands also, but somehow on Jamaica they seemed larger, more numerous and more vicious. In 1534 the Spanish built a dreary little capital, St. Jago de la Vega, on an alluvial plain 13 miles inland from the south coast. The nearby land was divided into plantations, and sugar cane was introduced. But the attempt at colonization was halfhearted, and by the middle of the 17th Century the Spanish crown had all but abandoned the island, leaving only about 1,500 settlers, 3,000 black slaves and a garrison numbering no more than 200 soldiers.

On May 10, 1655, a British fleet dropped anchor in what later became Kingston Harbor and sent ashore troops, who within 24 hours put to rout what Spanish defenders they could find. Yet for the attackers Jamaica was at best a sorry consolation prize. The British force had sailed from Barbados with the bold intention of seizing Santo Domingo, the capital of Spanish Hispaniola. But the aggressors had badly botched the job and, after being easily repulsed, decided to swoop down upon helpless Jamaica as a means of saving face.

What neither the Spanish nor the British understood at the time—though both would know it soon enough—was that Jamaica was a key to control of the Caribbean. More than 140 miles long from east to west and 50 miles across at its broadest point, Jamaica blocked the southern sea approaches to the Windward Passage between Cuba and Hispaniola; it would serve Britain as a wedge between the two Spanish islands. Holding a central strategic position almost equidistant from Cartagena, Panama and the tips of the Yucatan Peninsula and Florida, Jamaica offered as well a splendid base for raids against both the mainland cities and the treasure galleons making their way to rendezvous at Havana.

The island possessed one of the world's great natural harbors, which the British would shortly render all but impregnable by heavily fortifying the reef that commanded and nearly enclosed the entryway. That spit of land had been named Caguaya by the Spanish; the British at first called it the Cagway, and a town by that name sprang up at the harbor's entrance. Later, as Port Royal, it would become the greatest buccaneering stronghold in the Caribbean, far outstripping Hispaniola's Tortuga and causing such grief to the Spanish crown that nightly prayers were said in Seville, calling on God's wrath for its destruction.

The fleet that captured Jamaica for Britain tarried no longer than abso-

Armed to the teeth with a musket, a brace of pistols and a sword, a dapper Henry Morgan stands calmly aloof as his buccaneers engage in furious battle with the Spaniards outside the city of Panama in this 18th-Century engraving

lutely necessary, and made sail for home after scarcely a month. To secure this new challenge to the Spanish Empire, the British left behind 12 small warships and a garrison of about 6,000 men. These were the dregs of the British Isles and Barbados, described by their erstwhile commander, Sir Robert Venables, as "the most profane, debauched persons that we ever saw" and by one of their own number as "hectors, and knights of the blade, with common cheats, thieves, cutpurses and suchlike lewd persons."

But among these caitiffs and cullions was a young—he was still short of his 21st birthday—Welshman of obscure origin whose name would ring, as with the clash of steel against naked steel, throughout the Spanish Main for the better part of three decades. His name was Henry Morgan—Harry to his friends, the very devil to the Spanish—and from Jamaica he would bring the age of the buccaneers to blood-red flower.

"I left school too young and have been more used to the pike than the book," said Henry Morgan in later life—and those are his first, last and only recorded words about his youth and upbringing. He was certainly born in Wales, probably in the village of Llanrhymny (after which he named his favorite Jamaica plantation), but possibly in Penkarne (which gave its name to another Morgan estate). The approximate year of his birth is known only because of a November 21, 1671, deposition in which he said he was then 36 years old. The name, occupation and social status of his father are unknown but Henry was almost surely raised in a military atmosphere. Two of his uncles were prominent soldiers, and they would play important if indirect roles in Henry Morgan's career.

One of the uncles, Thomas Morgan, described by a contemporary as "a little, shrill-voiced choleric man," was something of an expert in the budding science of siege artillery. During England's Civil War Thomas chose the Parliamentary side and, as a major general, became second-in-command to George Monck, who had been appointed by Oliver Cromwell to subjugate Scotland. Years later, when General Monck turned his coat, overthrew the Parliamentary regime and placed Charles II on the throne, he was, as Duke of Albemarle, in a position to perform favors for Thomas Morgan—and Morgan's kinsmen, including Henry.

The other uncle, Edward Morgan, was a mercenary officer in the unceasing conflicts then besetting Europe. While in Germany during the Thirty Years' War, he wooed and married the daughter of the Baron von Pöllnitz, Governor of the city of Lippstadt. Unlike his brother, Edward cast his lot with the Royalists in England's fratricidal struggle, and when his cause was lost he went into exile with his in-laws in Germany. Finally redeemed by Thomas Morgan's influence with Albemarle, Edward would help bring Henry Morgan to the favorable attention of Jamaica's authorities.

As murky as Henry Morgan's boyhood in Wales was the manner by which he came to the Caribbean. The buccaneer chronicler John Esquemeling said that young Morgan had been snatched out of a waterfront "place of entertainment" and taken as an indentured servant to Barbados, where he won his freedom by volunteering to join the expedition to Hispaniola and Jamaica. Other versions of his early history,

Morgan's base of operations on the Spanish Main was the snug harbor of Port Royal, Jamaica, shown on the lower half of this page from a 1684 English atlas. The general map of the area, depicting the Caribbean islands and coasts of Central, South and North America, is far more accurate than the maps that were in use a century earlier (pages 16-17).

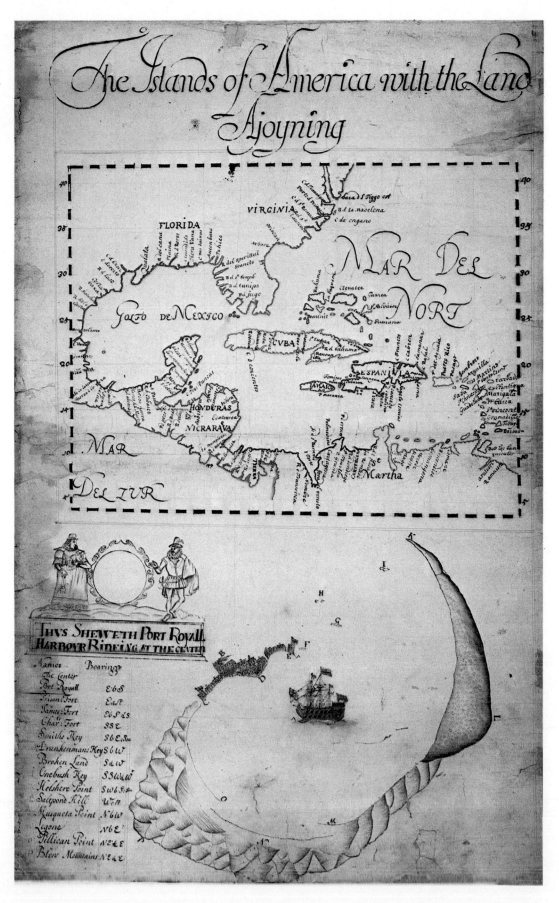

The Islands of America with the Land Ajoyning

VIRGINIA

FLORIDA

MAR DEL NORT

GOLFO DE MEXICO

CVBA

MAR

ESPANIVLA

JAMAICO

HONDVRAS

NICRARAVA

DEL IVR

S.ta Martha

THVS SHEWETH PORT ROYALL. HARBOVR RIDEING AT THE CENTER

Names	Bearings
The Center	
Port Royall	E.b.S
Prison Fort	East
James Fort	E.b.S.½.S
Char: Fort	S.S.E
Smithe Key	S.b.E.¾.e
Prankenmans Key	S.b.W
Broken Land	S.a.W
Onebush Key	S.S.W.¾.W
Kelshere Point	S.W.b.S.½.
Sallpond Hill	W.¾.n
Mugueta Point	N.b.W
Ligone	N.b.E
Pellican Point	N.E.¼.E
Blew Mountains	N.E.¼.E

equally likely, are that Morgan signed with the expedition, either in England or Barbados, to escape imprisonment for brawling, or because he had been found out as a "malignant," as the Puritans called Royalist sympathizers, or because he wished to escape an outraged father whose daughter Morgan had soiled.

In any case, the important points are that Henry Morgan almost surely accompanied the force that captured Jamaica, that he was hardy enough to survive the pestilence that mowed down many others and that he found the place congenial to a man much given to violent action.

He was not a large man, but he was lean and strong, with a Welshman's swarthy complexion, a prominent nose, sensuous lips and dark, arrogant eyes. In personality he was difficult to judge. His tongue carried both a lilt and a lash—he "always communicated vigor with his words," wrote Esquemeling, and "infused such spirits into his men as were able to put every one of them instantly upon new designs." There seems little doubt that he was driven by loyalty and love for England; yet he consistently turned his patriotism to his personal profit. Though lawless, he was evidently something of a sea lawyer, and he rarely sailed forth on his maraudings without an authorizing document—even if of dubious pedigree. Renowned for the wolfish ferocity of his assaults, he also possessed a foxlike cunning, and some of his greatest triumphs resulted as much from guile as from the open test of arms. Finally, and perhaps most important, although he apparently took a perverse pride in his lack of schooling, Henry Morgan had an immense capacity for learning through bloody experience.

The opportunities for a liberal education lay all about him. Though the Spaniards had little use for Jamaica, they could not abide an English bastion virtually at the heart of their empire, so they maintained a number of guerrilla bands along the island's north coast. There were perhaps 500 men in all, reinforced and supplied from Cuba, under Don Cristobal Arnoldo Yssasi, son of a former Governor of Jamaica and brother to the Spanish lieutenant general in Cuba.

Suppressing these Spaniards was a job at times for just about every able-bodied man in the English settlement, and Morgan most certainly was among the forces sent against Yssasi. The tactics that were employed in this deadly little war contained elements that Morgan later perfected: swift approaches by sea to the general area occupied by the enemy, undetected landings in some hidden harbor, stealthy overland marches to a Spanish encampment, and savage surprise attacks with no quarter given or asked.

The guerrilla actions continued for three years, until in the spring of 1658 the British spotted three Spanish vessels unloading cannon on the north coast. Some 600 hastily assembled Britons descended on the guerrillas, who had foolishly concentrated their forces; though Yssasi himself escaped, the Spanish were virtually wiped out.

The commander of this expedition was a little pepper pot from whom Henry Morgan could learn much. He was Commodore Sir Christopher Mings, who had captained a frigate in the invasion fleet and had decided to make his fortune in Jamaica. Mings was a fine seaman with a keen appetite for Spanish treasure and a flawless instinct for finding it. In

The spectacular successes of English Commodore Sir Christopher Mings while ransacking the Spanish Main during the mid-1600s set the pattern for raids for the next 40 years. His specialty was to go ashore undetected, attack from an unexpected quarter at an unexpected hour, plunder swiftly and slip away before the Spaniards regained their senses.

1659 he decided to attempt the most difficult—and unexpected—voyage in the West Indies, beating southeast into the prevailing trade winds to strike at the Spanish Main near its easternmost Venezuelan extremity. The South American coast was only 600 miles distant on a direct line, but by the time Mings, in the *Marston Moor*, accompanied by two other ships, had finished tacking across the Caribbean, he had traveled more than 1,000 miles.

For his first target Mings chose Cumaná, the center for Spanish pearl fisheries along the Venezuelan coast. Sweeping in without warning, the British raiders routed the astonished settlers and sacked the city, reaping rich rewards. Mings next sailed west for 250 miles to fall on the silver entrepôt of Puerto Cabello, where the yield was somewhat disappointing. But then, 125 miles farther west at Coro, a small and supposedly insignificant town, Mings had a marvelous stroke of luck. At the approach of the British, Coro's inhabitants fled into the woods—and led Mings straight to a cache of silver. There were 22 chests of the stuff, each weighing about 400 pounds and marked for the King of Spain. All told, they contained some 1.5 million pieces of eight, then worth about £375,000. It was a haul of monumental proportions, more than had been taken on any single raid since Francis Drake had seized the treasure ship *Cacafuego* nearly a century before. Even when shared with his company, the loot was enough to make Mings rich for life.

There is no direct proof that Henry Morgan accompanied Mings on this lucrative excursion. But his presence seems entirely likely in view of the fact that shortly thereafter he had, without other known means, enough capital to purchase his own small ship. The first documentary record relating to Morgan, a commission as a privateer signed by Jamaica's Governor Thomas Windsor, shows that Captain Henry Morgan was owner of one of the 10 ships sailing with Commodore Mings on September 21, 1661, against a major Spanish bastion—Santiago, Cuba's second largest port, near the eastern tip of the island.

The operation turned into a classic piece of improvisation. The little fleet set sail from Port Royal under cloudy skies with a light easterly wind, rounded Negril Point at Jamaica's western end and slowly clawed toward Santiago, 150 miles northeast. But the wind soon turned sulky, now dying, now puffing fitfully as the ships struggled along, rarely making more than three knots. An unexpected southwest current of up to two and a half knots cut their actual speed to a knot or less, sometimes taking them back toward Jamaica when the wind failed entirely.

Finally, after 15 frustrating days, the fleet neared its destination and Mings called his captains to a council of war. It was decided to sail audaciously straight into Santiago harbor and grab the Spaniards directly by their beards. On October 5 Mings at last sighted the massive fortifications of the Castillo del Morro, high on a cliff guarding the entrance to the harbor. The passage itself was no more than a long, narrow slot—in places, only 60 yards wide—between the Sierra Maestra walls, which fell sheer to the sea.

It would be suicide to try an assault through this deadly corridor. With remarkable facility Mings switched plans. Turning his fleet west, he sailed two miles along the coast, as far as the mouth of the San Juan

River. There, out of sight of the Spaniards, he put his 1,300 men ashore.

That night Mings and his men forced their way through the forest to attack Santiago from the rear at dawn's first light. "The path was so narrow," Mings wrote later, "that but one man could march at a time, the way so difficult and the night so dark that we were forced to make stand and light fires"; he then sent forth "guides with brands in their hands to beat the path."

At daybreak Mings and his men charged into the town. The astonished Spaniards were routed—including Don Cristobal Arnoldo Yssasi, the same Yssasi who had opposed the English on Jamaica and now, as Mings delightedly reported, "fairly ran away."

Mings knew how to loot. For five days his men toiled in what could only have been a labor of love—carrying chests of silver and barrels of sugar and wine to the English ships, now anchored in the harbor. The guns of the Castillo del Morro were shoved off a precipice into the sea. From the great fort's magazine Mings took 700 barrels of gunpowder; he distributed them at strategic intervals around the edifice, and lighted fuses. "Truly it was so demolished," Mings later wrote. "The greater part lies level with the foundations." On October 22 drums rolled and guns boomed in salute as Christopher Mings came home past the Cagway with his fleet, his booty and six Spanish ships captured at Santiago.

For nearly two more years, Mings—and Henry Morgan with him— made the Spanish Main miserable for its owners. But in the summer of 1663 the feisty commodore was recalled to England, where he stayed until he was killed in a battle against the Dutch three years later. Meanwhile Morgan, having learned his lessons well, struck out on his own in an exploit that was to propel him to buccaneering eminence.

The maturing of Harry Morgan began as a joint venture with four other captains, about whom little is known save for their surnames and nationalities—the Englishmen Morris, Freeman and Jackman, and the Dutchman Marteen. But Morgan soon became the recognized leader. In 1663 the five sailed from Jamaica, carrying documents of highly dubious validity: privateers' commissions bearing the signature of Governor Windsor, who by now had been back in England for nearly two years. Just as Mings had done on his Cumaná expedition, Morgan and his confederates sought Spanish towns that had long gone unmolested, where garrisons had grown indolent through inaction and cannon balls had become so encrusted with rust that they would no longer fit into their guns.

The five ships, carrying perhaps 200 men, sailed northwest around the Yucatan Peninsula of Mexico, where they caught a strong current that helped carry them about 400 miles westward. Even while staying far enough off the coast to avoid being flung onto the shore by one of the vicious storms that frequently blew down from the north, Morgan's men kept a sharp eye out for the muddy waters that signified the mouth of the Grijalva River. Their destination was Villahermosa, capital of the province of Tabasco, some 50 miles up the river. The buccaneers finally found the Grijalva, but in a short time they discovered that their problems were only beginning.

Though the river was navigable, by sailing up it to Villahermosa Morgan would have had to sacrifice the surprise fundamental to his tactics. Instead, he stopped at an Indian village about three miles upstream, hid his ships and enlisted some Spanish-hating guides to lead him around the swamp that stretched for 20 miles on both sides of the river.

With the help of the Indians, Morgan and his men finally reached Villahermosa and sacked the town, taking all the plunder they could carry away. But when they returned to the mouth of the Grijalva, having marched no fewer than 300 miles, they were faced with a calamity. To his horror, Morgan discovered that his ships had been taken away by a powerful Spanish scouting party that had stumbled onto the hideaway and had overwhelmed the skeleton crews. Morgan was stranded.

But not for long. Two Spanish barks accompanied by four cargo canoes—seaworthy sailing craft of up to 40 feet in length—soon entered the Grijalva, blissfully unaware of the desperate buccaneers lurking nearby. As the barks and canoes passed close to shore, Morgan and his men burst from the bush, swarmed aboard and seized the craft.

Now Morgan again had transportation as well as loot, and any reasonable man would have headed home as quickly as possible. But that was never Morgan's way. Instead, sailing and paddling for all they were worth, the buccaneers labored eastward to the tip of the Yucatan Peninsula, then took a southerly course across the Gulf of Honduras and finally made anchorage at Monkey Point, on the eastern edge of what is now Nicaragua. Since leaving Jamaica, they had traveled more than 2,600 miles—and they were only now arriving on the threshold of their crowning achievement.

Morgan meant to locate and capture the near-mythical city of Gran Granada, reputedly an original repository of Aztec treasure and now, under the Spaniards, a rich agricultural and silver-mining center. The buccaneers knew only that it lay somewhere far up a malignant jungle river, somewhere across cruel mountains, somewhere on an enormous and bountiful lake. Morgan enlisted some Indian guides who said they could take him there, and he was determined to go.

According to an official account by a new Governor of Jamaica, to whom Morgan reported when he eventually returned home, the buccaneers loaded their captured canoes with provisions and with their Indian guides worked their way up the north fork of the San Juan River, traveling 111 miles before they finally came to "a fair laguna, or lake of sweet water, full of excellent fish, with its banks full of brave pastures and savannahs, covered with horses and cattle, where they had as good beef and mutton as any in England." This was Lake Nicaragua.

Morgan's men, "hiding by day under cays and islands and rowing all night, by the advice of their Indian guides, landed near the city of Gran Granada," continued the report. "This town is bigger than Portsmouth with seven churches and a very fair cathedral, besides divers colleges and monasteries, all built of free stone, as also most of their houses." The buccaneers swooped upon Gran Granada—the modern city of Granada in southwest Nicaragua—not in the glooming hours but while the sun was shining down on the complacent city. Morgan and his men "fired a volley, overturned 18 great guns in the Parada Place, took the sergeant-major's house wherein were all their arms and ammunition, secured in the Great Church 300 of the best men prisoners, abundance of which were churchmen, plundered for 16 hours, discharged the prisoners, sunk all the boats and so came away."

How much the loot amounted to is not known, but it was enough to return Morgan to Jamaica a hero and a wealthy man.

Jamaica had advanced toward prosperity by leaps and bounds during Morgan's two-year absence. Although the economy initially fed on the treasures taken by the buccaneers, it found a more lasting base in the island's alluvial plains, which were ideal for growing sugar cane *(page 133)*. Sugar quickly became Jamaica's most important resource. From the first small shipment to England in January of 1660, the industry grew rapidly, until exports were in the hundreds of tons by 1665. And rum, sugar's deliciously intoxicating by-product, was also much in demand as an item of trade with England.

Port Royal's waterside now bristled with wharves, and the bowsprits of dozens of ships jutted across cobblestone streets. Carpentry stalls and sail lofts, grog shops and brothels stood chockablock. And there were three markets where a buyer could see his meat slaughtered before his eyes (thus being assured that it had not already spoiled in the tropical heat) or could watch as a slave splashed through a shallow pan to capture a six-pound spiny lobster. From the 4,000 or so survivors of the initial expeditionary force, the population of Jamaica was swelling year after year as a steady stream of ships arrived bearing impecunious and ambitious newcomers.

Of more immediate interest to Morgan than Jamaica's booming growth was the fact that during his absence his Uncle Edward Morgan, the Royalist veteran, had come to the island as Lieutenant Governor. Edward had been given the post because of his brother's longtime association with General Monck, now the Duke of Albemarle, to whose changing loyalties the King owed his scepter. The new Governor, Thomas Mody-ford, was Albemarle's cousin, and he and Edward Morgan got along splendidly. Soon after arriving in 1664, Modyford wrote to the Secretary of State that he was "infinitely obliged to his Majesty for sending so worthy a person to assist me, whom I really cherish as my brother."

So highly did Modyford think of his deputy that in the spring of 1665 he selected Edward Morgan—by now well past his prime—to lead an expedition against the Dutch island of St. Eustatius. (England, turning with the wildly shifting political winds that blew during that period, was now temporarily at peace with Spain and at war with the Dutch.) Edward Morgan was in the forefront of the force landing on St. Eustatius but, as Modyford later explained, "the good old colonel leaping out of the boat and being a corpulent man, got a strain, and his spirit being great he pursued over earnestly the enemy on a hot day, so that he surfeited and suddenly died."

Upon leaving England, Edward Morgan, a widower, had been accompanied by his four daughters and two sons; of these the oldest daughter had died aboard ship of, as Modyford later wrote with maddening brevi-ty, a "malign distemper by reason of the nastiness of the passengers." The surviving sisters automatically assumed high rank in what passed

Enduring riches from the "Noble Juice of the Cane"

"We at present," wrote a jubilant Englishman from the West Indies in 1690, "exceed all the Nations in the world in the true Improvement of that Noble Juice of the Cane." He might have also said that sugar growing outstripped buccaneering as a way to wealth. In fact, even such consummate raiders as Henry Morgan grew richer from their plantations than from plundering.

Sugar cane was not native to the New World. It traveled from Asia to the Mediterranean and was transplanted to Santo Domingo by Christopher Columbus in 1493. Dutch and Portuguese settlers built up a thriving sugar industry in Brazil, and English planters introduced the cane to their Caribbean colonies in the mid-1600s.

It was a complex and exacting industry, requiring so many workers that from 1671 to 1684 Jamaica alone imported 1,500 slaves per year. After harvesting, the cane was sent to a grinding mill and crushed to extract the sweet juice. The juice was boiled and thickened to syrup in huge vats, then piped to cooling trays in which sugar crystals formed atop a thick brown residue of molasses—which was distilled into a fiery rum called kill-devil.

Mismanagement could ruin an entire crop. Unless planting was staggered, the cane ripened all at once and spoiled before it could be processed. And unless rats were controlled, they could eat whole fields of cane.

But the English colonists learned their lessons well. By 1680 the planters of Barbados alone were sending sugar to England worth more than all the exports of all the North American colonies combined. The sugar growers' fortunes were so great as to give rise to the term "rich as a West Indian planter." And it was a durable wealth that grew from generation to generation. When William Beckford—a son and grandson of Jamaica planters—died in 1770, he had an annual income of £100,000, and he left an estate of £1 million in England and Jamaica.

At a Caribbean sugar mill, slaves feed the cane into an ox-powered grinder, from which the juice flows to a holding tank flanked by boiling vats. Though this 17th Century French engraving depicts an open-air operation, most of the mills were enclosed, and the grinding and boiling took place in separate buildings.

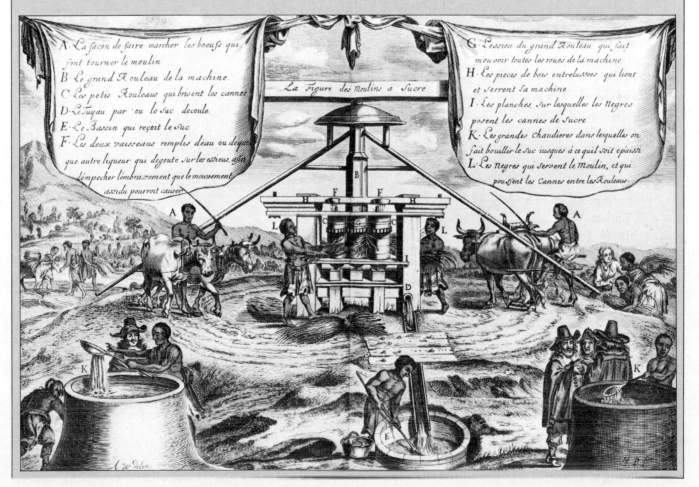

for Port Royal society and Henry Morgan, back from his successful raids and much the dandy in finery stolen from Spanish grandees, married his first cousin Mary Elizabeth, probably late in 1665 or early in 1666.

A wife was only one of the appurtenances and honors the 30-year-old Morgan now found himself possessing. As the nephew of Modyford's deceased friend and lieutenant, Morgan naturally found favor in the eyes of the Governor, who appointed him colonel and commander of the Port Royal militia. Moreover, his recent triumphs had won him stature among the buccaneers of the Brethren of the Coast, that loose coalition of sea rovers first organized on Hispaniola in the 1640s and now active on Jamaica. The elected leader of the brethren was a battle-worn old marauder named Edward Mansfield. But in 1666 he was somehow captured by the Spanish and, as the chronicler Esquemeling put it with considerable relish, "death suddenly suppressed him and put an end to his wicked career." As their new admiral the Brethren of the Coast selected Harry Morgan of Port Royal.

Thus Morgan, who had sailed off on his first independent buccaneering venture less than three years before, was now a man of great parts in Jamaica, confidant and aide of the Governor, married to a pillar of island society, and both commander of the King's defenses at Port Royal and leader of the town's freebooters. It was a remarkable turn of fortune for a man who may well have arrived on the Main as an indentured servant.

By now England and Spain were warring again, and among Morgan's first acts as admiral of the brethren was to draw up a list of Spanish strongholds he meant to loot and level: Havana, Portobelo, Veracruz, Cartagena, Maracaibo, Panama. This was ambition beyond possible accomplishment. But when he was done, Morgan would have achieved enough of it to merit permanent fame as a scourge of the Spanish Main.

His first opportunity came quickly enough. By the summer of 1667 Port Royal abounded in rumors that the Spanish in Cuba were gathering a fleet to recapture Jamaica. Governor Modyford therefore commissioned Morgan to assemble a fleet, scout Cuban waters and "take prisoners of the Spanish nation" who might provide him with information of the plan to attack Jamaica.

Morgan's call went out to Tortuga and other havens frequented by buccaneers, and by March 1668 a dozen ships, carrying some 700 men, had assembled at Twelve League Cays, one of the hundreds of tiny island groups off south central Cuba. The ships were a sorry-looking lot, enough to make a proper naval officer wince at the sight. They ranged from the *Dolphin*, a 50-foot sloop of eight guns, down to single-masted pinnaces scarcely larger than longboats. Henry Morgan's reputation as a seaman has suffered by comparison with his recognized abilities as a fighter. Yet in the course of his career he safely led scores of just such frail craft across vast reaches of a sea in which devastating hurricanes were spawned and where deadly coral claws often lurked inches beneath the surface.

Now, in the turquoise waters of Twelve League Cays, the buccaneering leaders held a council befitting their basic status as individual entrepreneurs embarking on a joint adventure. Morgan, who had not the slightest intention of limiting himself to his commission, had it in mind

Henry Morgan's raiders (right) launch a furious attack against the Spanish defenders of Puerto Príncipe, Cuba, in 1668. Armed with cannon and forewarned of the attack, the Spaniards put up a stubborn, four-hour fight but yielded when Morgan threatened to burn the city and slaughter everyone in sight.

to strike at Havana. But several of the others had been imprisoned there at one time or another, and they had a healthy respect for its defenses. It was finally decided to attack Puerto Príncipe, a hide-trading center that lay about 45 miles inland, northeast of Twelve League Cays. Unfortunately for the buccaneers, a Spanish prisoner was aboard the ship where the council was held, and he understood English. He escaped by jumping over the side and made his way to Puerto Príncipe. He warned the citizens, who managed to hide most of their valuables before Morgan and his men could make the difficult march through dense forests and across rolling hills. So, though the town was easily taken, it yielded booty worth only 50,000 pieces of eight, or £12,500—an amount, Esquemeling wrote, that "caused a general grief."

Admiral Morgan was off to a wobbly start—but one he would soon redeem. High on his list of prospective prizes was Panama's Portobelo, one of the main collection points for Spanish treasure. But its defenses were formidable. The castle of San Felipe, known as the Iron Fort, stood guard at the entrance to the mile-long harbor; two other forts, San Gerónimo and Triana, protected the town itself. In all, more than 60 cannon bristled from the Spanish works. And for excellent reason. One Englishman who had been there a few years before reported seeing mule trains arriving from Panama "laden with wedges of silver; in one day I told 200 mules laden with nothing else."

For Morgan the temptation was irresistible. In May 1668 he gathered 460 men and sailed south from Jamaica with nine ships. The vessels towed or carried on their decks 23 canoes of the sort he had become so familiar with during his Gran Granada adventure. Fearing desertions, Morgan at first said only that they were off on a secret mission. Not until he had sighted the solitary 1,700-foot mountain of Pilón de Miguel de la Borda near the mouth of the Chagres River did he inform his captains that their destination was Portobelo.

There were startled protests. The place was too strong. But Harry Morgan, calling upon his Welsh way with words, stifled the outburst by appealing to both courage and cupidity. "If our numbers are small, our hearts are great," he cried, "and the fewer we are, the better shares we shall have in the spoils."

Morgan had no intention of attacking the Iron Fort from the harbor side. Instead, he and his men took to the canoes, paddled along the coast to a point several miles from Portobelo, landed at 3 a.m. and plunged into the jungle that lay between them and San Gerónimo. That Spanish garrison of 130 men, taken by surprise, was easily overwhelmed. In the captured fortress the buccaneers found 11 English prisoners, chained to the walls of the dungeon and barely alive amid vermin and their own excrement. To Henry Morgan as to others in that remorseless age, atrocity could be answered only by further atrocity: he locked his Spanish prisoners, about 55 of them, in a central room and, as Esquemeling described it, "set fire to the gunpowder (whereof they found a great quantity) and blew up the whole castle in the air, with all the Spaniards that were within."

After San Gerónimo was destroyed, Morgan sent a detachment overland to the Iron Fort, whose guns were pointing seaward and whose defenders quickly succumbed to the buccaneers' furious assault. The remaining bastion, Triana, which lay within Portobelo itself, was a much tougher nut, if only because it was commanded by Don José Sánchez Ximénez, a soldier in whom courage and obstinacy were equal. Before approaching the fort, Morgan rounded up as many Spanish priests and nuns as he could and used them as a living shield, behind which his men advanced with scaling ladders. But if he thought Sánchez would shrink from firing into God's ordained, he was badly mistaken, and an unknown number of the helpless captives were killed.

Still, Morgan's men reached and swarmed over Triana's walls. "No surrender!" shouted Sánchez, flailing about with his sword and felling several of his men who sought to flee. Admiring his opponent's bravery, Morgan halted the fighting and offered quarter to Sánchez.

"I do not hang such as you," he called.

Sánchez declined, and almost immediately fell dead in a hail of shots fired by the buccaneers.

Portobelo was Morgan's. His men looted the town for 31 days, "committing all manner of debauchery and excess," according to Esquemeling. During Morgan's month at Portobelo, a Spanish force of 3,000 men marched across the Isthmus from Panama to recapture the city. But the Indians, Spanish-hating as always, alerted Morgan. He led 100 buccaneers into the jungle, where—although they were outnumbered 30 to 1—they ambushed the Spaniards at a narrow pass, killed several and managed to scatter the rest in terror. Morgan's band returned to Portobelo, hurriedly emptied the town of the remainder of its valuables and embarked for Jamaica.

Port Royal burst into noisy celebration when Admiral Harry Morgan and his little fleet returned carrying treasures then valued at nearly £100,000. It was far less than Mings's haul from Venezuela in 1659 but still a grand amount for the times.

At 33 Morgan ranked second on Jamaica only to Governor Modyford—if indeed he gave place to anyone. "The planters and men in power caressed Morgan," wrote a chronicler of the period. He had every incentive to settle down, including a recently purchased plantation and a wife to whom he was devoted—if not faithful. But his followers were faring poorly. According to the same chronicler, the denizens of Port Royal's brothels and grog shops "contrived every kind of bait to drain his associates of their money. They were very liberal and in a short time came clamouring to their Captain to put to sea."

Thus on January 2, 1669, Morgan found himself with 12 ill-assorted vessels and 900 men at a council of war at Ile-à-Vache—Cow Island to the buccaneers—off the southwest coast of Hispaniola. Morgan himself was aboard a newly acquired source of vast pride: the 26-gun frigate *Oxford*, which Modyford, doubtless with the powerful help of his cousin the Duke of Albemarle, had obtained from the British Admiralty. This time Morgan felt no hesitation in announcing his objective—the great Spanish bastion at Cartagena. And when he did, such was now his esteem among the disputatious buccaneers that no one offered so much as a murmur of protest.

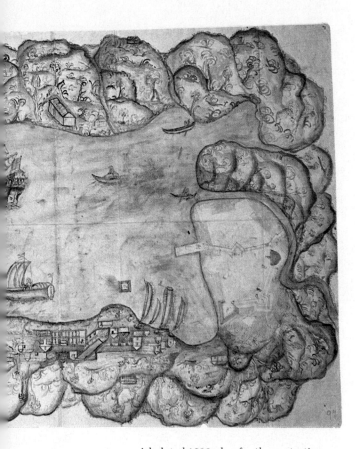

A belated 1688 plan for the protection of gold-rich Portobelo, Panama, shows the entire area well guarded by two forts near the mouth of the harbor, with a large redoubt to protect the town itself. Morgan had sacked the place two decades before, bypassing the harbor forts by attacking the town from the rear, where it was virtually without defenses.

The decision made, Morgan invited his captains to dinner. While they seated themselves in the great cabin, members of the crew caroused on the foredeck, consuming copious quantities of rum. And as darkness fell, candles in lanterns were lighted. But rum, candles and open kegs of gunpowder—the buccaneers were never tidy shipkeepers—proved a fatal combination.

Suddenly a tremendous explosion ripped through the *Oxford*. Of the 200 seamen, all but six were killed. Richard Browne, the *Oxford*'s surgeon, reported the scene in the admiral's cabin: "I was eating my dinner with the rest when the main masts blew out, and fell upon Captains Aylett, Bigford, and others, and knocked them on the head." Browne, hurled into the water, saved himself by clinging to a piece of the mizzenmast. By a freak of the explosion, all the guests seated on the opposite side of the table from Morgan were killed; Morgan and those seated with him survived with scarcely a scratch.

Throughout the Spanish Americas word of the *Oxford*'s destruction was received as a stroke of divine intervention. At Cartagena the city's patron saint, Nuestra Señora de la Popa, was given special credit. Wrote the buccaneer-explorer William Dampier: "Any misfortune that befalls the privateers is attributed to this lady's doing, and the Spaniards report that she was abroad the night the *Oxford* was blown up, and that she came home all wet."

Morgan scoffed at such nonsense. He quickly reorganized his force and—since his casualties, particularly of officers, had clearly rendered him too weak to attack Cartagena—he began casting about for another target. Any perplexities he may have had were resolved by a French captain who had joined him: the man had sacked Maracaibo with Francis L'Ollonais three years before and now professed, said Esquemeling, that he "knew all the entries, passages, forces and means how to put in execution the same again."

With 650 men and eight ships—a few of the battered sloops had deteriorated in the turbulent Caribbean—Morgan sailed into the Gulf of Venezuela, keeping well toward the middle of the broad entrance so as to remain beyond sight of the Spanish watchtowers ashore. At its southern end the deep gulf narrowed, like the waist of an hourglass, into a shallow channel that led to the Lake of Maracaibo. To attack the city of Maracaibo, Morgan would have to pass through the channel. To his chagrin he discovered that the Spaniards, having profited from the lessons of the L'Ollonais raid, had built a fort on a small island not 300 yards from the entrance to the channel.

There was no choice for Morgan but to take the bastion. He put his buccaneers ashore on the little island. Using sand dunes as cover, they crept toward the fort. At 3 p.m. a vicious wind blew up, whipping sand into the attackers' faces—but equally obscuring the defenders' vision. Shortly after dark, Morgan himself crawled to the walls of the fort and discovered a gate left open by the Spaniards, who had fled from the place only minutes before. Bursting in, Morgan spotted and stamped out a slow fuse. It had been cut to burn 15 minutes—and in only five minutes more it would have reached the fort's magazine.

But the alarm had been given. By the time the buccaneers finally arrived at Maracaibo, they found it, in Esquemeling's words, "without any person in it, for all were fled before them into the woods." Yet Morgan was determined, and for the following eight weeks he remained in the region, seizing the opportunity to raid Gibraltar, another lakeside town whose inhabitants fled into the jungle when they sighted Morgan's marauders.

At both Maracaibo and Gibraltar the buccaneers scoured the countryside and routed the citizens out of their hiding places. One by one the Spaniards were forced to disclose the whereabouts of their valuables, and Morgan's men gleefully went to collect them—in an amount estimated at about £50,000 in money and gems, in addition to a fortune in slaves and merchandise.

Finally, in mid-April, having pillaged and pleasured to their hearts' content, Morgan and his men started back to the Gulf of Venezuela—and into a crisis that would force Harry Morgan to call upon all the cunning at his command.

Awaiting Morgan at the gulf end of the connecting channel were three large Spanish war galleons, any one of which could have blasted Morgan's flimsy fleet straight out of the water. Under the command of Vice Admiral Alonso del Campo y Espinosa in the 48-gun *Magdalen*, the ships had been sent to the Main by the King of Spain, who had issued specific orders to bring Morgan's depredations to an end. Now they stood at stalemate: Morgan was bottled inside the lake, but the Spanish ships were too deep-drafted to pass through the channel and exterminate the buccaneers.

For a full week the deadlock continued. And then, late on the afternoon of April 30, Don Alonso saw Morgan's fleet thrusting through the shallow channel and approaching him in single file. The admiral was understandably delighted, and his confidence was in no way diminished when darkness fell and the pirates, as he called them, anchored just beyond range of his guns.

At daybreak the Spanish admiral again saw the buccaneer squadron moving toward him. It was evident that Morgan meant to lead with his strength. The first ship bristled with men and guns. Secure in his overwhelming superiority, Don Alonso permitted the enemy ship to come close alongside, intending to pulverize it with a single broadside. But the delay was fatal: as the buccaneers' ship drew to within a few yards of the *Magdalen*, wisps of smoke curled up from its hold—followed by an explosion of flame that instantly spread to the *Magdalen*.

Morgan's fireship—for such it was—had been cleverly disguised as a warship. At the portholes, instead of guns, logs had been inserted; and the decks—as Esquemeling described them—"were handsomely beset with many pieces of wood dressed up in the shape of men with hats and *monteros*, and likewise armed with swords, muskets and bandoleers." But inside, this phantom warship was packed with powder and brimstone, together with palm leaves coated with tar. The English crew had only to put a torch to her; as they made a hasty departure, she exploded in a rain of fire that made an inferno of the Spaniards' flagship.

Her stern consumed by fire, the *Magdalen* soon sank—but not until Don Alonso had escaped to the island fort, which had been retaken by

Trapped inside the harbor at Maracaibo, Venezuela, in 1669, Henry Morgan's flotilla (background) boldly takes on the heavily armed Spanish warships blocking the narrow channel to the sea. At right in this fanciful contemporary engraving, a fire ship sent in by Morgan explodes in a burst of flame, wreaking death and destruction on the Spaniards.

the Spanish during Morgan's absence. The captain of the second Spanish ship, the 38-gun *Santa Louisa*, panicked and ran his galleon aground. And in the wild confusion buccaneers boarded and captured the 24-gun *Marquesa*, which Morgan commandeered as his flagship.

But Morgan's difficulties were far from over: he still had to pass under the guns of the fort, where Don Alonso had now assumed command. To Morgan's offer to exchange Spanish prisoners in return for safe passage, Don Alonso replied: "I shall never grant your request, but shall endeavor to maintain that respect that is due unto my King, according to my duty."

Very well. Harry Morgan would again resort to trickery. For hours he sent boat after boat, each loaded with armed men, to the island's far side, where the buccaneers were concealed by mangroves. On their return trips to Morgan's ships, the boats appeared empty except for their oarsmen; in fact, they were still filled, though now the men hid behind the gunwales. With growing alarm Admiral Alonso del Campo y Espinosa watched and counted—until, convinced that Morgan meant to launch a massive land attack from the island's inshore side, he ordered his cannon trundled away from the seaward side to meet an assault. That night, without setting their sails, Morgan's ships weighed anchor and silently drifted past the fort on a favorable tide. When the Spaniards came to their senses, the buccaneers had spread their sails and were running into the distance before a gathering land breeze. In mocking farewell, Henry Morgan fired seven shots in the general direction of the fort.

On May 17, 1669, Admiral Henry Morgan in the captured *Marquesa* led his triumphant fleet, bearing booty valued at 250,000 pieces of eight, or £62,500, into the great harbor enclosed by the old Cagway. The celebrating buccaneers rolled barrels of wine into the streets, forced all passing men to drink and, according to a local historian, found an "excellent diversion to wet the ladies' clothes as they went along and force them to run from the showers of wine." But the news given Morgan by Governor Modyford was less exhilarating: a truce existed between England and Spain, and there would be no more buccaneering expeditions—at least for a while.

Morgan turned his enforced shore time to profit, scouting about Jamaica until he selected 836 acres in what is still known as Morgan's Valley, for which he was given a King's patent, a royal grant that entitled him and his descendants to ownership of the land in perpetuity.

By the summer of 1670, as might be expected, the truce had begun to unravel, thanks mostly to Spanish desire for revenge against Morgan's raids. Several English ships were seized and, along the unprotected coasts of Jamaica, Spanish marauders landed and attacked plantations. Without waiting for messages to travel to and from England, Modyford declared war on his own.

In a commission issued July 22, Morgan was authorized "to Land in the enemy's Country as many of his men as he shall think needful and then accordingly take, destroy and dispose of; and to do and perform all manner of exploits." Thus did Admiral Henry Morgan set out upon his last and greatest adventure.

So great was Morgan's fame by now that almost 2,000 buccaneers on

36 ships, by far the largest such assemblage yet seen in the Indies, answered the call to rendezvous near Cape Tiburón, Hispaniola, on December 2, 1670. Largest of the vessels was Morgan's new flagship, the 22-gun frigate *Satisfaction*. Of the remaining ships, 13 carried 10 guns or more; the five smallest mounted no guns, but they could still transport armed men of fierce disposition. At the customary council of war, Morgan seems to have left open the question of where the buccaneers should first strike. But he could only have been delighted when his captains selected the city of Panama.

Panama! The heart of Spain's New World. The citadel on the Isthmus' Pacific coast. The treasure house of gold and silver. Drake had dreamed of taking it, but not even that great captain had been able to fulfill his vision. The prize remained inviolate—beckoning to Henry Morgan.

His fleet left Cape Tiburón on December 8 and in a week covered the 575 miles to the flyspeck island of Old Providence, about midway between Jamaica and Portobelo. Once a favorite buccaneers' anchorage, the island had recently been captured by the Spaniards. Upon Morgan's arrival the island's Governor surrendered and asked only that Morgan stage a face-saving show with unshotted cannon. Morgan was happy to oblige, and he now had a base 300 miles from the mouth of the Chagres River, whence he would launch his strike against Panama.

From Old Providence Morgan sent an advance party of 470 picked men to storm the castle of San Lorenzo, which guarded the mouth of the Chagres River, up which the expedition would have to travel on its approach to Panama. The buccaneers reached the fort on December 26, and found that an attack by sea would be out of the question: the bastion's powerful guns outranged the ships' cannon. So the buccaneers left their sloops in a sheltered cove and sliced through the jungle for an assault by land. They took the fort, but only after a savage fight that lasted almost 24 hours and cost the buccaneers more than 100 casualties. Nevertheless, the road to Panama lay open.

From the mouth of the Chagres to the village of Venta de Cruces, itself a hard day's march from Panama, was a direct distance of only 25 miles. Yet such were the serpentine twists and turns of the sullen river that the trip took 75 miles by boat.

Leaving behind 400 men to garrison the San Lorenzo fort and thereby cover his rear—Morgan had learned a bitter lesson at Maracaibo—the admiral and 1,400 buccaneers started upriver in seven shallow-draft sloops and 36 riverboats and canoes. But the rainy season had come to an end, the river was consequently low, and at least five times they were forced to portage their heavy craft. Finally, after four days, they gave up and set out on foot through a jungle of towering trees, bamboo thickets, tangling vines and tearing thorns, swamps of rotting, stinking vegetation, biting insects, alligators, and terrifying snakes whose venom could kill within minutes.

Almost every tortured step of the way had to be hacked out with machetes. The men traveled light—arms and ammunition took precedence over even food and water—hoping to seize provisions at Venta de Cruces. But word of their coming had preceded them. They found the village empty and in flames, torched by its own inhabitants. The hungry buccaneers had already marched for seven dreadful days. It was too late for them to turn back. They could only move on into the perpetual gloom of the forest.

At about noon two days later, January 17, Henry Morgan and his men staggered out of the jungle onto a broad savanna. Morgan's advance guard climbed a hill, known forever after as El Cerro de los Bucaneros, and saw for the first time the gleaming blue Pacific, with the sun-varnished city of Panama resting beside the wide bay, a sight for the eyes and spirit to feast upon.

But there below them they saw something else, something even more to their present tastes: at the foot of the hill, hundreds of cattle were grazing placidly in grass as high as their withers. The starving buccaneers fell upon the animals and, recounted Esquemeling, "such was their hunger that they more resembled cannibals than Europeans at this banquet, the blood many times running down from their beards onto the middle of their bodies."

Glutted by beef, the buccaneers continued their march and in early evening came upon the enemy. Arrayed in line on the savanna before them, as if planning to fight a classical battle in the wilds of Central America, were the Spanish forces—600 cavalry and 2,100 foot soldiers—under Panama's Viceroy, Don Pérez de Guzman. The two opposing forces bivouacked for the night, and when Don Pérez awoke the next morning, he discovered that two thirds of his men, terrified by accounts of the brutality of the buccaneers, had fled back to Panama. Pérez realized that now he was no match for Morgan in the flat, open grassland, so he gathered those of his troops that remained and headed for Panama. There he rallied an impromptu army of 1,700 from among the citizens, and waited for Morgan to bring on the buccaneers.

Pérez formed up his forces east of the city, with his artillery in front. Behind the guns, he himself commanded the center; a squadron of cavalry covered his left, while his right was secured—or so he supposed—by a steep hill. His plan was to wait until the buccaneers charged his center, then blast them with his cannon. As the buccaneers reeled from the effects of the barrage, the cavalry would gallop ahead to scatter the enemy. Then Pérez meant to throw into the battle an extraordinary force—"two great herds of oxen and bulls," as Pérez described them, "driven thither by 50 cow keepers on purpose to disorder the enemy." After the cattle had been stampeded into the enemy, Pérez' infantry would move forward to mop up.

But Pérez was completely outgeneraled. Morgan, his own force divided into three with himself commanding the center, quickly spotted the flaw in the Spanish position: he could reach the hill on his left, and from that vantage point storm the Spaniards on their undefended right flank. Moreover, Morgan's detachment might be able to reach the hill unseen, since the sun was glaring into Spanish eyes and a light breeze was wafting smoke from preliminary gunfire across their front, further obscuring their vision. Morgan sent 300 men to capture the hill.

At that point an impetuous Spanish cavalry commander, unable to wait for Don Pérez' plan to unfold, led a wild charge against the buccaneers' center. Morgan's men coolly formed a square and broke the

charge, felling the rash commander in the process. Now Pérez was committed. "Come on, boys!" he cried. "Follow me!" Then, as he later related the experience, "I went directly to the enemy, and hardly did our men see some fall dead and others wounded, but they turned their backs and fled, leaving me there with only one Negro and one servant that followed me." The Spanish had, in fact, been taken in flank by Morgan's detachment, which, having seized the hill, had swooped down into the battle at precisely the right moment.

Pérez somehow escaped the English and, desperately trying to recoup, signaled his cow keepers to unleash the cattle. But like everything else for the Spaniards that day, the stampede proved a dismal failure. Esquemeling later described the action: "The greatest part of the wild cattle ran away, being frightened with the noise of the battle. And some few that broke through the English companies did no other harm than to tear the colors in pieces; whereas the buccaneers, shooting them dead, left not one to trouble them thereabouts."

Pérez and the remnants of his army fled into the hills, and by 3 o'clock in the afternoon Morgan and his men had entered Panama. But their sweet triumph soon turned to bitter disaster. A fire started in a home, and soon the city was ablaze, the cedar and superbly worked rosewood houses, the magnificent churches and even the King's stables that housed treasure-bearing mules all fueling a giant conflagration. How the fire started is unknown—but for the buccaneers, who were counting on booty and ransom, it was a calamity.

"There we were," wrote Morgan to Modyford afterward, "forced to

In this imaginative composite of the battle for Panama in 1671, Morgan's outnumbered but doughty buccaneers repulse a spirited charge by Spanish cavalrymen (right foreground), and drive off rampaging steers and oxen (center) stampeded into the English ranks by Spanish drovers. The city of Panama, shown in flames, actually did not catch fire until after Morgan's victory.

The new city of Panama, shown here on a delicately tinted Spanish map of the period, was five miles southwest of the original gold and silver entrepót, which burned when raided by Morgan and his buccaneers in 1671. Planned around a large central plaza, the rebuilt city was guarded on three sides by the sea and was well fortified against overland attacks across the Isthmus of Panama.

put the fire out of the Enemies houses; but it was in vain, for by 12 at night it was all consumed—that famous and ancient City of Panama, which is the greatest mart for silver and gold in the whole world."

Much of Panama's wealth had been hurriedly carried away by ship when the Spaniards first learned of Morgan's impending attack. More treasure was lost in the firing of the city. But during the 20 days that the buccaneers picked through Panama's smoking ruins, they collected a tidy enough sum—valuables worth some 400,000 pieces of eight, or about £100,000. Still, by the time the spoils were divided according to the articles signed at the beginning of the expedition—£10,000 to the King's brother, the Duke of York, who was also Lord High Admiral, £6,666 to the King, and £1,000 to Morgan—only about £50 apiece filtered down to the rank and file.

There was, inevitably, loud grumbling. Esquemeling years later wrote that the buccaneers thought Morgan had withheld much of the loot from them. But there is no evidence of it, and it is unlikely on the face of it. The cardinal buccaneer rule was fair division of the spoils, and Morgan was a buccaneer to the core.

Yet now Morgan's glory days on the Spanish Main were drawing to a close. Upon his return to Jamaica he found that the political winds had once again shifted. The Duke of Albemarle was dead; Modyford and Morgan no longer had a great friend at court. Worse yet, at least from Morgan's viewpoint, England and Spain had signed the Treaty of Madrid on July 18, 1670, prohibiting either party from pillaging and privateering in the Indies. Since the treaty for the first time officially recognized English holdings in the Caribbean, it was a diplomatic triumph for Charles II—but it would put a crimp in Morgan's style.

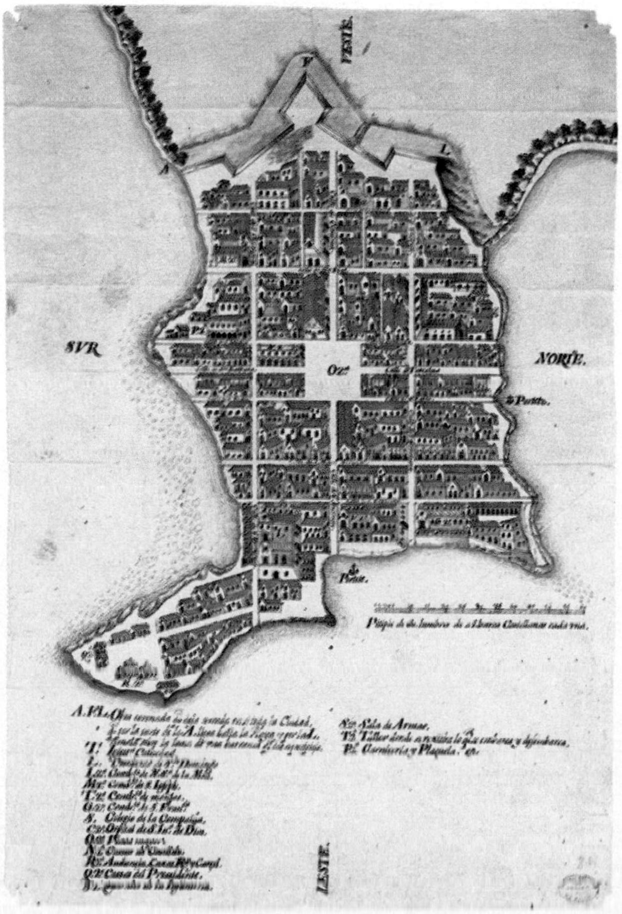

News of the treaty did not reach the Caribbean until May 1671, long after Morgan had embarked on his Panama raid. But now the Spanish Ambassador in London was outraged and called the raid a flagrant violation of the peace. He demanded that both Modyford and Morgan be punished and he threatened to overturn the treaty if they were not.

The King buckled. Modyford was deposed as Governor and, on August 15, 1671, he was placed under arrest on the frigate *Assistance*. He was taken to England and clapped into the Tower of London, where he remained for two years. Morgan, too, was returned to England, but not until April 4, 1672, when he was taken as "his Majesty's prisoner" on board the ironically named *Welcome* for a 12-week voyage home. Though technically under arrest, he was not confined on the ship or when he reached England. The reason is unclear, but it was probably that Henry Morgan was a popular hero, the talk of London coffeehouses, the toast of the taverns, the man who had singed the beards of the dons.

Within a year the King's advisers had taken to consulting Morgan about the West Indies, and the force of Morgan's personality had evidently not diminished an iota. Even Charles II was impressed; in August 1673, when Morgan submitted a memorandum to him outlining Jamaica's military weaknesses, the King decided that he wanted Morgan back in the Caribbean. In an astounding reversal of fortune, Morgan was designated Lieutenant Governor of Jamaica on January 23, 1674. And soon thereafter he knelt before his monarch, received the touch of a blade upon his shoulders and arose as Sir Henry Morgan, Knight.

He returned to Jamaica almost exactly three years after he had left it, and by every right his twilight years on the island should have been golden ones. He had a title. He was rich (he was granted a royal patent for another 4,000 acres, giving him a total of 6,000 and making him one of the island's wealthiest planters). But the sedentary life did not become Harry Morgan.

He spent his days and nights roistering from tavern to tavern, boasting loudly of his past exploits, denouncing old enemies and making new ones, being carried home in a stupor. On May 14, 1682, he was relieved as Lieutenant Governor. In 1683 he was ousted from membership in Jamaica's governing council for his "passions and irregularities."

His doctors told him to cut down on his drinking; instead, he increased it. "His belly swelled," wrote one physician, "so as not to be contained in his coat." His legs became bloated, too, and he was hardly able to move from the hammock in which he rested by day on the veranda of his mansion in Port Maria, across the island from Port Royal. Toward the end he called upon the services of a Jamaican witch doctor who, according to the disapproving English physician, gave him enemas of urine and "plastered him all over with clay and water."

On Saturday, August 25, 1688, the captains of the English warships *Assistance* and *Drake,* then anchored off Port Royal, were ordered to fire memorial salutes. The captain of the *Assistance* wrote in his log: "This day about eleven hours morn'g, Sir Harry Morgan died." He was 53.

Nearly four years later, the morning of Tuesday, June 7, 1692, was oppressively still and sultry. Some of Port Royal's citizens later remarked that the ceaseless waves were no longer breaking against the old Cagway. By noon the Reverend Dr. Emmanuel Heath, rector of St. Peter's Church—a building Henry Morgan had largely financed—having already read prayers "to keep some show of religion among a most ungodly debauched people," had repaired to a nearby tavern to sip a glass of wormwood wine with Jamaica's Acting Governor John White. Suddenly, Heath later wrote, "I found the ground rolling and moving under my feet, upon which I said, 'Lord, sir, what is this?' White replied very composedly, being a very grave man: 'It is an earthquake, be not afraid, it will soon be over.' "

The Acting Governor was a poor prophet. As the tremors increased, Heath ran toward Fort Morgan, which had a wide open courtyard surrounded by walls. "I thought there to be securest from falling houses," he said, "but as I made towards it, I saw the earth open up and swallow a multitude of people, and the sea mounting in upon us over the fortifications." Heath survived by making his way to the harbor and boarding a sloop, just as the sea engulfed the wharf and all the shops on it.

Another survivor told of "whole streets sinking under water with men, women and children in them; and those houses which but just now appeared the fairest and loftiest in these parts were in a moment sunk down into the earth, and nothing to be seen of them." And still another witness lived to report the most ghastly sight of all—that of persons

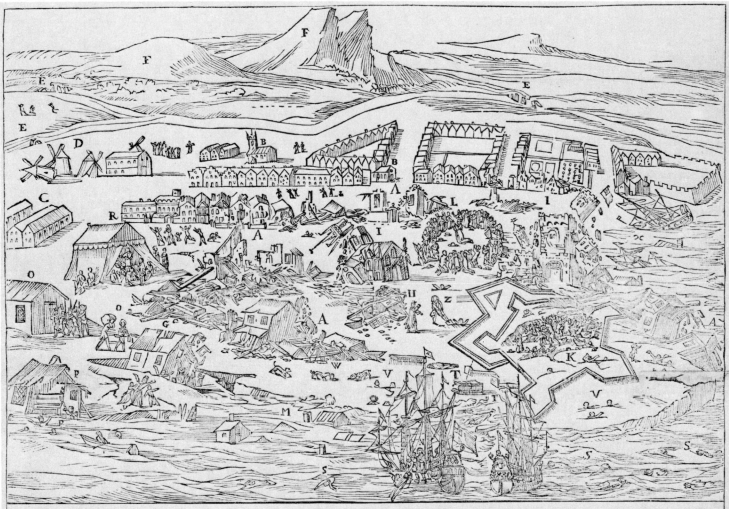

The EXPLANATION.

A. *The Houses Falling.* B. *The Churches.* C. *The Sugar-Works.* D. *The Mills.* E. *The Bridges in the whole Country.* F. *The Rock and Mountains.* G. *Captain Ruden's House sunk first into the Earth, with his Wife, and Family.* H. *The Ground rolling under the Minister's Feet.* I. *The great Church and Tower falling.* K. *The Earth Opening and Swallowing Multitudes of People in Morgan's Fort.* L. *The Minister Kneeling down in a Ring with the People in the Street at Prayers.* M. *The Wharf covered with the Sea.* N. *Dr. Heath going from Ship to Ship to Visit the bruised People, and do his last Office to the dead Corpses that lay Floating from the Point.* O. *Thieves Robbing and Breaking open both Dwelling Houses and Ware-Houses during the Earthquake.* P. *Dr. Trapham, a Doctor of Physick, hanging by the Hands on a Rack of the Chimney, and one of his Children hanging about his Neck seeing his Wife and the rest of his Children a Sinking.* Q. *A Boat coming to save them.* R. *The Minister Preaching in a Tent to the People.* S. *The dead Bodies of some Hundreds floating about the Harbour.* T. *The Sea washing the dead Carkasses out of their Graves and Tombs, and dashed to pieces by the Earthquake.* V. *People swallow'd up in the Earth, several as high as their Necks with their Heads above Ground.* W. *The Dogs eating of Dead Mens Heads.* X. *Several Ships Cast away and driven into the very Town.* Y. *A Woman and her two Daughters beat to pieces one against the other.* Z. *Mr. Beckford his Diging out of the Ground.*

Much of the Jamaican town of Port Royal sinks beneath the waves in this woodcut from a London broadside about the catastrophic earthquake that destroyed the British settlement in 1692. Contemporary accounts said some 2,000 people died—many lost in gaping fissures that cut through the town.

whom "the earth received up to their necks and then closed upon them and squeezed them to death with their heads above ground, many of which the dogs ate."

More than 2,000 people died on that day, and one third of Port Royal crumbled away and sank into the sea. In one fluky and perhaps symbolic incident, a tidal wave raised by the quake carried a ship on its crest into what was left of Port Royal and deposited it safely in a marketplace. The vessel was French, a prize recently taken from the nation with which England was now at war—and whose privateers would dominate the next Caribbean era now that English power had been dealt a devastating, though temporary, setback.

And Harry Morgan's grave, on a plot seized by the sea, now lay five fathoms deep.

Chapter 6

The sacking of Cartagena: a last, bold stroke

French regular army troops allied with a force of buccaneers wheel up heavy artillery for a major attack on the Spanish stronghold of Cartagena in 1697.

n an age and area notably deficient in chivalry, Jean Baptiste du Casse, Governor of Louis XIV's rowdy little enclave of Saint Domingue—the western section of Hispaniola that had been taken by default from the Spanish—was a true cavalier. "He was a tall, thin man," wrote an admiring contemporary, "who was gentle, polite, and respectful, and who was never false to himself. He was very obliging and had a good deal of wit, with a certain natural eloquence; and, even as to matters outside his calling, pleasure and profit were to be had in hearing him expound. He loved the state and good for the sake of good, which has become an extremely rare thing." Remarkably, this paragon of drawing-room virtues was a vastly ambitious fighting man as well. In fact, fighting and conquest were his life's work. Du Casse began his career in the perilous slave trade, and left his lasting mark on the Spanish Main as a leader of buccaneers.

Jean Baptiste du Casse was born in 1646 near Bayonne in southern France. Although he himself never displayed the slightest interest in the Church, reformed or otherwise, his family was Huguenot and du Casse was thus barred from preferment within Catholic France; instead, he found employment with the Compagnie de Sénégal, an enterprise of private shareholders set up to exploit the resources of Africa's west coast—including, especially, human beings. When the Dutch-held island of Goreé, a slaving center off Dakar, fell to a French fleet in 1677, du Casse, then 31, established his company's agents there and set about extending French interests in the area.

In 1680 he sailed from Senegal across the Atlantic to Saint Domingue with a shipload of slaves. There he encountered long-standing planters' complaints about the quality of the chattels furnished them by the Compagnie de Sénégal. Returning to France, he equipped a ship on his own, selected a prize lot of slaves in Africa and journeyed back to Saint Domingue, where he sold his cargo to the planters' satisfaction—and his own considerable profit. He used his earnings to fit out a privateer and, while sailing home to France, captured a large Dutch merchantman. He took care to divide his profits with the crown, which so pleased Louis XIV that the King overcame his religious bias to the extent of appointing du Casse a lieutenant in the French Navy.

For almost a decade, sometimes under official orders, sometimes on his own, but always with at least the tacit approval of his monarch, du Casse continued to enrich the coffers of Louis XIV by capturing English, Dutch and Spanish merchantmen. Then, early in 1691, du Casse learned that Saint Domingue's Governor Tarin de Cussy had been slain during a Spanish raid on the French holding. Du Casse immediately wrote to Count Pontchartrain, the French Minister of Marine, urging that French forces on Saint Domingue be strengthened. "The question of Saint Domingue," he said, "is the most important facing His Majesty outside his kingdom, from the standpoint of the enterprises that can be fashioned there against Spain."

The letter came to the attention of Louis XIV—and how his eyes must have glittered when they saw the word "enterprises," a euphemism carrying the promise of plunder. In the maelstrom of European politics,

Jean-Baptiste du Casse, who began his career as a slave trader and eventually became an admiral in the French Navy, gestures with his right arm, symbolically sheathed in steel in this early-18th Century portrait. The billowing sash at his hip denotes his rank as a flag officer.

Spain, England, Holland and Austria were now leagued against France in a war that was rapidly draining Louis's treasury down to its last livres. The Sun King, as he styled himself, was almost bankrupt—and more eager for prize money than ever. Du Casse was forthwith given a frigate and two smaller ships, and ordered back to duty in the West Indies—as Saint Domingue's new Governor.

Du Casse was under no illusions about the character of the people he had to govern. Saint Domingue, du Casse wrote shortly after his arrival in August 1691, was "composed of the refuse of all the kingdom, men without honor and without virtue." That was not much of an exaggeration. Among the thousands of immigrants who had come to the island during the three previous decades, there were some honest, earnest settlers working to build a viable sugar and tobacco economy. But the place was as rough and lawless as any frontier society, filled largely with cheats, thieves, brawlers and fortune seekers of every description. With every man out for himself, there was little sense of community and even less of service to the general weal. The local militia in the opinion of du Casse was utterly hopeless. "Men bear arms here," he growled, "as if they were at a carnival."

Actually, the only real fighting men in the place were French buccaneers, who were content to tolerate the growing colonial enterprise so long as no one interfered with their pursuits. Previous French administrators, and now du Casse, were happy to grant them status as privileged rogues. In return the buccaneers agreed to serve the colony in time of danger and help beat off the almost constant attempts by Spain to oust the French from Saint Domingue. Once the buccaneers discovered that du Casse was a man to be respected, and that he had aggressive intentions toward both the English and the Spanish, they accepted him—and only him—as their commander.

To du Casse the June 7, 1692, earthquake that leveled Port Royal and sent Henry Morgan's body to the sandy Caribbean bottom appeared a heaven-sent opportunity to bedevil the English. During the ensuing months rarely a week went by without small parties of French buccaneers landing to harass Jamaica's shaken and enfeebled English colonists. The scale of the attacks grew. In December 1693 du Casse sent 170 buccaneers to raid St. David, near Port Royal; they pillaged the place and stole 370 slaves. The next April a 400-man force set out in six small vessels; however, they thought better of the project upon sighting a British warship, and decided, in the words of an observer, that "they would only get broken bones."

Nevertheless, two months later du Casse himself led 1,500 men in 22 ships against Jamaica. He had it in mind to seize the entire island, and began by pillaging and burning in Jamaica's southeastern section around Port Morant and Cow Bay. Sailing west, the French passed the devastated Port Royal and landed on the island's south central coast at Carlisle Bay, where they remained for a month, burning 50 sugar plantations and capturing some 1,300 slaves. But then the English attacked with about 950 men, and du Casse abandoned his plans to annex the island. Gathering up the booty, he and his band of buccaneers sailed back to Saint Domingue.

But hectoring the British, profitable and pleasurable as that pastime may have been, was far from being the summit of du Casse's ambitions: his grandest project was to conquer the rest of Hispaniola, to fling the Spanish from their oldest possession and to rule it himself from the city of Santo Domingo. By the summer of 1696 he was ready to launch this campaign. But then he received a distressing letter from his mentor, Pontchartrain, instructing him to call off his plan and to bide his time until the arrival of a certain Baron de Pointis. The baron would be at the head of a powerful fleet, and du Casse was to place himself at the nobleman's convenience. Du Casse immediately protested by return courier. But his pleas for independent command were met only by another disturbing letter, requiring him to round up all his buccaneers and place them at Pointis's disposal.

Born in 1645, Jean Bernard Louis Desjeans, Baron de Pointis, was egotistical, arrogant, mulish, greedy and, as it turned out, a cheat on the grand scale. But he was also a seaman of high order and a first-rate fighting man. An experienced naval officer, he had served well against the pirates who plagued the Barbary Coast of the Mediterranean.

Like du Casse, Pointis had an ambitious goal: the conquest of Cartagena, the great wintering port for Spanish treasure galleons on the Main. He also had a detailed scheme for this project—one he had evidently stolen from its originator, an unfortunate Huguenot merchant, the Sieur Petit, who had been cast into the Bastille for his anti-Catholic activities. In happier days Petit had dwelt and done business for a while in Cartagena. Seeking release from the Bastille, he produced details of the city's defenses and specific proposals for its capture.

The fate of the Sieur Petit is unknown, but the Baron de Pointis somehow got wind of the project and adopted it as his own. He approached Louis XIV. If the King would lend him the ships and the men, then Pointis would undertake to storm Cartagena and return a handsome profit to the crown. To make the proposition even more attractive, all other expenses would be covered by public subscription, with investors receiving a share of the spoils. Since it would cost him so little, the Sun King was delighted to accept.

The baron fitted out a fleet of nine heavily armed frigates, four lightly armed corvettes and several transport vessels. Some 2,000 sailors and another 2,000 soldiers boarded the vessels and the expedition got under way at Brest on the Atlantic-washed tip of France's Finisterre peninsula. Because France was at war with England, a British blockading squadron under the command of Vice Admiral John Neville had been lying off Brest for some time. Pointis, flying his own admiral's flag from the frigate *Sceptre*, made his break at dawn on January 7, 1697, and succeeded in sailing his fleet past the British with the loss of only one ship. Details of the escape are unclear. But outwitting Neville could scarcely have been difficult, judging from the Englishman's subsequent performance as he slogged across the Atlantic and throughout the Caribbean in unavailing pursuit.

Held back by hard winds and stopping along the way for provisions, Pointis did not anchor at Saint Domingue until the end of February. By then some of the buccaneers whom du Casse had dutifully assembled

Wearing a self-congratulatory smile, the cunning Baron de Pointis, mastermind of the French conquest of Cartagena, is shown in this period engraving before a hilltop view of his troops assaulting that city in 1697. For his feat, King Louis XIV conferred on him a knighthood in the prestigious Order of St. Louis.

had wearied of waiting. They were restless men, and this was a season when Spanish galleons were under sail on the Main. Only 700 buccaneers remained, along with 170 colonists and local militia and a number of blacks, bringing du Casse's force to about 1,000 men. These men Pointis proceeded to alienate by announcing, as he later pridefully recalled, that they would find him "a commander to lead them on, but not as a companion of their fortune." And he added that "they must submit themselves to the same rules as the men on the King's ships." Unless the buccaneers obeyed him, he said, he would burn their ships "even to the poorest boats."

These buccaneers had sliced off men's ears with considerably less provocation, but du Casse somehow managed to mollify them. Moreover, du Casse loyally submitted to Pointis's insulting demand that he, the Governor of Saint Domingue, sail with the expedition not as a co-commander but as the mere captain of a buccaneering ship. There was, however, one point on which du Casse was adamant: the buccaneers must receive their legitimate share of all booty. Since there was roughly one of du Casse's men for every four of Pointis's regulars, the buccaneers would get one fifth of the spoils to divide among themselves according to their custom. Pointis gave his word.

Jean Baptiste du Casse and Jean Bernard Louis Desjeans, Baron de Pointis, were indeed a most peculiarly matched pair. And yet between them, despite dozens of disagreements and the venomous hatred with which they came to regard each other, they would find both glory and gold in the last and perhaps the greatest exploit of the buccaneers on the Spanish Main.

In late March the French fleet, now boasting seven buccaneer craft, 13 royal warships and six to 10 smaller vessels, departed from Saint Domingue and laid a course almost due south across the Caribbean to the coast of South America. The passage was uneventful, and about two weeks later, on April 13, this powerful armada arrived off Cartagena, renowned as the Queen of the Indies.

It required the merest glance at Cartagena's glowering fortifications for Pointis to see how inadequate the Sieur Petit's crude paper drawings were compared with the reality. The massive defenses before him had been a-building for nearly 150 years, ever since the 1560s. As work progressed in the 1580s, the expenses of construction had become so great that, according to legend, Philip II once sat staring intently westward until a courtier inquired, "What is it that Your Majesty is looking for?" The reply came, "I am looking for the walls of Cartagena. They cost so much, they must be visible from here."

The fortification of Cartagena had gained new urgency after 1586, when Francis Drake proved the defenses still inadequate by capturing the city. Now, a century later, as Pointis and du Casse gazed at the stronghold that held the fabled riches of Potosí and gems from the Colombian highlands, they could begin to see how the Spanish engineers had skillfully imposed Cartagena's man-made defenses on the formidable impediments provided by nature.

Cartagena was on the northwestern coast of the rounded top of South

America, almost 200 miles northeast of the point where the continent is joined to Central America. The city lay at the north end of a deepwater bay, nine miles long and four miles across at its broadest, that was sheltered by arms of land and open to the west (map, pages 156-157). Resting squarely athwart the entrance of this natural harbor was a hilly and densely wooded island named Tierra Bomba. Originally, two narrow channels leading into the harbor—Boca Grande (Big Mouth) to the north and Boca Chica (Little Mouth) to the south—had flanked Tierra Bomba. When Drake conquered Cartagena, he anchored in the bay just inside Boca Grande and there disembarked his troops for the short march along the Caribbean beaches to attack the city. Cartagena would not yield so easily to du Casse and Pointis. In the five score and 11 years since Drake's raid, the city and the bay had been heavily fortified. Boca Grande had been filled in and now served as a causeway linking Tierra Bomba with the walled city.

Thus the only passage into the harbor was Boca Chica. But this opening was so narrow and shallow that Pointis wrote, "There's no sailing through it, but you must warp your ships along by their anchors and cables." That was hyperbole; Spanish vessels, including large treasure

Pinnaces and fishing vessels ply the waters before Cartagena's narrow harbor entrance, blocked by a stout chain and guarded by a turreted fortress in this 1690 engraving. Cartagena's defenses were famous, but Baron de Pointis, planning an attack in 1697, found them "even greater than they were reputed to be."

fleets, routinely passed in and out under sail. But Boca Chica was indisputably narrow and the channel treacherous for strange vessels without benefit of local pilots. And its traverse had been rendered suicidal for an enemy by the construction of a Spanish stronghold, Fort San Luis, on the southern side of Tierra Bomba, with 33 guns commanding the passage. Before Pointis and du Casse could hope to reach Boca Chica with their fleet, they would have to capture Fort San Luis. There were four more forts on the inner shores of the bay, and the walls of Cartagena itself were massive and studded with heavy cannon.

Pointis was in a hurry, having it in mind that England's Admiral Neville would soon catch up with him. (In fact, the hapless English pursuer was now dawdling around Barbados, awaiting intelligence of Pointis's whereabouts.) Studying the formidable defenses, Pointis at first decided not to force the harbor entrance but to go ashore outside the bay and attack Cartagena from the beaches, deploying du Casse's buccaneers in the van as shock troops. But the sea's bottom shelved so gradually as to make it impossible for ships to approach within cannon range of the city from the ocean side; moreover, a giant surf built in the wide shallows, making it dangerous and exceedingly difficult to land even small boats. When Pointis and du Casse attempted to reconnoiter the beaches, their boat swamped in the surf and nearly capsized; only by furious bailing and great good fortune were they able to get it out through the breakers again and escape. Obviously this was not the way. Even the pigheaded Pointis was forced to conclude, as he later wrote, that "the sea upon all this coast, and in all seasons, is a natural invincible rampart; Cartagena is approachable only by the harbor."

Noon of April 15 found Pointis anchored in deep water off Boca Chica, ready to launch his strike. Again du Casse and his buccaneers were assigned to lead a landing party, although this time they were preceded by 80 black slaves, who would spring any trap the Spanish might have laid. The landing force was to seize Fort San Luis (which the French called Fort Boucachique because of its position on Boca Chica). Du Casse and the blacks, paddling light, shallow-draft boats, slipped through Boca Chica, hugging the far shore and drawing no fire from the fort, and then landed in several places protected from the surf. Woods lay close to the shore, affording the Spaniards perfect cover for an ambush. But the way was clear, and soon du Casse raised a white flag as a signal for Pointis to send the French soldiers ashore in shallops. Then, while the blacks with machetes slashed a half-mile trail toward the rear of the fort, the fleet diverted the Spanish garrison with a bombardment.

Surprisingly, considering the imposing look of the fort, the bombardment drew only desultory return fire. One reason was that the fort's guns were mounted on flimsy cedar carriages that kept breaking down. "Only our yards and rigging suffered a little," Pointis later noted, "and three men were killed or wounded."

Pointis joined du Casse ashore and prowled the perimeter of Fort San Luis. Next day, entrenching equipment and some light artillery were landed, and in the afternoon a Spanish vessel, sailing from Portobelo and unaware of the dark events that were transpiring, arrived at Boca Chica and was captured. From a Franciscan monk on board came disappointing news: the Spanish treasure galleons, which Pointis had hoped to find at Cartagena, were still at Portobelo. Du Casse, who was familiar with the Spanish schedules, had predicted as much and had been scoffed at by Pointis for his pains.

Nevertheless, the attack was to proceed. It was decided to use the Franciscan monk as a go-between to demand the surrender of the fort. To properly awe the friar for this mission, Pointis employed a ruse reminiscent of that used by Henry Morgan when he pretended to be sending men ashore at Maracaibo: Pointis paraded most of his 5,000 troops and buccaneers in a circle through the woods so that the naïve Franciscan was counting the same men a second and third time. "If the matter had depended on him only," wrote Pointis of the friar, "the fort would have surrendered at that very instant."

As it was, the attackers did vastly outnumber the defenders, and to a far greater degree than anyone on the French side might have imagined. In a sense, the very strength of Cartagena's outer works spelled the city's doom; so confident were the Spanish that the mere sight of the fortifications would discourage any invader that they neglected to provide the bastions with sufficient troops to man them effectively. Fort San Luis, for example, had a garrison of only 150.

Despite the friar's tale of the disparity in numbers, the fort's commander kept up a heavy, effective fire. As he was momentarily expecting a reinforcement of 300 men, he declined to surrender. But when the reinforcements arrived, in two large boats from Cartagena, they met fierce resistance from the French troops and were finally put to flight by a wild machete charge from du Casse and his buccaneers. At that the fort's flag was lowered. "In a moment of time," wrote Pointis, "the gate was opened, and old Sancho Jimeno, who had been Governor for above 25 years, came and delivered the keys into my possession." The cost to the French had been only 50 men killed—but among the wounded was du Casse, who had been struck in the thigh by a fragment of rock when a cannon ball narrowly missed him.

Pointis now held the key to Cartagena, but the door was a long way from open. He knew that the citizens of Cartagena would flee into the interior with their valuables at the first sign of attack. Pointis meant to cut them off by sending a force inland to approach Cartagena from the rear while he and his main force attacked from the harbor side. The inland expedition was a dirty job, and Pointis naturally assigned it to du Casse's buccaneers, although du Casse himself was down with his wound and unable to lead. The buccaneers were accustomed to working in the bush, "where each of them," wrote Pointis, "carries his own provisions, and lives upon what he kills."

From Cartagena a single road led into the interior, twisting through a swamp. Any force heading along that road toward Cartagena, as the buccaneers must now do, would first be brought up short by a steep-sided pinnacle of volcanic rock where, as on a pedestal, stood the convent of Nuestra Señora de la Popa, the patron saint of Cartagena.

Heavily fortified, La Popa was an awesome obstacle. And as if that were not enough, the buccaneers would have to rely for fresh water on what little they could carry with them. Over the decades Cartagena's authorities had repeatedly vetoed suggestions that an aqueduct be built to carry water from the interior; under siege conditions such a structure could not be defended and would only help an enemy. Cartagena's own water supply came from the clouds: there was hardly a flat surface above ground level that was not connected by pipe to one of the thousands of cisterns in the city. If the water therefrom was sometimes a little putrid, it was far healthier than that from puddles and brackish bogs outside the walls.

The buccaneers were reluctant to enter the small boats that would take them from Tierra Bomba to the mainland and the march on La Popa. With du Casse incapacitated by his wound, Pointis had appointed a leader from his French officers who, according to Pointis himself, had not "acquired either the esteem or love of anybody." The buccaneers, Pointis continued, "could not be persuaded that he had any right to command them." Pointis later claimed that he lashed the men aboard with his tongue, threatening to burn their ships and abandon them if they did not obey; far more likely, the well-respected du Casse, incapacitated though he was, talked his ruffians into doing as they were directed. After all the arguments, La Popa itself was anticlimactic: the Spanish had deserted the place, although not until after a train of 110 mules, fleeing from Cartagena laden with gold and gems, had passed through.

The bloodless fall of La Popa pinpointed the fatal flaw in Cartagena's defenses. For all their technical genius, Spanish engineers could not account for human nature, and the myriad fears by which it is afflicted. Each of the forts leading to the gates of Cartagena was built to withstand protracted sieges. But each was separate—and alone. Cut off from and unable to communicate with the other forts or with the main Spanish force inside the city, the defenders were victims of their own imaginations. And so they ran. It happened at Boca Chica and La Popa, and it would happen again.

With La Popa their own, the buccaneers moved to the next fort in line, San Lázaro, constructed on the only solid ground within cannon shot of Cartagena. There they were joined by Pointis and his French regulars, who had been having a more frustrating time of it than du Casse's men.

The bellicose baron had meant to pass through Boca Chica once the fort was secured and sail right up the bay to bombard Cartagena. But that was easier said than done. The city lay on the northern shore of a lagoon that served as an inner harbor. The narrow entryway was guarded by opposing sandspits, reaching toward each other like closing tongs, on which the Spanish had constructed defenses. On the eastern tongue stood little more than manned bulwarks, but on the western side of the lagoon entrance stood the imposing Fort Santa Cruz. This fort would have to be taken before Pointis's ships could make their way into the lagoon. Thus Pointis decided to march 1,700 men across the causeway that had been formed between Tierra Bomba and the mainland. He would then be in position to take one of the sandspit bastions, Fort Santa Cruz, from the rear, after which he could move his fleet into the inner harbor and lay siege to the city itself.

While the fleet moved up the bay toward Fort Santa Cruz, the land force approached the bastion cautiously—and with good reason, since du Casse later estimated that a mere 300 Spanish could have held the position for days and perhaps weeks. But again, to Pointis's perfect astonishment and vast relief, the Spanish were gone.

Putting a skeleton force in Santa Cruz so that it could not be retaken by the Spaniards, Pointis did not immediately return for his fleet, which was now waiting in the bay just off the fort. Instead, he quickly marched his force of 1,700 men toward the city. The townspeople were congregated on the walls, from which, he wrote, they "quietly looked on us." Among them was the Governor, Don Diego de los Rios y Quesada, who, wrote Pointis, "answered my drum that he was ready to defend himself better than we could attack him."

Pointis soon learned that the Governor was right: the area where Pointis had drawn up his army was all sand or marshland, too unstable to mount cannon. Frustrated again, Pointis ordered his men reembarked in the ships to cross the lagoon and join the buccaneers where they lay hidden in the woods outside Fort San Lázaro. The fort would have to be captured and Cartagena taken from the rear.

San Lázaro, occupying a commanding position atop a steep hill, was enough to give pause to even the most reckless attacker. The crenelated walls were so devised as to provide an interlocking pattern of cannon fire, and the masonry of the entire edifice was massive.

But the French soon discovered that the eminence on which the fort stood was so densely covered with thicket that they could creep unseen to the very foot of the walls. Hacking a tunnel-like path through the brush, they prepared to mine the walls with gunpowder and blast their way in. Small-arms fire broke out, but to bring their pieces to bear, the defenders had to lean over the walls, and the French snipers picked them off. At the same time, Pointis called in a stentorian voice—which he made sure the Spanish could hear—for scaling ladders to be brought up.

As at San Luis, La Popa and Santa Cruz, Spanish nerves began to fray, and in the loneliness of their isolated fort the defenders sought a strangely pathetic comfort. The French heard a solitary bell begin to toll. "At first," wrote Pointis, "it struck only now and then, keeping sounding more and more by degrees, until at length it rang full out, when their fear gave them occasion to think they would be attacked on all sides." Suddenly the gates of the fort flew open and the Spaniards came pouring out, racing pell-mell down the road to Cartagena. Pointis let them go. San Lázaro was his.

Now, at last, the French commander brought up his ships to begin a bombardment of Cartagena's immediate environs. On the morning of April 21 a steady fire was commenced against the massive limestone walls of Getsemaní, a fortified island suburb over which a road led across two bridges to Cartagena's main entryway, the Gate of the Half Moon. Cartagena also came under fire, but the defenders fought back furiously. Pointis reported that one French ship was forced to withdraw after it was "shot through with several balls and ready to sink." Pointis's chief engineer was badly wounded, and the admiral himself was hit in the abdomen with a piece of grapeshot. To Pointis, the wound was "more painful than dangerous," but he was immobilized and thereafter directed the

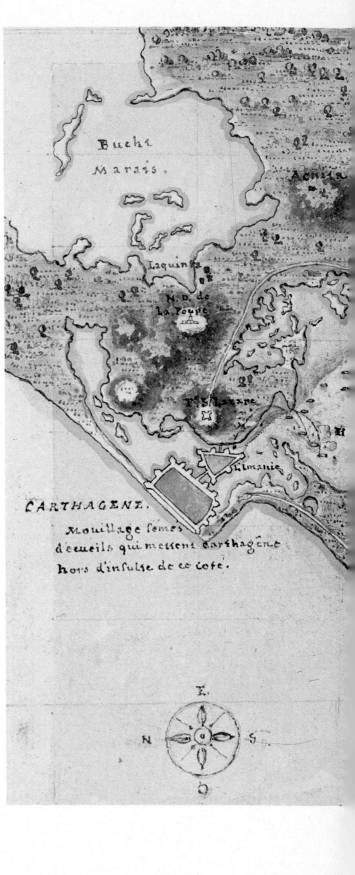

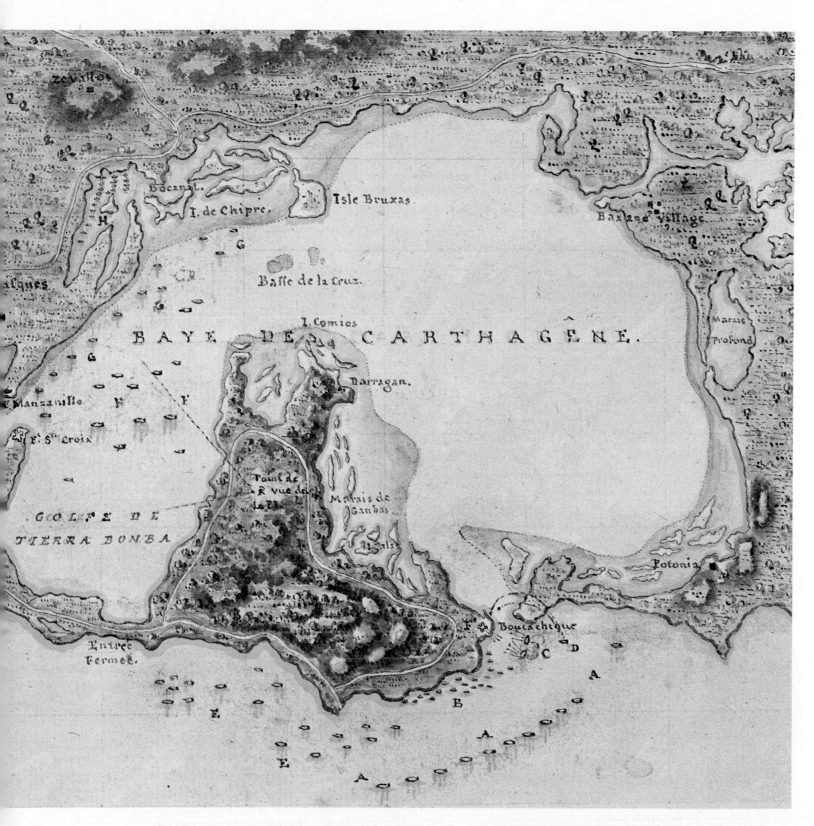

This contemporary map illustrates the tactics used in the French attack on Cartagena. The buccaneers' vessels (E) and Admiral Pointis's fleet (A) first massed outside the bay's entrance. While some ships (C, D) were detached to bombard Fort San Luis (identified here on the French map as Boucachique), troops went ashore (B) and captured it from the rear. The ships then sailed in and the soldiers marched to Fort Santa Cruz (St. Croix), where they met their fleet (F) and took the bastion. Meanwhile 650 buccaneers landed at two places (H) and joined Pointis to attack Fort San Lázaro (St. Lazaro) and the city.

attack while being carried from place to place on a makeshift stretcher.

The most powerful weapons Pointis had brought from France were six great artillery mortars able to fire 24- and 36-pound balls. Pointis named them the Royal Battery in honor of his sponsor, Louis XIV. Merely manhandling these monsters ashore and setting them in place consumed the better part of a week. Meanwhile the bombardment with lesser cannon went on. Unrelenting in his contempt for du Casse and his buccaneers, Pointis could be generous in praise of his own officers. When the siege guns were finally in place and had commenced their terrible work, Pointis wrote, "Gombaud played the mortars, which he had been exercised in from his youth. One would have thought the bombs had been placed by hand."

On the evening of April 29, after only a day of thundering bombardment by the mortars, the first breach appeared in the walls of Getsemaní. Du Casse, who had recovered from his wound sufficiently to return to battle, reported to Pointis that he thought the position could be taken quickly and easily if the French moved before the Spaniards had time to redeploy their troops and plug the breach. With the French regulars giving fire in support, du Casse led the buccaneers in a howling, headlong charge that swept through the breach and carried the day. Scores of Spaniards were slain. Pointis later admitted that du Casse had been the first man over the rubble of the broken wall, but the spiteful admiral could not refrain from adding: "Not so nimble as the rest, despite all his good will, du Casse had so much trouble to climb it that he was out of breath by the time he got to the top, where he thought he should never recover his wind." Pointis neglected to mention that du Casse had suffered two more flesh wounds during the savage attack.

With Getsemaní overrun, only the walls of Cartagena stood between Pointis and fulfillment of his audacious dream, and he later wrote that he felt himself for the first time "rid of all uneasiness for the success of the action, which may, with modesty, be termed very bold, and very extraordinary for seafaring men."

Cartagena's Governor, having seen what the great guns of the Royal Battery could do, sent word that he would surrender under certain conditions. The terms required that the Spanish would not be ill treated in any way; the churches were not to be despoiled; the citizenry might keep their personal possessions. These conditions were far more generous than those customarily granted, and the Baron de Pointis was by no means a charitable man. But he had information that 2,000 Spanish reinforcements were marching from the hinterland (in fact, they had turned back upon hearing of Getsemaní's fall), and there was always the specter of the British Admiral Neville and his squadrons lurking somewhere beyond the horizon.

Pointis granted the terms. On May 6, 1697, Don Diego de los Rios y Quesada rode out through the Gate of the Half Moon in full-dress uniform, leading the Spanish garrison and the townspeople for the formal surrender. All told, almost 3,000 Spaniards were in the melancholy procession. Pointis, still in pain from his wound, was also on horseback to receive them. He later recalled, "We two, the Governor and I, were upon our horses and, having saluted me with his sword and some ex-

Struck by decree of Louis XIV, this gold medal commemorates the victory of the French at Cartagena. One side of the medal bears the likeness of "Louis, Most Christian King," and the reverse depicts a ravaged maiden, symbol of the fallen city. The legend, "Part of the Plundered Treasures of the Spanish," indicates that the gold used to cast these medals came from Cartagena.

pressions of civility, he continued his way and the garrison all marched out before sunset."

But as soon as the ceremonies were done, Pointis repaired once more to his couch and issued orders for the treasure to be collected with all possible speed, so anxious was he to get clear of Cartagena. Well aware that much of the wealth of the city had been hidden, and believing that he had little time for a thorough search, he decreed that $1/10$ of all declared wealth could be kept by the owner—or by anyone giving information on hidden sums. Knowing their fellow citizens to be more greedy than honorable, and fearing that they might lose everything unless they cooperated, the Cartagenans brought their riches to Pointis in wagonloads, and the baron gloated: "Tilleul, who was charged with the treasure, was not able to weigh the silver fast enough."

By Pointis's questionable reckoning, the total take came to some eight million livres (du Casse estimated closer to 20 million), and as quickly as it was collected and weighed it was stowed aboard the French warships. By now the rainy season had arrived, and with it mosquitoes, yellow fever and other plagues. In just six days 800 Frenchmen, nearly one fifth of the original force, were infected and most died. Few of the stricken were buccaneers. Those men, "being accustomed to these climates, were no more infected with the unhealthiness of the air than the natives that are rarely touched with it," noted Pointis. He chided his second-in-command to hurry along the collection and loading of treasure.

When the fleet was at last ready to sail, the buccaneers, who had so far seen not so much as a livre to call their own, demanded not simply a fifth but a one-fourth share of the loot, then and there. Presumably, they had taken a head count and upped their demand because of all the French dead. The seemingly aghast Pointis replied from his sickbed that the buccaneers had never been promised even one fifth of the whole treasure. They had agreed to share man for man with the French regulars— and the regulars were being paid on the basis of $1/10$ of the first million and $1/30$ of the subsequent millions. The buccaneers could have a fourth of that. The rest went to pay back the investors and to the King.

By that accounting, the buccaneers would divide some 40,000 livres instead of the 1.6 million to four million (depending on whose word for the total was accepted) that they deemed their due. Pointis was especially indignant at du Casse for insisting that he honor the financial pledge he had made at the outset of the Cartagena expedition. "I must acknowledge," the admiral wrote, "I was a long time before I could comprehend that his misapprehension should carry him so far as to imagine that the credit of so many people was used, much address employed, great sums of money collected and expended, and so long a voyage undertaken to give a fourth of what it produced to the Governor of Saint Domingue and a troop of *banditti*, the greatest part of them idle spectators of a great action."

With those sentiments, on May 31 Pointis sailed out of the bay. He retained only 10 ships to transport the treasure and his battered and much-reduced expeditionary force. He burned his remaining vessels, which only further infuriated the already enraged buccaneers, some of whom wished to give chase and attack the flagship. For the final time du

Casse restrained them, promising to "go and present your claims to the King." Intent on keeping his word, he too departed for Saint Domingue, from which he planned to take passage for France. Close behind him sailed the buccaneer squadron.

But there were those among the cheated buccaneers who held that a sure thing was better than a promise. After going only a few leagues, four captains brought their ships about and headed back to the prostrate city. This time there were no terms given and, with unrestrained rape, torture and the sacking of churches and homes, the buccaneers made clear their intent not to leave before the sum of five million livres was paid them. It says something of Pointis's haste in departing that he had left behind more than enough to meet the brigands' demands. And for the last time in the history of the Caribbean, a significant force of buccaneers set sail with booty-laden ships.

Meanwhile Pointis, who had regained his health at sea, decided to make directly for the channel between Cuba and the Bahamas. He thought thereby to give the slip to the English, who he imagined, since they had not caught up with him at Cartagena, would be awaiting him off Saint Domingue. In fact Neville, with a combined English and Dutch fleet, was sailing south to intercept him, and in the darkness of the night of June 6-7 the two fleets interwove just south of Jamaica like the strands in a long splice. At daybreak the French counted 29 enemy sail around them. The odds against the French were nearly 3 to 1, and eight of the largest English ships, each the equal or the better of Pointis's flagship, the *Sceptre*, were in a body and had the weather gauge of the French.

"Dismal misfortune," as Pointis put it, replaced the luck that had so far graced his enterprise. "What an alteration for me in particular!" Pointis reflected. "The taking of Cartagena seemed to have acquired me a pleasing distinction; and being enriched, I had, at my return, a prospect of glory and pleasures, all that now passed like a shadow; and I had before my eyes the destruction of a flourishing squadron, which I had the honor to be entrusted with." He was stricken by "despair in the remainder of my life, which after a long imprisonment, I must have passed in obscurity."

What he did not know was that the English ships were woefully undermanned. Neville hesitated to attack for an entire day as he sought to marshal his whole force and descend on the French in a mass. The delay was costly, for during the night Pointis neatly reversed course. By the next dawn he had put considerable distance between their fleets. Crowding on sail in an attempt to catch up, a number of the English ships lost their rigging. In the end the French simply outsailed them.

Riding the Gulf Stream north, Pointis reached Newfoundland, where he put in to Conception Bay for water and provisions. There he learned of a squadron of eight English men-of-war in the port of St. John's, less than 25 miles down the coast. Seizing the initiative, Pointis headed south and found the enemy still in port. He later explained: "Apparently some reflection of the force and largeness of our ships had prevented them from coming out. I was contented to show myself and offer them battle, which seeing they did not answer, we steered for the coast of France." Toward the end of August the French sighted yet a third Eng-

At the head of his ragtag crew, a buccaneer leader demands hidden treasure from a kneeling captive in this re-creation by Howard Pyle of the 1697 sack of Cartagena. The buccaneers, who had helped the French pillage the place a few days before, were returning for a second looting visit because they felt the French had cheated them out of their share the first time around. This time they threatened to blow the leading citizens to smithereens if enough booty were not produced.

lish fleet, this one near the Scilly Isles just off the tip of England. Pointis fought a running battle through the course of a long afternoon, and when night came he was able to sail away. There remained only the British blockade of French ports to run. To Admiral Pointis, that posed no more of a problem than his original escape. On the dark night of August 28, his fleet slipped unseen through the loose net of patrolling British into the haven of Brest. Pointis had been gone just one week less than eight months, and he carried a fortune in his holds.

In September 1697 France signed the Treaty of Ryswick, making peace with Spain, England and Holland. Under the terms of the pact, Spain formally recognized French possession of Saint Domingue; no mention was made of the French colonies on Martinique, Guadeloupe and Saint Kitts, which in French eyes amounted to tacit recognition. Nor was any mention made of the Dutch or English colonies, which in the eyes of those nations solidified their claims. In return, all three pledged to help the Spaniards suppress buccaneers in the Caribbean and the Gulf of Mexico. Henceforth buccaneers who sailed the Caribbean in their small ships to prey on other seafaring men would do so without commission as privateers, outlawed as common pirates by all nations and facing an almost certain fate on the gibbet if they were caught.

Jean Bernard Louis Desjeans, Baron de Pointis, lived in France until his death in 1707. He was wealthy and he was much admired for his great deed, but he was unbeloved—as if he cared a fig.

Jean-Baptiste du Casse also returned to France, where he was made a knight of the Order of St. Louis, was promoted to admiral and was assured by Minister of Marine Pontchartrain that "His Majesty is as satisfied with your conduct as you could possibly desire." As he promised, du Casse fought for and finally won a settlement of 1.4 million francs, to be distributed among the buccaneers Pointis had bilked. But, in the end, the buccaneers would have virtually nothing to show for their adventures. They had lost nearly everything they had looted from prostrate Cartagena. On their way back to their stronghold on the island of Hispaniola, they had run afoul of Neville's squadron and lost four ships—two of which carried the bulk of their plunder. And most of the money won for them by du Casse simply and quietly disappeared for expenses and in graft on the way to the West Indies.

Toward the end of his life, du Casse might have reflected on the curious tricks politics and fate play on men. In 1708, with Spain and France now allied, Admiral du Casse was detached for service with the Spanish fleet, his old enemy. His assignment, fantastic as it may seem, was to convoy the Spanish treasure fleet from Veracruz to Seville, and to draw on his vast experience to protect it from the pirates then swarming in the Caribbean. That first year he lost only two vessels to the brigands, and the next year he got the entire convoy through without a scratch.

For his remarkable feat du Casse was awarded one of the highest honors within the power of the King of Spain to give—the Order of the Golden Fleece. No act could better have signified the passing of the day of the buccaneers on the Spanish Main. Du Casse died in 1714 at the age of 69, the last of the great buccaneering leaders.

An ornately illustrated engraving from a French almanac commemorates the 1697 signing of the Treaty of Ryswick by France, Spain, Holland and Britain, which brought at least a temporary peace to the Spanish Main. Under an inscription declaring an end to the war, the French diplomatic entourage deliberates; around them are scenes of victorious engagements in Belgium (top), at Cartagena (left) and in Spain (bottom).

A new era of naval warfare on the embattled Main

Although the dawn of the 18th Century on the Spanish Main saw an end to the wild individualism of the privateers and buccaneers, it brought no peace for the Spaniards in their beleaguered colonial cities and on board their threatened treasure galleons. Spain remained rich; her enemies remained envious. And now that the Dutch, the French and the English had all established their own island colonies in the Caribbean, they could—and did—use them as bases from which to mount full-scale assaults with large, well-organized war fleets, flying their national emblems and commanded by ranking captains and admirals.

It was the English who struck hardest at Spain's increasingly feeble defenses in the New World. In a succession of European wars, Britain always seemed to find herself on the side opposite that of Spain. And Britannia never failed to use the hostilities on the European side of the Atlantic as a golden opportunity to belabor and pauperize Spain on the other side of the ocean.

In 1739, while Britain and Spain were, as usual, at war, Vice Admiral Edward Vernon was sent to Jamaica with a force of nine major men-of-war, including four 70-gun ships of the line. His orders from the British Admiralty were "to destroy the Spanish settlements in the West Indies and distress their shipping by any method whatever."

He mounted attacks on Portobelo and Chagres. These were stunning blows against Spain, and major reinforcements were sent from Britain to enlarge Vernon's successful Caribbean squadron. By 1741 he was in command of no fewer than 30 ships of the line and 90 other vessels manned by 15,000 seamen. Vernon sailed his great fleet first to bombard Cartagena, then Santiago de Cuba. The Spaniards stoutly defended their key cities on the Main, but they were becoming prisoners inside their own fortifications and their treasure fleets sailed in ever-growing peril.

Back home Vernon and his fellow admirals were national heroes. Englishmen, moreover, could vicariously experience the smoke and thunder of the faraway combat in the work of an artist named Samuel Scott, whose meticulous recreations appear here and on the following pages. Better than any words, these paintings dramatized the Royal Navy's disciplined men-of-war, which were putting an end to Spanish dominion in the Caribbean and were, as on other seas, launching the golden age of the British Empire.

An incandescent detonation of her powder magazine destroys the heavily armed Spanish galleon San José off Cartagena before the guns of the British man-of-war Expedition on May 28, 1708. The San José's royal cargo was lost, but the Expedition and three sister ships (right) managed to disperse the more numerous Spaniards (far left) and capture a second galleon laden with silver ingots, millions of pieces of eight, and bundled cacao.

Bombarding the stone-walled Iron Fort guarding the entrance to the vital harbor of Portobelo—the main Caribbean terminus of treasure shipments that came across the Isthmus of Panama—the British force the city to surrender in November 1739. To the surprise of the Spaniards, Admiral Vernon did not pillage and burn the town, but he removed its brass cannon, spiked its iron guns, seized its powder and shot, and then left with the contents of its treasury.

Belching smoke and shot, two British men-of-war (left) take on seven heavily armed Spanish galleons off the north coast of Cuba on October 1, 1748, while five other British warships (far right) tack into the wind to close with the Spaniards. The British were trying to break through to reach a gold- and silver-laden treasure fleet that they thought was assembling at Havana. In the desperate seven-hour battle that ensued, the Spaniards fought off their enemies in spite of the loss of two of their war galleons.

Bibliography

Andrews, Kenneth R., *The Spanish Caribbean*. Yale University Press, 1978.

Arciniegas, Germán, *Caribbean: Sea of the New World* (translated by Harriet de Onis). Knopf, 1946.

Barrientos, Bartolomé, *Pedro Menéndez de Avilés: Founder of Florida* (translated by Anthony Kerrican). University of Florida Press, 1965.

Benson, E. F., *Sir Francis Drake*. Bodley Head, 1927.

Boxer, C. R., *The Dutch Seaborne Empire, 1600-1800*. Hutchinson, 1965.

Burney, James, *History of the Buccaneers of America*. Swan Sonnenschein, 1891.

Cooper-Prichard, A. H., *The Buccaneers*. Cecil Palmer, 1927.

Corbett, Julian S., *Drake and the Tudor Navy*. Longmans, Green, 1899.

Esquemeling, John, *The Buccaneers of America*. Dover, 1967.

Haring, C. H.:
The Buccaneers in the West Indies in the XVII Century. Archon Books, 1966.
The Spanish Empire in America. Harcourt, Brace & World, 1963.

Hart, Frances Russell, *Admirals of the Caribbean*. Houghton Mifflin, 1922.

Herring, Hubert, *A History of Latin America*. Knopf, 1968.

Kemp, P. K., and Christopher Lloyd, *The Brethren of the Coast*. Heinemann, 1960.

Manucym, Albert, *Florida's Menéndez: Captain General of the Ocean Sea*. St. Augustine Historical Society, 1965.

Marx, Robert F., *The Treasure Fleets of the Spanish Main*. World Publishing, 1968.

Newton, Arthur Percival, *The European Nations in the West Indies 1493-1688*. Barnes & Noble, 1967.

Parry, J. H.:
The Age of Reconnaissance. Weidenfeld and Nicolson, 1963.
The Discovery of South America. Paul Elek, 1979.
The Spanish Seaborne Empire. Knopf, 1970.

Parry, J. H., and P. M. Sherlock, *A Short History of the West Indies*. Macmillan, 1966.

Payne, Edward John, ed., *Voyages of the Elizabethan Seamen to America: Select Narratives from the "Principal Navigations" of Hakluyt*. Oxford, 1893.

Peterson, Mendel, *The Funnel of Gold*. Little, Brown, 1975.

Pike, Ruth, *Enterprise and Adventure*. Cornell University Press, 1966.

Pointis, Sieur, *An Authentick and Particular Account of the Taking of Carthagena by the French in the Year 1697*. Olive Payne, 1740.

Pope, Dudley, *Harry Morgan's Way*. Alison Press, 1977.

Roberts, W. Adolphe:
The Caribbean. Bobbs-Merrill, 1940.
The French in the West Indies. Cooper Square Publishers, 1971.

Rumeu de Armas, Antonio, *Los Viajes de John Hawkins a América*. Escuela de Estudios Hispano-Americanos de Sevilla, 1947.

Sir Francis Drake: An Exhibition to Commemorate Francis Drake's Voyage around the World 1577-1580. British Museum Publications, 1977.

Williamson, James A.:
Hawkins of Plymouth. Barnes & Noble, 1969.
Sir John Hawkins: The Time and the Man. Greenwood Press, 1970.

Wilson, Derek, *The World Encompassed*. Harper & Row, 1977.

Wright, I. A., *Spanish Documents concerning English Voyages to the Caribbean, 1527-1568*. Hakluyt Society, 1928.

Wright, Louis B., *Gold, Glory and the Gospel: The Adventurous Lives and Times of the Renaissance Explorers*. Atheneum, 1970.

Acknowledgments

The index for this book was prepared by Gale Partoyan. The editors wish to thank the following: Richard Knight, consultant; Philip Bosscher, consultant (pages 96-101); John Batchelor, artist, and William A. Baker, consultant (pages 32-35); Peter McGinn, artist (end-paper maps); and Richard Schlecht, artist, and William A. Baker, consultant (pages 42-51).

The editors also wish to thank: In the Netherlands: Amsterdam—Rijksmuseum; Rijksmuseum Nederlands Scheepvaart Museum; The Hague—Algemeen Rijksarchief; Martin de Vries, Photographer; Rotterdam—Atlas van Stolk. In Switzerland: Lausanne—Jacques Berger, Curator, Musée Cantonal des Beaux-Arts. In Colombia: Cartagena—Alejandro Obregón, Calle de la Factoria; Josefina Delvalle Jimeno, Director, Seccional Cartagena, Corporación Nacional de Turismo-Colombia; Denis Nahum, Club de Pesca; Eduardo Lemaitre, Palacio de la Inquisición. In Germany: Babenhausen—Markus Graf Fugger; München—Baron Hubert Freiherr von Welser. In the United Kingdom: London—P. Higgins, D. H. Turner, Sarah Tyacke, the British Library; R. Williams and P. Moore, the British Museum; Wendy Baron, Department of the Environment; J. W. Picton, Museum of Mankind; Annie Hood, Joan Moore, Pauline Stocks, National Maritime Museum; Plymouth—Commodore J. H. Carlill, H.M.S. Drake; M. V. Attrill and James Barber, Plymouth City Museum and Art Gallery. In Spain: Madrid—Don Manuel Carrión Gutiez, Subdirector, Biblioteca Nacional; Don Fermín Muñoz, Secretary to the Duchess of Alba, Liria Palace; José María Zumacalarregui, Director, Museo Naval; Seville—Doña Rosario Parra, Director, and Doña María del Carmen Galbe, Secretary, Archivo General de Indias. In Mexico: Veracruz—S. Romero. In France: Dieppe—Henri Cahingt, President, and Claude Féron, Association des Amis du Vieux Dieppe; Paris—Henri Marchal, Curator, Musée des Arts Africains et Océaniens; Hervé Cras, Director for Historical Studies, and Denise Chaussegroux, Researcher, Musée de la Marine. In Haiti: Cap Haitien—Walter Bussenius and Robert Morgan; Limbé—Dr. William Hodges, Hôpital Bon Samaritain.

The editors also wish to thank: In the United States: Washington, D.C.—Anacostia Neighborhood Museum; The Moorland Springarn Research Center, Howard University; Joseph Young, Museum of History and Technology, Smithsonian Institution; New Haven, Connecticut—Department of Afro-American Studies, Yale University; St. Joseph, Louisiana—the Reverend Edwin C. Webster; Baltimore, Maryland—Dr. Richard Price, Department of Anthropology, The Johns Hopkins University; Minneapolis, Minnesota—Dr. Stewart Schwartz, Chairman, Department of History, University of Minnesota; New York, New York—Martha M. de Narváez and Lydia Dufour, Hispanic Society of America; Elizabeth Roth, Prints Division, and Sheila Curl, Rare Book Division, New York Public Library; Newport, Rhode Island—Library of the Naval War College; Providence, Rhode Island—Thomas R. Adams, Director, Susan Danforth, C. Daniel Elliott, Laurence Hardy, Samuel Hough, Susan James, John Carter Brown Library, Brown University; Arlington, Virginia—Daniel Koski-Karel.

A particularly valuable source of quotations was *Harry Morgan's Way* by Dudley Pope, Alison Press, London, © 1977 by Dudley Pope. Other important sources of information and quotations were *The Buccaneers of America* by John Esquemeling, Dover, 1967; *Voyages of the Elizabethan Seamen to America*, edited by Edward John Payne, Oxford, 1893; and *An Authentick and Particular Account of the Taking of Carthagena by the French in the Year 1697* by Sieur Pointis, Olive Payne, 1740.

Picture Credits

The sources for the illustrations in this book are shown below. Credits from left to right are separated by semicolons, from top to bottom by dashes.

Cover: Rare Book Division, The New York Public Library, Astor, Lenox and Tilden Foundations. Front and back end papers: Drawing by Peter McGinn.
Page 3: Courtesy Richard Knight, England. 6-15: Derek Bayes, courtesy of the owner, Miss M. L. A. Strickland, and the Department of the Environment, London. 16, 17: By permission of the British Library. Harley MS3450. 18: Réunion des Musées nationaux, Paris. 20: Courtesy American Museum of Natural History. 21: Hispanic Society of America, New York. 22: Photo Bibliothèque nationale, Paris. 24: Library of Congress—William L. Clements Library, University of Michigan. 25: William L. Clements Library, University of Michigan. 28: Museo del Oro, Bogotá—Mike Burgess, © Times Newspapers Ltd., courtesy Museum of Mankind, London; Museo del Oro, Bogotá—Museo del Oro, Bogotá; Foto Rudolf, courtesy Hernan Borrero Collection, Bogotá. 30, 31: Rare Book Division, The New York Public Library, Astor, Lenox and Tilden Foundations. 32-35: Drawings by John Batchelor. 36: Hispanic Society of America, New York. 38: Photo Bibliothèque nationale, Paris. 39: Lauros-Giraudon, courtesy Service Historique de la Marine, Vincennes. 40, 41: Archivo General de Indias, Seville. 42-51: Drawings by Richard Schlecht. 52: Derek Bayes, courtesy National Maritime Museum, London. 54: By permission of the Master and Fellows, Magdalene College, Cambridge. 55: Bodleian Library, Oxford. 56, 57: Rare Book Division, The New York Public Library, Astor, Lenox and Tilden Foundations. 59: Derek Bayes, courtesy Trustees of the Walter Morrison Collection, Sudeley Castle, Gloucester. 60, 61: By permission of the British Library. Cott.Aug.1.i. 62: Library of Congress; Derek Bayes, courtesy the British Museum. No.1898.1.15.22. 63: Rijksmuseum Nederlands Scheepvaart Museum, Amsterdam—Photo Bibliothèque nationale, Paris. 65: By permission of the British Library. 143.a.11. 66, 67: Archivo General de Indias, Seville. 68: Photo Bibliothèque nationale, Paris. 70: Salmer, courtesy Museo del Prado, Madrid. 72, 73: Derek Bayes, courtesy National Maritime Museum, London. 74: National Portrait Gallery, London. 76-81: Rare Book Division, The New York Public Library, Astor, Lenox and Tilden Foundations. 84: National Portrait Gallery, London. 86: By permission of the British Library. C.114.c.21. 88: Library of Congress. 89: Derek Bayes, courtesy City Art Gallery and Museum, Plymouth. 90, 91: National Maritime Museum, London. 93: Courtesy the British Museum. 95: Photo Bibliothèque nationale, Paris. 96, 97: Rijksmuseum, Amsterdam. 98, 99: Derek Bayes, courtesy National Maritime Museum, London. 100, 101: Salmer, courtesy Museo del Prado, Madrid. 102: Howard Pyle Collection, Delaware Art Museum. 104: Photo Bibliothèque nationale, Paris. 106, 107: Rijksmuseum Nederlands Scheepvaart Museum, Amsterdam. 109: Museo del Prado, Madrid. 110: The John Carter Brown Library, Brown University. 111: Photo Bibliothèque nationale, Paris. 112: Library of Congress. 115: The John Carter Brown Library, Brown University—Photo Bibliothèque nationale, Paris. 116: Library of Congress. 118: Photo Bibliothèque nationale, Paris, except center, Library of Congress. 119: Photo Bibliothèque nationale, Paris. 120, 121: Library of Congress. 123: Lauros-Giraudon, courtesy Musée Carnavalet, Paris. 124: Rare Book Division, The New York Public Library, Astor, Lenox and Tilden Foundations. 127: By permission of the British Library. Add. MS5415G.7. 128: Derek Bayes, courtesy National Maritime Museum, London. 133: The John Carter Brown Library, Brown University. 134: Photo Bibliothèque nationale, Paris. 136, 137: Archivo General de Indias, Seville. 138, 139: Library of Congress. 142: Photo Bibliothèque nationale, Paris. 143: Archivo General de Indias, Seville. 145: By permission of the British Library. 719.m.17(15). 146, 147: Photo Bibliothèque nationale, Paris. 149: Bulloz, courtesy Musée de la Marine, Paris. 150: Photo Bibliothèque nationale, Paris. 152: Courtesy Kenneth M. Newman, The Old Print Shop, New York. 156, 157: Réunion des Musées nationaux, Paris. 158: Photo Bibliothèque nationale, Paris. 161: Howard Pyle Collection, Delaware Art Museum. 163: Photo Bibliothèque nationale, Paris. 164, 165: National Maritime Museum, London. 166-171: Derek Bayes, courtesy National Maritime Museum, London.

Index

Printed in U.S.A.

SILVER MINE

SUGAR PLANTATION

HAVANA HARBOR

MORGAN AT SAN LORENZO

NORTH AMERICA

FLORIDA

Fort Caroline

St. Augustine • Anastasia Island

GULF STREAM

GULF OF MEXICO

STRAITS OF FLORIDA

BAHAMA ISLAN

Havana

BAHAMA CHANNEL

CUBA

Puerto Príncipe

Tampico

Cape St. Anthony

Twelve League Cays

Santiago de Cuba

Guanajuato

GULF OF CAMPECHE

Campeche

GREATER

JAMAICA

Tenochtitlán (Mexico City)

Veracruz

Jalapa

San Juan de Ulúa

MEXICO

Villahermosa

YUCATAN

Negril Point

Kingston

CARIBBEAN

SEA

GULF OF HONDURAS

Acapulco

GUATEMALA

Puerto Caballos • San Pedro

HONDURAS

EL SALVADOR

NICARAGUA

• Gran Granada

Old Providence

Cartagen

Lake Nicaragua

Portobelo

Nombre de Dios

San Lorenzo • PANAMA

COLO

Panama City

Isle of Pines

GULF OF PANAMA

DARIEN

PACIFIC OCEAN

ANDES MOUNTAINS

ECUADOR

SAN MATEO BAY

• Tumbes

GULF OF GUAYAQUIL

PERU

Cajamarca